WITHDRAWN

Abandoned to Their Fate

In the series Health, Society, and Policy, edited by Sheryl Ruzek and Irving Kenneth Zola

Abandoned to Their Fate

Social Policy and Practice toward Severely Retarded People in America, 1820–1920

Philip M. Ferguson

Temple University Press
PHILADELPHIA

Temple University Press, Philadelphia 19122
Copyright © 1994 by Temple University. All rights reserved
Published 1994
Printed in the United States of America

The paper used in this publication meets the minimum requirements of American National Standard for Information Science — Permanence of Paper for Printed Library Materials, ANSI Z39.48-1984

Library of Congress Cataloging-in-Publication Data
Ferguson, Philip M.
    Abandoned to their fate : social policy and practice toward severely retarded people in America, 1820–1920 / Philip M. Ferguson.
        p.   cm. — (Health, society, and policy)
    Includes bibliographical references and index.
    ISBN 1-56639-154-7 (cl : alk. paper)
    1. Mentally handicapped — Government policy — United States — History.   2. Mentally handicapped — Institutional care — United States — History.   3. Alms-houses — United States — History.   4. Asylums — United States — History.   5. Rome State Custodial Asylum for Unteachable Idiots (N.Y.) — History.   I. Title.   II. Series.
HV3006.A4F39   1994
362.2'0973 — dc20   93-21887

Contents

Acknowledgments

I owe many thanks to many people for their active support and steady patience in helping me complete this book. Keith Hoffman, Steve Slachta, and the rest of the administrative staff then at the Rome Developmental Center generously gave me access to the early case files and other archival materials at their facility. Equally important, they made sure that I had an adequate place to study this material. I thank them for their help. The book (and the dissertation that preceded it) has taken longer to finish than I ever envisioned when I began. I need to thank Irv Zola of Brandeis University and Janet Francendese at Temple University Press for their encouragement and patience as various deadlines passed and new ones were set. Throughout the process, Doug Biklen and John Briggs, both at Syracuse University, always seemed to find just the right balance of supportive tolerance and gentle prodding when the work looked almost dormant to me. From the very first moment when I started mumbling about some sort of historical study of people with severe disabilities, Steve Taylor, also at Syracuse, has been enthusiastic about my research, quick to respond to my writing, and right on point with his questions and critiques. He has both my thanks and my respect.

For the last eight years, I have worked on this project while employed at the Specialized Training Program (STP), Division of Special Education and Rehabilitation, University of Oregon. During that time, first Tom Bellamy, and then Rob Horner, used the position of director of STP to create a working environment with enough freedom and flexibility to allow me to finish this project. I appreciate their tolerance. Richard Parker generously helped with some of the tables, and Linda Wicklund and Priscilla Phillips helped immensely in typing and formatting various parts of the manuscript.

Finally, my family: My parents, Clyde and Loree Ferguson, have supported my educational endeavors all of my life. When it came to this book, they gradually learned to quit asking what was taking so long, but I know they must have wondered. My one regret is that my father did not live to see the publication of this book. I need to publicly acknowledge my indebtedness to Dianne Ferguson. As a colleague in special education, she has been my closest reader and my most probing critic. When there were few around with the interest or knowledge to discuss with me some esoteric point about institutional development in the nineteenth century, she unfailingly listened, responded, challenged, and praised. Beyond her substantive involvement, Dianne has provided me with a professional example of how to combine careful scholarship, effective teaching, and personal advocacy in a field that needs more of all three. On a more personal level, she has sustained her support in more ways than I can name. My son Ian will not read my thanks to him, so I shall find other ways to let him know how much he has taught me and how proud I am of him. In a very real sense, he is at the heart of this work.

Introduction

This is a study of the history of American social policy and practice toward severely retarded people. Covering the 100-year period from the beginning of Jacksonian reform to the end of World War I and the Progressive era allows me to emphasize events and patterns that are often overlooked. By starting in 1820 in the era of Jacksonian reform, the story can demonstrate the importance of the almshouses in the history of custodialism for mentally retarded people. It was in this decade, with the influential surveys of Quincy in Massachusetts (Quincy, [1821] 1971) and Yates in New York (Yates, [1824] 1901), that the spread of almshouses beyond the major cities began. By ending around 1920, the story can include the worst of the eugenics panic and its effect on people with the most severe disabilities.

Much of this account focuses on developments in New York State, and the last half of the study looks closely at the early history of one institution in upstate New York. When it was officially closed in 1989, the institution was called the Rome Developmental Center, but its original name, the Rome State Custodial Asylum for Unteachable Idiots, reflects the initial intent of the facility: to house specifically the most severely retarded portion of the population. My initial interest in this institution, however, came not so much from its official name or from an academic awareness of its specialized history. Those discoveries came later. My interest began on a personal level through a young man I had met named Peter. I first thought of the Rome Developmental Center simply as the place where Peter had lived so much of his life. In many ways I still think of this study as Peter's story more than Rome's, or New York's.

PETER'S QUESTIONS AND THE OUTCOME OF REFORM

When we first met, Peter was 17.[1] For the last 16 of those years he had lived in large state institutions, mostly the one at Rome, New York. The labels used to describe Peter range from laughable euphemisms to offensive slurs on his very humanity. "Medically fragile," "vegetable," "severely/profoundly retarded," "idiot," "multiply handicapped," "custodial": some of the terms are official argot, and some used to be but are now colloquial. Tomorrow's playground insults are often foretold by today's professional diagnoses. As for Peter, he could not walk or talk—either officially or colloquially. He could not sit up unsupported. He was fed through a tube that plugged into his stomach. His frequent seizures were powerful enough to knock him out of his specially adapted wheelchair if he was not strapped in. Peter's eyes seldom stopped flicking about long enough to focus on anyone. His hands seldom moved at all. He had a spindly body twisted by muscles that never relaxed, and by years of therapy never received. He was shaped like a human question mark. For me, though Peter opened my questions, he did not mark their end.

Peter died several years ago without leaving the institution. The questions that live after him all concern how relatively unaffected he was by the momentous reform efforts of the past two or three decades that have effected many significant improvements in our society's attempts to support disabled individuals in general, and severely mentally retarded individuals in particular.

Perhaps the single best way to summarize the change is to remind ourselves that for the first time since the eugenics movement of the Progressive era (Haller, 1984; Reilly, 1991), mental retardation and developmental disability have gained general recognition as a social problem. Disability issues are once again a regular part of the public agenda. The difference, of course, is that the reforms this time seek to increase the freedom and dignity of disabled people, not to limit them further through "segregation and surgery" (Tyor, 1972). What the periods share is a sense of broad social concern that the issue requires public attention and political action. In Mills's terms (1959), a "private trouble" of being mentally retarded (or knowing someone who was) became a "public issue."

Even those directly involved in these latest reforms need to remind themselves of the recentness of their most dramatic triumphs. Most of the federal involvement in services for developmentally disabled Americans has occurred in just the last 15 years. Over one-half of all the federal funds ever spent on mental retardation and developmental disability has been spent since 1979 (Braddock, 1987, p. 183). Not until 1980 did all the various portions of the 1975 Education of All Handicapped Children Act (further amended since then and now called the Individuals with Disabilities Education Act, or IDEA) become fully operational. It was this legislation that, for the first time, legally guaranteed all school-age children in our country, regardless of disability, access to a "free, appropriate, public education," in the "least restrictive environment" possible. The deinstitutionalization movement stopped the growth of large, public institutions for mentally retarded people in 1967, and the population of these facilities has declined steadily ever since (Lakin, 1979; Lakin, Hill, and Bruininks, 1988; Lakin, Hill, Hauber, Bruininks, and Heal, 1983; White, Prouty, Lakin, and Blake, 1992). In January 1991, New Hampshire became the first state in the country since 1848 to operate no large public institutions (of 16 or more residents) as part of its developmental disabilities service system (Braddock and Mitchell, 1992). At a much more embryonic stage, the federal government's vocational support policies have begun over the last decade to encourage the development of real employment opportunities in integrated settings, instead of segregated, sheltered workshops or "day activity" programs (Bellamy, Rhodes, Mank, and Albin, 1988; Kiernan and Stark, 1986; Rusch, 1986; Wehman and Hill, 1981). Brought together under the banners of "normalization" (Wolfensberger, 1972), "community integration" (Taylor, Biklen, and Knoll, 1987), and "disability rights" (Scotch, 1984), these and other changes at all levels of government and in most areas of public awareness have constituted a truly major effort at social reform (Berkowitz, 1984, 1992). The most recent manifestation is the passage of the Americans with Disabilities Act, commonly referred to as the "civil rights act" for people with disabilities (Scotch, 1989). As the result of all this effort at the policy level, accompanied by impressive advances in medical interventions and instructional technologies, many mentally retarded individuals are undeniably better off than they were 10 or even 5 years ago.

However, against this backdrop of overall change, the comparative lack of improvement in the lives of most people, like Peter, with the most severe and multiple disabilities assumes an even starker contrast. The numbers threaten to overwhelm an otherwise uplifting sense of reform. According to the several major studies, there are *fewer*—not more—mentally retarded students in regular classrooms in America, and *more*—not fewer—in totally separate schools now than in 1975 (Biklen, 1988; Danielson and Bellamy, 1989; Singer and Butler, 1987). Certainly some of this situation merely reflects the entry of some students with the most severe disabilities into the education system, students who had been excluded from any public school setting, segregated or integrated, before 1975. Nonetheless, it is still startling to learn that for the 1989–90 school year, a recent analysis of federal education data reported that 73 percent of all school-age mentally retarded children were being educated either in separate buildings (12 percent) or in separate classrooms from their nondisabled peers ("Retarded Students," 1992).

Although many people have returned to their communities, over 80,000 people remain in large state institutions (White, Prouty, Lakin, and Blake, 1992), the vast majority labeled severely and profoundly retarded (Lakin, White, Prouty, Bruininks, and Kimm, 1991). "Privatization" of residential services associated with this period accounts for an additional 50,000 people or so, many of whom have simply moved from large public institutions to large private ones. By 1988, more than 60 percent of the individuals with mental retardation living in formally designated out-of-home placements still resided in facilities of 16 or more residents (Braddock and Mitchell, 1992). Despite the official federal policy of deinstitutionalization, in 1988 the single largest source of federal support for people with developmental disabilities (the so-called ICF/MR program to reimburse states for health care costs) was still targeting more than 80 percent of its funds (approximately $2.85 billion) for their care in large, congregate care facilities (Braddock and Mitchell, 1992). In effect, the past 25 years have seen the "ghettoization" of institutions:

facilities that are more costly (Braddock, 1987; White, Prouty, Lakin, and Blake, 1992), more segregated (Lakin, Hill, and Bruininks, 1988; Lerman, 1982), and more professionally respectable (Crissey and Rosen, 1986a; Henning and Bartel, 1984) have increasingly been reserved for people with both physical and mental disabilities or with severe behavioral problems.

Finally, there are the dismal figures for vocational services. The "supported employment" initiative in developmental disabilities has a shorter history than the deinstitutionalization reform. However, it has the distinction of specifically targeting people with severe disabilities (Bellamy, Rhodes, Mank, and Albin, 1988; Wehman, 1988; Will, 1984). Nonetheless, the same patterns of differential results according to level of disability are already clear, and they follow perhaps predictable lines (Ferguson and Ferguson, 1986). Recent studies of the individuals with disabilities now working in supported employment settings have found that only 3 to 10 percent of the total were labeled as having severe or profound disabilities (Buckley and Bellamy, 1985; Kregel and Wehman, 1989; McGaughey, Kiernan, Lynch, Schalock, and Morgenstern, 1991; Wehman, Kregel, and Seyforth, 1985). By contrast, some 57 percent of the people in nonvocational, segregated day programs were so labeled. For people with multiple disabilities, the situation is even bleaker (Goetz, Lee, Johnston, and Gaylord-Ross, 1991). For most severely disabled young adults, not to mention their families, the notion of better-paying, productive, integrated, supported jobs remains simply a professional promise obscured by the looming reality of life at home or in the asylum with nowhere to go (McDonnell, Wilcox, Boles, and Bellamy, 1985; Wehman, 1992; Zollers, Conroy, Hess, and Newman, 1984). For most of the Peters of this world, reform has yet to arrive.

The questions here, however, go beyond numbers. Why have the reform efforts met with so little success in improving the lives of severely, multiply disabled people? Is it just a case of unheeded calls for change, a reform movement mired in a bureaucratic slough? The more troubling question about Peter's unchanged life goes beyond such pragmatic considerations of professional inertia and 1980s realpolitik to a more basic consideration of human value and social structure. Has the movement itself been somehow misdirected or left incomplete for this population? Have the calls for change left something unsaid, not merely unheard? Or, finally, the most dismal prospect of all, has there been— will there always be—some people such as Peter, inevitably untouched by reform, betrayed even more by physiology than by fiscal conservatives?

Increasingly, progressives within the field of developmental disabilities are beginning to reassess the concepts and policies that have driven the reforms of the past two decades (Ferguson, Hibbard, Leinen, and Schaff, 1990). Terms borrowed from other spheres of life or from other social movements now seem to some critics to have unintentionally misstated the message of community integration and participation that reformers envisioned. The legal notion of "least restrictive environment" has thus been used in defense of programs of the most segregative character (D. L. Ferguson, 1987; Taylor, 1988; Turnbull, 1981). After years of disavowing most of what was done in the name of "normalization" (a concept he is credited with popularizing in America), Wolfensberger even disavowed the name itself (Wolfensberger, 1983). Supporters should probably have known that any neologism as awkward and bulky as "deinstitutionalization" would come to cover a panoply of programmatic sins that had little to do with community life (Scull, 1984; Taylor, 1992). Even work reform in the direction of "supported employment" runs the risk of overemphasizing personal productivity so as to unintentionally perpetuate the social exclusion of those who remain unproductive (P. M. Ferguson, 1987; Ferguson & Ferguson, 1986).

The issues go deeper than ill-chosen labels for well-chosen goals, however. The effort to bring people back into the community has talked about how all people with cognitive disabilities could be productive citizens (Will, 1984). Yet, what kind of economic context could ever define as productive people who are as massively disabled as Peter? What vocational functions could Peter have served that society could not do without or do better? If Peter simply did not fit into a society based on the marketplace and ubiquitous competition, then why the fight by reformers to get him back into that society? Peter seems to have failed the very test that reformers established for gaining a place in the community. The effort to bring mentally retarded children into the public schools has emphasized that all children can be educated. Yet, how useful is it to think of what Peter needed to learn—to hold his head up, to respond to sound, to swallow—as education in the same sense that calculus and creative writing are for other students his age? The vision of what would have been a fulfilling life for Peter can seem almost as blurred as his unfocused eyesight. What seems clearly visible, however, is an institutional existence that was abusive and inhuman during his worst years; sterile, soporific, and impersonal when he was lucky. While the reform questions go unanswered, even a sanitized, euphemized, and downsized version of the institutional choices inflicted on Peter seems profoundly wrong.

All of the questions about the future of reform in developmental disability policy led me ineluctably to a consideration of earlier efforts. How had Peter come to live his life in that warehouse of a home? How had such institutions become the "placement of choice" for severely disabled people? What exactly did the term "severe retardation" mean in the first place? Peter, of course, is just the instance, the personal embodiment, of a class of people whose history seems as vague as its future. Were earlier generations of severely and multiply disabled individuals also largely untouched by the reform efforts of their time? If they were, are there patterns in the incremental failures of those past reform efforts that are instructive for the current attempts to do better? The chapters that follow try to answer these questions.

ORGANIZATION OF THE STUDY

This book breaks roughly into four parts. The first chapter serves as an orientation to the topic. It lays the conceptual groundwork for the interpretation of events and context that subsequent chapters develop. In Chapter 1, I present the outlines of an argument about the dimensions of chronicity, and suggest the potential relevance of the historical questions to current policies and reform initiatives. I also discuss there the slippery issues of prevalence and other demographic matters for mental retardation in the nineteenth century.

Chapters 2 and 3 shift the focus to specific developments in the Northeast, New York State in particular. Chapter 2 discusses the prominent role that almshouses in the first half of the nineteenth century played in the lives of retarded people. Chapter 3 then examines the development of the specialized congregate idiot asylum, including the words and actions of Samuel Gridley Howe and Hervey Backus Wilbur, founders of the two earliest public idiot asylums in the United States. These two men are generally viewed rather one-dimensionally, as benevolent reformers whose good intentions and visionary experiments were frustrated by subsequent generations of lesser bureaucrats and penurious legislators. From the perspective of "incurable idiocy," this overwhelmingly favorable portrayal needs significant modification.

The third segment of this book is the case study of the Rome Custodial Asylum that constitutes the bulk of Chapters 4, 5, and 6. Chapter 4 focuses on the years just before and just after Rome opened its doors in 1894. The superintendent, John Fitzgerald, and his young assistant, Charles Bernstein, in charge of an inadequate facility, had an intolerable mandate and an uncertain professional status. Chapter 5 continues the examination of Rome through the first eighteen years of Bernstein's tenure as superintendent. Bernstein is a fascinating figure in the history of institutions in this country. Unfortunately, he has been largely overlooked in favor of some of his less progressive colleagues (such as Fernald and Goddard). Chapter 6 examines case files drawn from the first 1,000 admissions to the Rome Asylum, from 1894 to 1902. What the files reveal has as much to do with those outside the institution as with those who lived and worked inside.

In conclusion, Chapter 7 summarizes the themes developed in earlier sections, and furthers the analysis of the dimensions of chronicity by tentatively suggesting its relevance to current reform efforts. Most important, it tries to anticipate some objections to the interpretation of individuals and events presented in this account.

A COMMENT ON LANGUAGE AND LABELS

I should try to justify the language used in this study, although some readers outside the disability community may consider what follows an unnecessary excursion into a fairly esoteric debate.

Language is seldom neutral. The words we use both reflect and create the meaning we intend to convey (Eisner, 1988, 1991). Various professional and advocacy groups in the area of disability generally, and mental retardation in particular, have thus focused a lot of attention on the language we use to refer to disabled people. As many in these groups will presumably not approve of some of the specific words and syntax that I use in this study, a brief explanation of my linguistic choices may be useful.

First, it is precisely because words are such active participants in the context of meaning and communications that throughout the book I use terms that were part of either the vernacular or the specific professional jargon during the period under discussion. Terms such as "idiot," "imbecile," "feebleminded," "lunatic," and "insane" cannot be avoided without losing some of the context and meaning of the nineteenth century era. Modern terms such as "severe retardation" or "mental illness" differ from the earlier labels in both sense (connotation) and reference (denotation).

Second, even when I use the modern terms, my syntax will bother some readers who are proponents of "people first" language. In the pages that follow, I regularly violate the preferences of some disability activists (mainly in the area of developmental disabilities) by using phrases such as "a severely retarded individual," rather than "an individual with severe retardation." I do so for several reasons. I think adjectives generally have less stigmatizing power than nouns, and seem less permanent. This study is partly about how a sense of permanency was involved in the concept of chronicity that developed in the nineteenth century. Mental retardation is a plastic concept that is inevitably shaped by the shifting forces of historical development and cultural prejudice. The exclusive reliance on nominal reference tends—to my mind—to harden and reify the notion into something more factual and objective than it really is. That is also why I avoid terms such as "the mentally retarded." Moreover, I think the whole strategy of shoving unwanted words back toward the end of a sentence is politically unwise. To my ear, the message of such sentence reconstruction is that "retardation" is such a terrible thing that it must be hidden as far as possible from the person to whom it is applied. I prefer the approach of other minority groups (including progressive segments of the disability rights community) who fight prejudice directly by accentuating their identity (and their solidarity) with such phrases as black activists, gay pride, women's rights. Perhaps the best example among disability groups is the Deaf community (the uppercase "D" is important). The Deaf pride movement has embraced the label as a sign of their unique historical and cultural heritage. There is nothing wrong with being mentally retarded except the barriers that society creates for people who have that label. When it is relevant to the conversation (and if it is not relevant, then why mention it at all, in any construction?) the label should be used with all of the openness, flexibility, and even confrontation that other minority groups have adopted for self-reference.

Finally, I find that the recommendation not to use adjectives in referring to individuals leads to some tortured syntax and awkward phrasing. There is too much of value that disability rights advocates have to say, for them to neglect the fluency with which they say it. People should not constantly have to stumble over our sentence structure to discover our message of social change. The stylistic problem stems from the rigidity of the "people first" construction. In some sentences, it works fine. In other contexts, it sounds terribly forced.

I doubt that these remarks will convince any on either side of this dispute, but I hope at least to demonstrate that my terminology is not an oversight. If despite this explanation my grammar and vocabulary still offend some readers, I apologize.

ABANDONMENT, NEW AND OLD

A few years ago a group of national leaders in the field of mental retardation opposed a court order that mandated community placements for many of the residents of an Alabama institution (Partlow) and that established a "right to treatment" for all those who remained. These prominent opponents argued that a sizable portion of the individuals still living in the facility should remain there because of their incapacity for change or dangerous behavior, and should not be "subjected" to further treatment or education efforts:

> Habilitation interpreted to mean deinstitutionalization or return to home/ community living is an unrealistic goal for the majority of residents in Partlow. Indeed, the behavior of many cannot reasonably be expected to improve *significantly* with training, even for living within the sheltered environment of an institution. . . . A meaningful program for these residents should insure that they live in comfort, with dignity, and with the full extent of enrichment that they are able to appreciate. (Partlow Review Committee, 1978, pp. 4, 5)[2]

More than 100 years earlier, the New York State Board of Charities, a monitoring arm of the state government, had made much the same argument and had divided retarded people into the same two general classes implied in the later statement.

> Experience shows that while there is an almost infinite variety in the forms of idiocy, shading, by degrees, from perfect intelligence to absolute fatuity, persons of this class may be broadly divided into two great divisions; those who can and those who can not profit by instruction. For those of the second class, nothing is needed but custody in a spirit of kindness. They should be properly housed, fed and clothed, and permitted to pass a comfortable physical existence. . . . The case should be plain and the necessity stringent, before a person is relegated among those who are to be *abandoned to their fate* [emphasis added]. But in a clear case such abandonment should be made. (New York State Board of Charities, *Annual Report*, 1868, p. xxxv)

The language changed in those 100 years. "Abandonment" became "enrichment," but both sentences mean that no effort at improvement is to be made. A cynic might argue that today's tone is less blunt, but the purpose is unchanged. The argument for continued institutionalization has remained remarkably the same: a chronic segment of the population remains supposedly beyond the pale of successful training and remediation. The failure of these residual few, said the experts then and now, is permanent, and so should be their custody. Defenders of today's institutions might choose fewer individuals than their nineteenth-century predecessors for inclusion in the category of chronicity. The category remains available; abandonment remains the outcome. Peter would have fit the category, no matter which experts made the assignments. Our society still seems to need a place to abandon its failures.

Chapter One Abandonment and Chronicity

The primary aim of this book is integrative, or contextual, in design. I describe the various dimensions of social structure and cultural meaning that have, in the recent past at least, worked interactively to shape our collective approach to people with the most severe cognitive disabilities. What was the official policy toward mentally retarded people at various moments in history, and how have those policies changed over time? Beyond the official pronouncements of any era, we benefit from interpreting the meaning of social discourse at all levels: from official utterance to informal behavior, from organizational structure to popular imagery. Practically speaking, this orientation means that the study ends up being less a history of severe retardation than a history of "incurable idiocy" or "custodial" feeblemindedness. Severe retardation is a modern term that overlaps, but is not identical to, the earlier terms that now sound so offensive. The point is to examine the variety of contextual factors—the strands of social discourse—that helped construct the meanings of idiocy and imbecility during the nineteenth and the early twentieth century. My hope is that such an examination of historical context may indicate the source and direction of influences on the social meaning of today's preferred category: severe retardation. To borrow a term from the social sciences, the book is an exercise in cultural hermeneutics (Geertz, 1980; Greene, 1986), where the texts being interpreted are social rather than literary.

THE CONTEXT OF FAILURE

Failure surrounds severe retardation. Obviously, the label itself implies a certain amount of personal failure, if only the inability to evade the attention of those with the power to apply the label. More typically, perhaps, the phrase usually connotes some lack of success in school, employment, or more functional categories like adaptive behavior and communication. The problems do not end with the individual's competence, however. There is also the repeated failure of society to achieve its stated goals for increased community participation of severely retarded people. Finally, at one level removed from the actual events, there is the academic failure of professional historians to tell the story of severely retarded people and the policies that most affected them (Grob, 1986). Failure on these levels is not a purely passive acceptance of defeat. One type of failure connotes opposition, however unsuccessful; another type results from unintended oversight or neglect; yet another is the failure produced by active omission: the kind of "aggressive surrender" that tries to hustle defeat into part of some larger triumph over an unwary foe. Failure, in short, has as many contexts and outcomes as success.

This study is a history of failure, in all of its outcomes, on all of these levels. Historians have failed to describe adequately how the failures of specific reform initiatives have repeatedly been explained as the result of the failure of severely retarded individuals to perform adequately. More precisely, the story that follows describes the uses of failure, as an organizational and conceptual category, to an emergent professional class in the area of mental retardation. This study argues that the central contextual development in the nineteenth century for severely retarded people is the professionalization of failure through the social construction and application of the concept of chronicity.

There was first of all a pattern of persistent exclusion in the cycles of nineteenth century reforms as they affected the field of mental retardation. That is, the reformers always ensured (or, at a minimum, unintentionally allowed) the continued existence of a residual population who could not be helped by their reforms. Membership in this residual category varied from reform to reform—tending to get smaller from era to era—but the category always remained, as a way both to explain the individual failures and to dramatize the contrasting successes. In the almshouses, the early small asylums, or the later congregate institutions, the need for a custodial class persisted across reform efforts of nineteenth century social welfare.

The second part of my argument is that this category of failure had three dimensions—economic, ethical, and aesthetic—that varied in emphasis and social origination. Each dimension played a part in ultimately justifying the outcome of social exclusion. Finally, central to the establishment of professional legitimacy by the leaders of the idiot asylums, the specialized version of therapeutic failure evolved as a fourth and final dimension by which to judge who belonged in the residual population. It was a dimension reserved for the diagnostic power of experts, and it had the effect of making custodialism a biological inevitability rather than a social arrangement. It transformed failure into chronicity.

DIMENSIONS OF CHRONICITY

Specific arguments about how various elements of perceived failure contributed to the overall notion of chronicity weave through the chapters that follow. First, I need to discuss the dimensions of the term "chronicity." As I intend to use the word in this book, chronicity connotes much more than a medical judgment that a condition or disease is incurable: the opposite of "acute" illness. Rather, I intend the much more general social status, within the realm of "charities and corrections," of being judged somehow "unfixable." The terms actually used to convey this judgment varied from category to category and included the more familiar medical areas "incurable," "incorrigible," "unteachable," "unproductive," "hopeless," and even "chronic" (usually in reference to insanity). The emergence of this broad distinction between the salvageable and the unsalvageable in the eighteenth and the early nineteenth century in America has been ably documented by several historians of social welfare (Katz, 1986; Scull, 1980). What I am doing is developing the category as applied to people viewed as idiotic. By using the term "chronicity," I hope to convey the sense of permanence about the judgment, and also to suggest the key role of medical superintendents in contributing an air of scientific objectivity to what was otherwise a commonsense notion of failure.

I argue here that for understanding the quality of life of people viewed as idiots or as low-grade imbeciles, at least in the period from 1820 to 1920, the status of chronicity is more central than retardation. Indeed, although I do not pursue such a course here, I would argue that the direction of future investigations in this area should be toward a history of chronicity that cuts across disability categories. As a field, disability studies needs to go beyond the disciplinary histories that limit themselves to one or another of the traditional disabilities within the human services (such as mental illness, epilepsy, mental retardation, or physical disability) to examine the common experiences of people placed at the lowest social and functional level of each of those diagnostic groups.

This study limits itself to chronicity in the lives of so-called idiots and imbeciles. It identifies four dimensions of chronicity, each of which applied its own criteria for success and failure and emphasized its own set of outcomes for those who came up short. Perhaps the best way of interpreting these dimensions is as separate strands of social discourse, with different vocabularies, different metaphors, different "ways of seeing" the phenomenon of chronic failure. There is a pattern that can be applied to each of the dimensions. For example, all four of the dimensions can be associated, at least for the sake of analysis, with a major category of historical development in the nineteenth century. Moreover, the meaning of failure within each of those spheres of social discourse and organization can be reconstructed out of similar elements:

1. The general perspective from which the failure is approached;
2. The type of criteria used to determine individual chronicity;
3. The terms or labels used to characterize individual chronicity;
4. The officially sanctioned result of chronicity.

Organizing the various dimensions according to these separate elements creates a convenient diagram (presented in Table 1.1) that

Table 1.1 Dimensions of Chronicity

Historical Sphere	Perspective	Criteria	Label	Outcome
Cultural imagery	Personal appearance	Aesthetic	Ugly, repulsive	Hiddenness
State control of social welfare	Social	Moral	Dangerous Burdensome	Custody
Industrial capitalism	Functional	Economic	Unproductive	Poverty
Professional specialization	Therapeutic, scientific	Medical Educational	Incurable Unteachable	Exclusion, rejection

summarizes the alternative ways in which chronicity was constructed in the nineteenth century. A brief discussion of the diagram according to the four dimensions follows, beginning with the top row of the table and working down.

Cultural imagery

As de Toqueville noted, individualism was a prominent feature of American democracy from its very first years. As the nineteenth century progressed, however, this political individualism combined with an expanding consumerism to yield a kind of broad cultural aesthetic that is even more familiar today. Increasingly there came to be a forceful cultural association of the outward appearance of health and prosperity with inward moral character and personal worth. Wealthy people looked materially prosperous because they were spiritually upright. Cleanliness was now "next to godliness." Bathtubs moved from the fancy hotel or spa to the private homes of the upper and professional classes (Eberlein, 1978). Health foods such as Graham's crackers and Kellogg's corn flakes flourished within the various sects of the public health movement in the middle of the century (Leavitt and Numbers, 1978; Reverby and Rosner, 1979). Beauty aids were popularized through newspapers and mail order catalogs.

Merchandizers were more than happy to convince the burgeoning middle class that the consumer culture allowed almost unlimited improvement upon one's natural endowments. Popular advertising promulgated images of feminine beauty and delicacy or masculine refinement and energy. The implicit message was that personal appearance was a personal responsibility. Propriety, that watchword of Victorian sensibility, came to include how one looked, not just how one behaved.

As logic and human nature might suggest, the prominence of personal appearance meant that ugliness became as important a judgment as beauty. The circus sideshow became an increasingly popular attraction (Bogdan, 1986, 1987, 1988; Fiedler, 1978; Gerber, 1992): aesthetic pornography for those who wished to glimpse what society said should be hidden. Applied to people with physical and mental disabilities, heightened attention to appearance made words such as "repulsive," "grotesque," "dirty," "slovenly" into accusations of moral and mental failure as well as the more obvious aesthetic transgressions. Congenital abnormalities showed the internal defects of mind in the external signs of repulsive habits (drooling, for example) or grotesque appearance (as in microcephaly). Proper society, of course, did not put such people on display; it hid them from sight, humanely, in the large public asylums. The proper outcome of aesthetic failure was permanent invisibility.

State control

Not only did people need to look good, they needed to behave well. If any trend marks the development of the nineteenth century, it is the increasing assertion of state responsibility to guarantee such proper behavior by its citizens. Over the last 25 years or so, social historians have described and debated the variety of social control mechanisms that characterized the evolution of the state public welfare and corrections systems in nineteenth-century America (Cohen and Scull, 1983; Gettelman, 1975; Mohl, 1971; Piven and Cloward, 1972; Platt, 1969; Rothman, 1971, 1980; Rothman and Wheeler, 1981). In general, however, there is agreement that, prompted by concern about social breakdown among the masses of immigrants and others in the lower class, upper and middle classes mounted reform efforts that increased the government role in policy and programs. Almshouses, specialized asylums, penitentiaries, outdoor poor relief, reform schools—all became widely adopted as the state replaced the family, church, and community as the primary agency responsible for the dependent classes. The debate centers around how benevolent or controlling these reforms actually were (Mayer, 1983).

If the perspective in this development was social, the criteria were overwhelmingly moral. As sociologist Stephen Spitzer has bluntly framed it, the concern of the state was what to do with the "social junk" and the "social dynamite" (Spitzer, 1975). Social junk included all of those weak, burdensome, helpless individuals whom society was duty-bound to protect and support through its welfare system. Social dynamite included all of those viewed as dangerous to society through criminal or immoral behavior. In their case, the state was duty-bound to protect and support the rest of society through incarceration and rehabilitation of offenders.

With increasing vehemence and moral judgment, state officials in the nineteenth century viewed mentally retarded people as burdensome, dangerous, or both. In either case, the justified outcome of failure to meet the standards of moral safety or independence was custody. The dual justification of custodialism became especially powerful in the official pursuit of institutionalization of lower-functioning retarded youth and young adults. Whether to protect them or to restrain them, the reasoning went, idiots and imbeciles should be removed from society.

Industrial capitalism

America became a modern industrialized nation in the last half of the nineteenth century. For those who took a functional or instrumental outlook on such a nation, there was a steadily increasing need for a pliant, productive workforce to keep the economy humming. The logic is still very strong in our culture: you "earn" your living by the work you do. To be unproductive in such a context was perhaps the worst indictment of all that could be made of an individual. To be judged permanently unproductive left one totally beyond the economic calculus by which individual worth was figured.

To some degree, the functional perspective of the marketplace came to subsume the social and personal perspectives of moral and aesthetic worth. That is, to label someone as unproductive became

a personal and social condemnation as well as an economic evaluation. What was truly "burdensome" and "dangerous" was disrupt-
ing the industrial arrangement by refusing to sell one's labor to
management, or by having no labor potential to sell. To be "useful," to have a function in society, one had to be a productive
worker (that is, producing or providing goods or services), or a
supportive spouse. For a significant portion of those people labeled
imbeciles or idiots, such a "single standard of honor" (Lasch, 1973)
meant chronic uselessness. It went without saying that it also meant
chronic poverty. As the following chapters will illustrate, despite
variations of moral discourse and professional specialization, chronicity in the nineteenth century remained an economic judgment more
than a medical diagnosis. The push to segregate the economically
dependent was a way to keep the marketplace not the individual,
healthy.

Professional specialization

One consequence of the development of the medical and educational professions in the nineteenth century was the rationalization of
individual failure in the midst of what was supposed to be a bountiful
economy. It was the emergence of specialists in mental disease and
special education that helped transform failure into chronicity for
those who became subjects of the new professionals. The positive side
of this therapeutic perspective was the scientific optimism that
suffused the work of reformers from Samuel Howe to Charles
Bernstein, from Dorothea Dix to Elizabeth Farrell (the founder of
the Council for Exceptional Children). Many people's lives materially improved as a result of reforms in the treatment and education of
disabled people. People previously judged to be unteachable were
successfully taught; people judged incurable were cured. There were
also failures, of course. Those who did not learn, or did not learn
enough, became more unteachable than before. Those who could not
be cured, even with the new treatments and regimens, became even
more incurable. The professions added two key elements to the
explanation of those who failed. First they contributed a sense of
permanence—inevitable, inescapable—that made a "patient's" failure chronic. Second, they made the failure objective, a matter of

science instead of art or morality. Medical superintendents of idiot asylums (and other institutions, as well) made the custodial abandonment of severely retarded people into a fact of nature rather than a value of society. Chronicity could explain the failure of reform; it was the victims who failed, not the reformers.

All of these four strands of discourse about chronicity will weave in and out of the discussion in the chapters that follow. Understanding their content and structure is the overall purpose of this historical account. I should add the caveat here that the strands are not intended as direct causal links between one event and the next. Nor do I mean to imply that any of the dimensions have totally negative connotations; the dimensions of chronicity were also the dimensions of success. There were winners as well as losers according to these measures of social achievement and adjustment. This history is limited to the losers, however, and to how society sanctioned their loss. The dimensions are meant to reconstruct the context of response and justification for the social abandonment of people with the most severe levels of retardation.

SOME ADDITIONAL THEMES

Within this larger argument about the emergence of chronicity, there are three amendments that I think need to be made to the existing chronology or periodization of mental retardation history. These amendments support the overall explication of the dimensions of chronicity, but I believe they can also stand on their own as significant components of a broader approach to mental retardation history than is widely available today. The concluding chapter will develop some additional comments about the overall pattern of change from 1820 to 1920.

The Persistence of Custodialism

In relation to the most severely retarded segment of the population, the nineteenth century cannot be understood as a brief golden age of experiment and reform followed by a gradual slide into custodialism. Such an interpretation of the rise of asylums in the middle of the century, popularized by scholars in mental retardation such as Kanner (1964), Wolfensberger (1975), and Scheerenberger (1983), places too much emphasis on the public pronouncements of a few reformers. When one begins with a focus on severe disability, the midcentury institutional "experiments" can be seen as somewhat self-serving endorsements of the status quo by the founders of the so-called schools. The reformers, while not without ambivalence on the matter, basically wanted the lower-functioning individuals to remain exactly where they were: socially abandoned to the private struggles of families, or justifiably incarcerated in the basements of local almshouses. The social policy toward those judged unteachable or incorrigible in the nineteenth century was uninterrupted in its custodial orientation. All that changed was the preferred location of the custody and its professional exploitation.

Comparisons with Mental Illness

If the history of mental retardation has been, so to speak, slow to develop, part of the reason has been the tacit assumption that the history of insanity in fact covered most of the important themes and events. Indeed, there are important similarities and comparisons. Most of the history of insane asylums in this country seems to presage the evolution of idiot asylums by 15 or 20 years. The professional debate over congregate, all-purpose institutions or separate, specialized facilities for acute and chronic insanity provides an important context for the similar debate that occurred among superintendents of the "idiot" asylums.

There are also important differences, however, that raise some interesting questions. The rates of institutionalization for the two populations, for example, differ dramatically. Even at the height of the eugenics era, less than 10 percent of the identified population of mentally retarded people was actually confined in large, public institutions. By the end of the nineteenth century, the comparable rate for mental illness was in the 70 to 80 percent range. Why the difference?

Varieties of Family Resistance

Another secondary theme that emerges repeatedly in the events discussed here, from the Jacksonian almshouse reform to the eugenics era 100 years later, is the resistance to state control and institutionalization demonstrated by the economically impoverished families targeted for such programs. As later chapters will discuss in more detail, many contemporary accounts and subsequent historical reports have claimed that the rise of institutional solutions to disability was, in part, a political and professional response to the pleas and demands of parents for relief from their caregiving responsibilities. Without denying that many families faced enormous hardships and themselves asked for assistance from their local and state officials, I can cite recurring instances of families who strongly resisted placing their disabled relatives outside the home, or, once they were institutionalized, actively pursued their release. The history of families of mentally retarded individuals turns out to be much more complicated and varied than the rather superficial accounts of the period in question.

THE QUESTION OF DEFINITION: WHO IS SEVERELY RETARDED, AND DOES IT REALLY MATTER?

It is a straightforward matter to say that I will be studying the story of severely retarded people. As already acknowledged, however, that statement is also misleading. It would be more accurate to describe this as a history of idiocy. It is difficult to specify exactly who was meant by the label of idiocy, much less how idiocy compares to today's severe retardation. Regardless of the historical method I use, the problem of defining the population remains a thorny one (Blanton, 1976). A brief summary of some of the aspects of this problem will serve as a backdrop for a description and defense of the definitional approach I chose to adopt.

The current consensus about the prevalence of mental retardation and developmental disability seems to hover in the 1 to 1.5 percent range (Kiernan and Bruininks, 1986; Mercer, 1973), although some estimates approach a 3 percent rate (Drew, Logan, and Hardman, 1988; Zigler and Hodapp, 1986). For a population base of 250 million people, the conservative 1 percent figure means that approximately 2.5 million people are assumed to be mentally retarded. Of this number, some 10 to 15 percent are believed to be severely or profoundly retarded. One recent estimate is that 10 percent of the mentally retarded population fall into the moderately to profoundly retarded category (U.S. Department of Education, 1989; Drew, Logan, and Hardman, 1988). Using the high figure of 15 percent would mean roughly that some 375,000 people are moderately, severely, or profoundly retarded. In 1989, some 132,000 mentally retarded people lived in large (16 or more beds) public and private residential facilities (Lakin, White, Prouty, Bruininks, and Kimm, 1991).[1] In other words, slightly more than 5 percent of the estimated mentally retarded population lived in large institutional settings. However, for the same year, if we look only at the people labeled severely and profoundly retarded who lived in formal residential programs (public or private), we find that over 31 percent—or 85,406—lived in large institutional settings. They represent almost two-thirds (64.4 percent) of the total mentally retarded population in such facilities (Lakin, White, Prouty, Bruininks, and Kimm, 1991). Given the population estimates for overall prevalence, and using admittedly rough numbers, almost one of every four people anticipated to be severely or profoundly retarded is in a large institutional setting (85,000 out of 375,000, or 22.6 percent). On the other hand, fewer than two of every 100 people labeled mildly or moderately retarded are in such facilities (46,000 out of 2.5 million, or 1.8 percent).

These numbers, however, suggest a certainty of identification that does not really exist. How to define terms such as "severely handi-capped" or "profoundly retarded" is a contentious subject in the general area of developmental disabilities. Some experts advocate strict usage of IQ scores by themselves as the best available determinant (Zigler, Balla, and Hodapp, 1984). Some, including the authors of the official American Association on Mental Retardation definition (AAMR, 1992), want to use measures of adaptive behavior as well

(Drew, Logan, and Hardman, 1988; MacMillan, 1982; Mercer, 1973). One might suppose that such definitional squabbles would disappear when confronted with the obvious physical and functional deficiencies associated with the lower levels of retardation. Such is not the case, and the difficulties multiply when the historical factors become part of the equation. There are at least four obstacles to definitional precision confronted by this study.

1. The terms "severe" and "profound retardation" were not in use during the years covered in this book. Furthermore, a simple transla-tion of the terms "idiot" and "imbecile" into modern terms of "profound" and "severe/moderate" retardation, respectively, would be enticingly convenient but hopelessly misleading and anachronistic. For example, "idiot" was used both as a generic term for all people viewed as mentally retarded, regardless of level, and as a diagnostic term for the lowest-functioning portion of the population. Even when used in the more restricted sense, "idiot" would refer to someone in the "bottom" half (functionally speaking), from the halfway mark all the way down to the bottom 10 or 20 percent only.

2. Just as it is hard to identify the population linguistically, it is also difficult to do so numerically (despite the figures cited earlier). Current prevalence rates for severe and profound retardation cannot be extrapolated back to the nineteenth and early twentieth centuries for many reasons. Prevalence is not simply a one-directional consider-ation under which improvements in medical care and general public health mean only that fewer organically impaired babies are born today and fewer children are left impaired from childhood diseases that are now largely controlled. The same general improvements in health care mean that severely retarded children survive infancy and childhood today who would have quickly perished in earlier years. The examples of Trisomy 21 and neural tube defects like spina bifida come quickly to mind. Consideration of the cumulative effects of increased environmental hazards (lead poisoning from the use of lead-based gasoline, for example) makes the situation impenetrably complex. It would be an exercise in obfuscation, then, to spend a lot of time speculating on whether a currently used prevalence rate of 1.3 per 1,000 general population for severe and profound

retardation is too high, too low, or just right for 1850, 1890, or 1920.

3. Even if it were feasible to apply retroactively the terms "severe" and "profound" retardation, there is a lack of consensus even today on the proper definition of those labels. Despite the "official" definition by the American Association on Mental Retardation, there are those who would use nothing but IQ scores (Zigler, Balla, and Hodapp, 1984); those who would use simply a percentage of the population (e.g., Sailor and Guess, 1983); and those (including the government) who would use functional criteria only (Kiernan, Smith, and Ostrowsky, 1986). There are even those who despair of the entire effort (Bogdan and Taylor, 1982).

4. Finally, there are at least two specific physical conditions that complicate the historical evaluation of retardation: cerebral palsy and epilepsy. Of course, both these conditions still complicate the lives of some people who are also retarded. In the nineteenth century these were devastating impairments. Cerebral palsy often affected the ability to communicate, and the problem was often seen as part of retardation. The status of epilepsy was even worse. Uncontrolled seizures were one of the most stigmatizing conditions of the nineteenth century. Separate institutions were established for people labeled epileptic (Dwyer, 1992). Some of these people were undoubtedly also retarded, but exact percentages are difficult even to estimate.[2] To a large extent, seizures were also prima facie evidence of retardation of the "worst" (meaning most incurable) kind.

Many of these problems are familiar to historians, especially historians of the social sciences. They are troubling, of course, but they come with the territory. The problem is possibly more discomforting to someone from the field of mental retardation, who may well expect at least the charade of precision that numbers can sometimes provide. Given all of the caveats discussed, there still are some general statements that can at least begin to orient the discussion.

Notions of Prevalence

It is clear that prior to the popularization of the intelligence test between 1910 and 1920, medical superintendents and other public welfare professionals believed the prevalence of mental retardation to be much lower than the most conservative of today's figures. Most public accounts endorsed the estimate of Walter Fernald, superintendent of the Massachusetts Idiot Asylum and a leader of the professional association for the field, that the prevalence rate for all feeblemindedness in the United States was 2 per 1,000 (Fernald, 1893; Ireland, 1900). The woefully inadequate 1890 census was uncritically accepted as supporting this by reporting some 95,609 feebleminded people out of a total population of slightly over 50 million. The report preceded the category of "moron" that intelligence tests made popular.

As discussed earlier, the current estimates of prevalence hover around the 1 to 1.5 percent range, or 10 to 15 per 1,000. However, the much lower estimates in the nineteenth century of the occurrence of retardation were balanced by a belief, or at least an official policy, that most such people belonged in institutions, and that many should remain there for life. As a result, most superintendents of institutions before 1910 argued that up to one-half of all retarded people were of the so-called custodial class. One professional of the era used just such a percentage to arrive at exactly how many feebleminded people should be lifelong inmates of public asylums: "Now if the experience of institutions for the feeble-minded shows that fifty percent of their inmates are, or eventually become, custodial cases of idiocy, it is fair to assume that those outside of institutions are in the same condition. Hence we think that according to the figures of the Tenth Census, there are at least over thirty-eight thousand custodial cases of idiocy in the United States" (Fish, 1891, p. 99).

Defining by Dimensions: Aspects of Chronicity

Again, the four dimensions of chronicity come into play as so many strands in defining feeblemindedness in the nineteenth century, especially the custodial classes. As mentioned, the three nonprofessional dimensions each involved one of our three basic value systems. The identification of retarded people sounded like nothing so much as a bad Western movie: the bad, the ugly, and the useless. Morality, aesthetics, or productivity: one or more is repeatedly involved in the efforts of experts to define the various types of idiocy and imbecility. Each of these dimensions may be conceived of as a continuum of social marginality. At one end were those whose deviance or failure was temporary and mild; these cases were amenable to rehabilitation in their ethics, their appearance, their employability. At the other end were those whose deviance or failure was hopelessly chronic, unimprovable. At some point, then, badness becomes incorrigible, ugliness becomes inhuman, and uselessness becomes untrainable. Temporary trouble becomes irredeemable failure. For these chronic cases, an atmosphere of permanence comes to envelop their lives on the edges of the cultural universe. Of course, the worst feature of a prognosis of chronicity is not that it is terminal, but that it is unending. The "condition" will not kill you, but it will follow you to your grave.

Mental retardation has a long association with sin and immorality. For most of the nineteenth century, the official view was that idiots were either the result of bad behavior (as by the parents), or the perpetrators of it. The more mildly retarded imbeciles were judged custodial for their danger to society and their moral degradation. They were condemned as bad. These individuals "possess excellent physical powers and are trained to a high degree of elementary capacity, but are yet so lacking in judgment and in the moral sense as to be unsafe members of the community, and, if discharged into it, contribute largely to the criminal classes, or, falling victims to the depraved, are adding to the bulk of sexual offence and to the census of incompetency" (Fish, 1891, p. 99).

The appearance of an individual was also thought to be a telltale sign of imbecility or idiocy, abhorred as ugly. The "physical stigmata of degeneration" (Barr, 1910, p. 23) became more prominent as the idiocy became more severe, a belief that combined nicely with racially based notions of social evolution as well.

> In considering physical characteristics of all mental defectives, the various ethnological types are easily recognizable: the dark skin, curled hair, and thick negroid lips of the Ethiopian; the prominent cheek bones and deep-set eyes of the American Indian; and the tawny skin, coarse hair and peculiar Chinese cast of countenance of the Mongolian. The Cretin, who is sometimes

confounded with the last named, may be distinguished by the short, squat figure and pendulous abdomen, wide mouth, flat nose, etc. (Barr and Maloney, 1920, p. 3)

For other experts, the racial reminders were combined with animal characteristics. "Certain idiots, in their physiognomy, habits, and demeanor, resemble in a still more specific manner *certain species of animals*. Some strongly resemble apes, . . . others forcibly remind us of swine" (Griesinger, 1867, p. 379; emphasis in original).

Finally, idiots were dismissed as useless. Indeed, the essential means of diagnosis was a curious mix of medical or educational experts making economic judgments. Perhaps the most damning identification of idiocy was that which defined it as the state of being "incapable of performing any useful task" (Tredgold, 1914, p. 93). Increasingly throughout the nineteenth century, this notion of uselessness was understood in terms of economic value. The total lack of productivity made idiots a negative economic drain on the state, the family, and even the institution that claimed to be their proper destination. At its most basic level, the uselessness was compared to infancy. Idiots were "those who by reason of physical infirmities, such as epilepsy and paralysis, associated with profound idiocy, are so dependent as to need the same protection as we administer to infancy" (Fish, 1891, p. 99).

Early in the nineteenth century, a label of idiocy or imbecility (or any of the other terms for retardation of any kind) automatically meant a prognosis of failure in at least one of the three dimensions identified. All retardation was deemed beyond hope. As the century progressed, however, specialized professionals began to make distinctions where none had been made before. Some feebleminded people were newly claimed as belonging on the trainable—the curable—side of the continuum. It is not that they were suddenly not seen as bad or useless or repulsive, but that some were now said not to be so permanently. With the emergence of that distinction, the process of professional categorization and prediction gradually became a separate dimension of clinical chronicity in addition to the other three. Moral, aesthetic, and economic judgments were now joined by medical (and educational) judgments as well.

Whether people were judged chronically bad, chronically useless, or even chronically ugly, it was the chronicity of the judgment that was crucial to its effect and that ratified social dismissal. Increasingly in the period covered in this study, it was this added dimension of professional prognosis that validated the label "beyond help" as applied to the individual failures in the moral, economic and aesthetic life of the community. The point is not whether people were in fact incorrigible or incurable, but that being perceived as such by people in controlling positions is what determined their membership in the "chronic" class. I am not studying all members of that class, only those drawn from the ranks of people viewed as mentally retarded. I claim, however, that the determinative status is chronicity, not retardation. The most revealing comparisons for these individuals are with chronically mentally ill people, from whom they were increasingly separated, not the mildly or moderately retarded people with whom they shared accommodations. Treatment and training developed a hundred variations as professional expertise became increasingly specialized; sanctioned abandonment always looked the same.

A Definitional Justification

None of this excursion into the notion of chronicity is meant to deny that my study begins and ends with the history of severely retarded people. What I have tried to argue in this chapter is that a proper historical investigation of severe retardation cannot look solely at the evolution of a concept, nor only at the lives of those historical figures we would today hold to embody that concept. The power of the concept of severe retardation must be understood in combination with an understanding of the people subjugated by the use of that concept, or the even more oppressive one of chronicity. Therefore, to use the crass language of the era to be explored, this study will look at all of those who were ever called idiots, as well as at idiots whatever they were called. That is, I intend to include all of those people who today would be described as profoundly retarded or severely multiply handicapped. But I will also include those assigned to the custodial (that is, chronic) class, regardless of their functional characteristics.

Indeed, a major point of this study is a deeper understanding of how the category of severe retardation has changed over time. Even a diagnosis as somatically based as "apathetic idiocy" had a significant social component, and it involved the value systems of a changing society. The complexities of the sense and reference, the connotation and denotation, of words are present even when the biological limitations seem most overpowering. The admonition of Wittgenstein for a half-century of philosophers applies just as well for our approach to severe retardation: "Don't ask for meaning, ask for the use."[3] Here, then, we will study "the use of uselessness" as a concept for those at the centers of power and as a curse for those at its margins.

Chapter Two The Legacy of the Almshouse

The nineteenth-century history of increasing government involvement in the lives of people judged mentally retarded begins with the rise of the almshouse. The role of the almshouses in the history of social policy toward severely retarded people (and all disabled people), however, tends to be overlooked in many accounts of the topic. For most of the nineteenth century, there were more so-called idiots living in these county and city institutions than in the large state asylums. For the most part, their treatment in these almshouses can only be described as abominable; a sort of passive neglect was the best they could hope for. Neglect was especially preferred as a treatment for those people judged to be both insane and violent (going by contemporary descriptions, some of these cases would today be labeled retarded or autistic). The notorious "crazy cellars" or dungeons held these poor souls: naked, chained, without heat or light.

However, beyond confining many idiots, the almshouse is important because it began in both policy and practice the approach to chronicity that later became the basis of asylum organization for severely retarded residents. The connection between the almshouse and the later asylums on this conceptual level has simply not been adequately examined. Making that connection allows one to see that the segmentation of idiot asylum history into eras of optimism followed by custodialism overlooks the thematic strands of medical incurability, economic uselessness, moral intractability, and aesthetic offensiveness that weave their way through the pattern of nineteenth-century practice. Those strands were first stitched together in the patchwork of county and municipal almshouses that arose throughout the Northeast in the first half of the nineteenth century.

It is certainly true that people had made the basic distinction between acute and chronic before the almshouses hit their stride in the antebellum years, even if all of the various dimensions of that distinction had not yet been elaborated. The Elizabethan Poor Laws, on which earliest colonial poor relief was based, made a crucial distinction between those sick, "impotent," and unable to work on the one hand, and those sturdy but idle souls able to work but unwilling. "Suitable" treatment followed. As early as 1751, the overseers of the poor in Boston contrasted the able-bodied paupers with the "distracted, helpless and infirm people" (cited in Jimenez, 1987, p. 55). Too many of the latter group, the overseers argued, kept the workhouse from being self-supporting. Furthermore, the American reformers knew their history well enough to identify the ancestry of such divisions of the poor as were "still presented to our notice" (New York State Board of Charities, 1869, Annual Report p. l).[1] What occurred in the early part of the nineteenth century was that this distinction became intensified and focused in the specific institutional form of the almshouse itself. Very quickly that distinction revealed the impossible dichotomy of purpose that masqueraded as a unified policy. "There should be one rule for every poorhouse: Support for the infirm and helpless; hard work for the sturdy and strong" (NYSBC, 1869, p. lviii).

Unfortunately, even those reporting on the dismal results and the contradictory nature of the almshouses saw the solution in further specialization and intensification of service. The contradiction perpetuated itself. Dorothea Dix, an indefatigable investigator and spokeswoman on the evils of the almshouse for insane and idiotic people, made the people housed in the "crazy cellars" the focus of her numerous appeals for legislative action. In 1844, Dix visited New York to plead the institutional case even though the state had already established one such insane asylum in Utica. Her report on her visits to the counties of New York State is similar to many others she gave, yet affecting in its starkness. Dix's description of the accommodations for "a gibbering idiot, or a cowering imbecile, or perhaps a murmuring half demented creature" (Dix, 1844, p. 110) is bluntly

worded despite her constant "feminine" demurrals of embarrass-
ment. The solution for Dix was not to return the sufferers to their
families with ample "outdoor" support. She criticized family care of
disabled relatives even more harshly than she did the almshouses.
Instead, Dix became one of the earlier supporters of purely custodial
state asylums for the incurably insane and idiotic (Dix, p. 67).

This chapter will examine how in the short span of about 20 years
the criticisms of a Dorothea Dix in 1844 came to replace the
solicitations of a John Yates (secretary of state for New York) in
1824 to establish county almshouses to control and reform the idle
poor. From this examination emerge three main points that lay the
basis for the interpretation of developments in the idiot asylums.

First, almshouses established the ultimately contradictory aims of
deterring laziness, yet caring for the helpless in one and the same
facility. The tension in this approach carried over into a clear, if
unannounced, resistance of many poor people to the state's latest
efforts to control their behavior. Poor families, including those with
mentally retarded dependents, were not passive recipients of whatever poor relief the state and counties decided to give them. Some
basic and sketchy demographics of those who lived in almshouses
and of the changing composition of the inmates suggest that both
state policy and the adaptability of the working poor affected the
nature and function of the almshouse.

Second, the outcomes of chronicity were first institutionalized in
the push of the almshouse movement for firmer distinctions between
the able-bodied poor and the "truly needy," to borrow a phrase from
a more recent era. The connection of chronic poverty with the
officially proclaimed hopelessness of clinical prognoses began a line
in the almshouse that one can follow down through the idiot asylums,
perhaps even to policy debates of our own day. The spread of the
wage labor system and commercial competitiveness in both urban
and rural parts of the Northeast becomes a key to understanding the
unavoidability of the connection.

Finally, the outcomes of remedial futility and economic poverty
together bolstered a third outcome of chronicity (not new in itself), in
the form of custodialism as not merely socially appropriate but also
morally laudable. Custodialism, as a form of care, became the

virtuous response of civic fathers to the reproachable sloth or burdensome incapacity of the chronic poor. The almshouse started an American tradition of formalized custodialism in its more vicious forms that tied economic failure and social deviance to moral categories and individual inadequacy.

These outcomes of chronicity functioned, then, as nonthreatening, reductionist explanations of systemic failure. The institutionalization of mentally retarded people in America began with the almshouses in the eighteenth and early nineteenth centuries, not with the first specialized idiot asylums of the 1850s and 1860s. The transition from the almshouse to the idiot asylum as the approved receptacle for poor idiots was, in fact, marked more by the continuities of the two models than by the disruptions. The almshouse system remains today largely in the form of nursing homes for elderly poor people. The legacy of its past, however, still influences the terms of debates on how best to serve disabled people. That legacy begins in the colonial era.

THE COLONIAL ERA

In colonial times the connection between poverty and mental disability was overt and unquestioned. Disability was simply one of the many possible versions of dependency. Society did not become involved unless the economic stability of the family was threatened. Indeed, for practical purposes, the important distinction was one of dependency, not disability. The community concern was for those who, for whatever reason, could not make their own way in the world nor be carried along by their families. Whether it was because you could not walk or talk, or were old or orphaned, widowed or homeless, the etiology of your indigence was seldom an urgent question. What mattered to the community was, first, whether you were a resident or or not; second, who would care for you; and third, how the provisions for care were to be handled.

In 1637, in what is probably the earliest surviving reference to idiocy among America's settlers, one Ambrose Harmor of the Jamestown settlement wrote a letter to England. He requested the Crown to provide him with an estate because of his extra burden of caring for "Benomie Buck, an idiot, the first in the plantation" (cited in Hecht and Hecht, 1973, pp. 174–75). In Massachusetts in 1680–81, extended court proceedings were conducted to determine whether the town of Taunton or Plymouth should bear the cost and responsibility of caring for John Harmon, a "decriped" pauper (Demos, 1970, p. 80). Even in these earliest days, the institutional solution to communal responsibility for feebleminded citizens can be found. Perhaps the first retarded person to be institutionalized in North America was one Pierre Chevallier, admitted in 1694 to the Hospital General Charon in Ontario as a 44-year-old "innocent." He remained there until his death in 1735 (Griffin and Greenland, 1981).

Maintaining the Family

The first line of relief was certainly the family. However, disputes were fairly frequent over where responsibility rested when family support failed. The prevailing attitude does not seem to have been particularly sympathetic. One source reports that some communities forced the town paupers to wear brightly colored badges on their shirts, emblazoned with the letter "P" (Schneider and Deutsch, 1941, p. 4). While the basic procedure was common, at least in the Northeast, specific decisions over the nature and source of support became increasingly problematic throughout the colonial period and even into the 1800s (Yates, [1824] 1901).

Should the family falter, the normal community response was first to provide the support needed to keep the natural family intact. The town saw the stability of the family as usually the least expensive means of support, and thus maintenance of the family was viewed as fiscally prudent as well as Providentially ordained. "The catalyst for community involvement was the threatened disruption of the family unit; when insanity imperiled social stability, traditional criteria and means of relief were used. The needs of the insane and the needs of society were not in conflict and both were best served through supporting traditional roles for the family" (Rosenkrantz and Vinovskis, 1979a, p. 191).

One common means of local support for disabled people, then, was direct support to the family involved, in the form of either straightforward cash payments or allocations of food and other supplies from the common stock kept by many communities for just such purposes. If such aid was not possible—because the person either had no family or was too disruptive to remain at home—then the person might be "bound out," or assigned to a designated guardian within another household in the community. In 1651, Roger Williams wrote a letter asking the Providence town council to make some such provisions for a woman who had become "distracted" (Rochefort, 1981b, p. 113). By 1742, the Rhode Island Colony had officially authorized town councils to assume full responsibility for the care of mentally disabled people and to name guardians of their estates as well as of their persons, when needed.

Sometimes the secular authorities came into conflict with the churches. Mary P. Ryan's account of life in and around Utica in the early nineteenth century (1981) shows how the various churches might step in with aid if they thought the town too hasty in breaking up a family through the binding-out process. Rural New York was still relying on the old colonial procedures in 1823, when the case of a Mrs. Startman is recorded in the minutes of the business meeting of Utica's First Presbyterian Church: "Mr. White reported that the town poor master would not extend relief to Mrs. Startman and family without the liberty of binding out her children" (cited in M. P. Ryan, 1981, p. 23). The church moved in with some direct support in an effort to keep the family together. Whether natural or assigned, then, the family unit was the centerpiece of local relief efforts.

> The actions of both the town and the church, in binding out children and the granting of relief, were supplementary to a basically household method of providing for the dependent population. . . . Neither required an independent agency or institution, be it an orphanage or a welfare bureau, to intercede in the relations of family, church, and town. Both relied on the household, either that of a subsidized widow or the one to which a dependent child might be bound out, as the basic location of this social service. The aged as well as widows and orphans could be accommodated within this system. (M. P. Ryan, 1981, pp. 23–24)

The Treatment of Strangers

Another feature of colonial poor relief, and one that became increasingly troublesome for municipalities to administer, was the method of determining the residency of a pauper and thereby the town responsible for his or her care. Settlement laws governing such determinations became increasingly complex until by the time of the Yates report on New York in 1824 some 1,800 paupers—including 600 children—were moved from one town to another through legal warrants, at an expense "far exceeding $25,000." The cost of appeals by receiving towns added $13,500. According to Yates, the total expenditures in transportation and legal fees would have supported 1,283 paupers for a year (Yates, [1824] 1901, p. 946). Jimenez (1987, p. 54) reports that in 1762, Boston officials even paid the entire cost of sending an insane pauper all the way back to Guernsey rather than assume responsibility for his care. Towns often accepted responsibility for their own citizens with some equanimity, if not generosity. Poverty was part of God's universe, an unavoidable element of the community. However, any possibility that the legal residency of the person might be assigned to another town would usually be thoroughly explored. Responsibility to help extended to one's neighbor, not to strangers.

In their efforts to shave costs or avoid new ones, towns even devised methods to restrict the numbers of indigents further. Poor strangers were "warned out" of town before they could become legal residents. Some civic leaders apparently showed their fiscal responsibility by spiriting disabled, poor residents into the next town at night. Klebaner (1976, p. 596) reports that Onondaga County in upstate New York commonly smuggled paupers into a neighboring county in a conspiracy between justices of the peace and overseers of the poor. "Many Massachusetts towns were alleged to engage in the happy practice of providing for the able-bodied state paupers (from whom labor could be gotten) while sending along the aged and infirm of this category to Boston" (Klebaner, p. 596).

Gradually, various direct or indirect subsidies of cash or supplies to families of the poor came to be known as outdoor relief. The term referred to any response that kept the poor person outside the almshouse. Technically, such remedies did not include binding out, which, together with apprenticeship, became increasingly impracticable under the growing reliance on wage labor. Outdoor relief became the target of reformist criticism as wasteful and indulgent of vagrancy. For the truly disabled person, outdoor relief was said to be simply inhumane. A new system, the almshouse, spread from the largest cities to dominate the secular systems of poor relief in the first years of the nineteenth century.

The picture we are left with of colonial treatment of insane and idiotic people is direct and uncomplicated, if not especially benevolent. The poor were seen mainly as an ordained part of the social structure. For the disabled population, poor or not, there was often little optimism about improving their condition. For the wealthy, though, this was simply a private trouble, not a public issue (Mills, 1959). If medical treatment was even available, it was usually harsh, ineffective, debilitating, or fatal. The disabled poor were surely visible in the community and were often maintained at home as well. As with the poor in general, however, coercion, control, and cost containment could easily overrule even the reverence for family stability (Rosenkrantz and Vinovskis, 1979a, p. 91). There was certainly a willingness to shun, segregate, and secure the most chronic, unproductive members of the colonies, especially if they were also disruptive in some way. Nonetheless, the public approach remained a local issue, with only the beginnings of larger governmental involvement through the occasional almshouses and hospitals.

THE RISE AND FALL OF THE ALMSHOUSE

A Haven for the Dying and Disabled Poor

Only in such large population centers as New York City (1736), Boston (1664), and Philadelphia (1732) did the alternative of the almshouse become a major factor in poor relief in the colonial period. However, where it did arise, the almshouse from the beginning was the acknowledged last resort for the most troublesome or disabled cases. In most of these early almshouses, the largest percentages of cases were seriously disabled or infirm.

Rothman (1971) analyzed the records of 50 admissions to the New York City almshouse from 1736 through 1746 (all that have survived out of probably 200 total admissions). "One-quarter of them were lame or blind, insane or idiotic; another quarter were not only very old but infirm, sickly, and weak" (p. 39). From this he concludes: "It is apparent that the institution held the exceptional case. The New York poor did not live in constant dread of the poorhouse" (p. 39). Even if the general, able-bodied poor had no such dread, however, one must wonder if the disabled pauper could have been free of such fear. This pattern continued for the other early almshouses, too. The "Book of Daily Occurrences" for the Philadelphia General Hospital (or Blockley, as it was better known) describes its youthful admissions in particular as cases of "feigned deafness, idiotic children, consumptive children" and other victims of disease or violence (Radbill, 1976, p. 752). Bellevue in New York and Kings County Hospital in Brooklyn also functioned, for most practical purposes, as free hospitals and orphanages for the poor (Klebaner, 1976, p. 207). Indeed, the poor were the only ones who would have used a hospital at all. Throughout the nineteenth century, for most Americans, "the word 'hospital' evoked emotions from fear to sheer terror. Hospitals were frequently associated with the poorest class and the makeshift pesthouses for victims of the much dreaded yellow fever and cholera epidemic" (Mottus, 1983, p. 1). By 1800, then, the almshouse of the large city was, both in fact and certainly in common perception, a home for hopeless causes. That status was to change fairly rapidly in the first 50 years of the new century.

The Jacksonian Reform Era

The big push for almshouses coincided with the rise in institutional solutions for all types of devalued, or simply nonproductive, groups of people. The period from roughly 1820 to 1850 saw a massive shift in the direction of both welfare and educational policy in the Northeast. The first school for the deaf, the first school for the blind, the first reformatory, the first large public insane asylum, the first idiot asylum, all got their start in this period in Massachusetts or New York.[2] Public education gained momentum and gradually became accepted by families of both the lower and the expanding middle classes (Katz, 1976). Elite boarding schools for children of the wealthy began in this period. The number of hospitals almost tripled between 1826 and 1850, from 17 to 49 (Mottus, 1983). And, finally, there were the almshouses.

The almshouse went from an unpopular last resort in a few large cities and towns to the common practice of counties and cities across the Northeast and Midwest. In 1824, three years after the famous Quincy report, there were some 83 almshouses in Massachusetts. By 1850, there were 204 (Klebaner, 1976, p. 74). When Secretary of State Yates surveyed poor relief in New York State in 1824, he found that 30 of the 130 cities and towns responding reported having an almshouse. Following Yates's suggestion to move to a county system, New York had almshouses in 56 of 60 counties by 1857, not counting the municipal almshouses that continued in some of the biggest cities (Report of Select Committee of New York Senate, [1857] 1976). In fact (though the law was repealed 25 years later), New York in 1824 mandated the establishment in each county of both an almshouse and a county superintendent of the poor (Schneider and Deutsch, 1941, p. 7). By the 1830s, a mill town district in Pennsylvania would not show a trace of any disabled poor remaining in the town.

> Members of [the indigent poor] class of people were not visible in Rockdale, however, because, being unable to take care of themselves, they were for the most part housed in the "House of Employment" at Media, several miles away. This lowest group, physically extruded from the community and supported at public expense . . . , included the insane, the mentally retarded, the chronically ill and handicapped, young orphans, some deserted wives or widows with children too young to work, and no doubt one or two who simply could not seem to manage without constant supervision. (Wallace, 1978, pp. 44–45)

The official and unofficial calls for the installation of an almshouse system of poor relief almost always made two points. First, the care of lunatics, idiots, the aged, and infirm was said to be much more humane with centralized and enlightened administration and housing. One of Yates's major criticisms was that "idiots and lunatics do not receive sufficient care and attention in towns, where no suitable asylums for their reception are established" (Yates, [1824] 1901, p. 952). The second type of argument was the more negative one that "outdoor relief" was needlessly extravagant and unavoidably supportive of the very habits that produced the able-bodied pauper's indigence. Quincy concluded that "of all modes of providing for the poor, the most wasteful, the most expensive, and most injurious to their morals and destructive of their industrious habits is that of supply in their own families" (Quincy, [1821] 1971, p.9).

The town of New Bedford, Massachusetts, reported that much the same reasoning lay behind their decision to open an almshouse in 1817, and the point again emerges that the two reasons were contradictory and antagonistic. On the one hand, custodial but kindly care was to be given to disabled people and the elderly. Yet on the other hand, conditions were to be severe enough to deter able-bodied poor from even applying for admission. Furthermore, the almshouses were also to be workhouses. Once inside, able-bodied poor were supposedly to work hard and long in facilities designed to house the chronically helpless and unproductive. The ultimate goal was to firmly separate the unproductive from the marketplace, leaving a working class "stripped for action" in the newly competitive society (Braverman, 1974; Katz, 1984; Katz, Doucet, and Stern, 1982).

Initially, there was at least partial success for the almshouses. There was little humanity or kindness in their custody of the helpless, but the poor tried hard to keep from being admitted. Even though outdoor relief was drastically curtailed from the 1820s through the 1840s, the almshouses continued to be populated largely by the chronically dependent classes of people. Yates termed them "permanent paupers" and found that almost two-thirds (65 percent) of the New York City inmates fit the description, including 56 idiots, 35 "palsey," and 32 "cripples" (Yates, [1824] 1901, p. 1011). The Massachusetts Pauper Abstracts from 1837 to 1860 show from one-third to one-half of inmates as "unable to perform any labor" (Report of the Special Joint Committee, [1859] 1976). In 1848, the main Philadelphia almshouse had a total of 1,588 inmates, but only 79

in male working wards. More than 700 resided in the hospital and
lunatic asylum, and 540 in the wards for old men, old women, and
incurable (Klebaner, 1976, p. 211). Even the records of a rural
county like Seneca, in the Finger Lakes region of New York, showed
that from the township of Seneca Falls, some 61 percent of the
native-born men were classed as having some physical or mental
disability from 1842 to 1847 (Altschuler and Saltzgaber, 1984, p.
582).

From the other perspective, both newspaper accounts and observ-
ers' notes from the period make it clear that there continued to be a
widely held aversion among the poor to going to the almshouse.

The Failure of Reform: Poverty and Chronicity

In a shift that began by the 1850s, most of the almshouses in New
York State expended most of their relief on temporary shelter to
able-bodied but unemployed people. Evidence suggests that in many
locales, the working classes came to use the nearest poorhouse as a
place of shelter in the winter or as temporary respite at other times
when they traveled around the state looking for work. Lunatics and
idiots still made up a sizable portion of the almshouse population, but
they and the elderly were the only ones to stay for long stretches of
time (Altschuler and Saltzgaber, 1984 p. 577).

Still, in an 1856 survey of "charitable institutions" around the
state, a New York Senate committee commented on the continued
disdain of the almshouse by most poor people. The tone of the
remarks shows the humanitarian side of social welfare policy. In fact,
the report in its entirety is a good example of the dichotomous
instincts of reformers of this era that are so strikingly depicted in
Rothman's *The Discovery of the Asylum* (1971) and that were at the
contradictory core of the almshouse model. The reformers' optimism
in the curative powers of social engineering was matched by the
darker fears of creeping chaos if the lower levels of society were left
to their own devices. The poor were to be both comforted and
controlled in the attitudes of those calling for more and more
segregative facilities. If those attitudes were to accomplish their goal
in practice, confinement had to be made more acceptable.

Poorhouses, if properly conducted, might be what they were originally designed to be, comfortable asylums for worthy indigence. To suffer them to become unsuitable refuges for the virtuous poor, and mainly places of confinement for the degraded, is to pervert their main purpose; and the present management of them is such that decent poverty is virtually excluded until the last extremity of pauperism is reached, when the necessity of supporting mere existence compels it reluctantly to seek the scanty comforts of a poor house rather than to suffer the horrors of starvation outside. (Report of Select Committee, 1857/1976, p. 6)

Most writings of this era were not nearly so beneficent in spirit; for most, the phrase "virtuous" or "decent poverty" bordered on oxymoron. Even here, however, the antagonistic logic is conveyed. In colonial times disability entailed poverty or dependence; Either family or state had to step in to avert destitution. By 1850, the logic had reversed. *True* or *justifiable* poverty entailed disability, at least in the sense of explanation. The economic system would not allow capacity and effort to go unrewarded. This was the credo of the new commercial capitalists. Poverty, therefore, was either the avoidable result of individual laziness or intemperance, or, if unavoidable, the empirical proof of chronic incapacity. The continued existence of gratuitous poverty in the new culture indicated natural, not social, deficiency. Most poverty was the justified result of evil or indolence, not virtue; what poverty remained was the residue of disease.

It was poverty that had to be explained now, not disability. The moral dimension augmented the economic and clinical dimensions. This moral augmentation is captured only two paragraphs below the passage just quoted. The ethical dichotomy of purposes was unnoticed by the writers, to be sure, and even more powerful because the contrast is unintentional: "Although pauperism is not in itself a crime, yet that kind of poverty which ends in a poor house, unless it is the result of disease, infirmity, or age, producing a positive inability to earn a livelihood, is not unusually the result of such self-indulgence, unthrift, excess, or idleness, as is next kin to criminality" (Report of Select Committee, [1857] 1976, p. 7).

In a survey of Connecticut towns in 1852, the General Assembly found only one town attributing its rise in paupers to unemployment (another town rather tautologically found the cause of its increase in paupers to be a growth of poverty). Almost all of the 130 other towns replying attributed their pauperism to intemperance or immigration (Report of the Committee, [1852] 1976). Indeed, the very use of the noun "unemployment" to mean forced idleness was not to occur in print in America until 1887 (Keyssar, 1986, p. 4). Given the era's moral understanding of heredity, even lunacy and idiocy, if not the direct results of vile habits, were the inheritance of intemperate parents. Pauperism was a moral choice, even a physical disease, as much as an economic outcome.

The Failure of Reform: A Description

The almshouse system in New York by 1860, then, embodied all of the ambivalence and contradiction inherent in the attitudes and practices of those in power toward the poor, disabled or not. The almshouse also shows the systemic effect of the rise of capitalism, with its boom-and-bust cycles and its need for a fluid but quiescent workforce (Scull, 1979, 1980). Most particularly, the almshouse shows that custodial incarceration of idiots did not begin in 1870 or so with the decline of the specialized asylums, but rather was the continuing practice, and even policy, from the first almshouse institutions. As always, perhaps the most amazing numbers are those of the retarded people who remained in the community, living with family or friends.

Some basic numbers

Before interpreting these developments at more length, some simple numbers are needed to indicate where mentally retarded people were located in the middle of the nineteenth century. Table 2.1 is a compilation of results from the New York Senate Survey of Charitable Institutions published in 1857. The survey covered all of the almshouses in the state, including the facilities in Kings County (Brooklyn) and New York City (Manhattan). The table shows numbers of inmates at almshouses in eight selected upstate counties, both urban (Albany, Erie, Monroe) and rural (Clinton, Schoharie, Seneca) as well as the two complexes in Brooklyn and New York City. The numbers for New York City are incomplete since the

Table 2.1 Inmate Distribution in Selected County Almshouses of New York State in 1856

County	Avg. No. of Inmates	Children under 16 Yrs.	Lunatics	Idiots	Total No. of Deaths (%)
Albany	350	80	73	4	71 (20%)
Broome	45	5	21	11	1 (2%)
Clinton	65	11	6	10	15 (23%)
Erie	300	75	71	11	83 (28%)
Monroe	360	75	28	8	46 (13%)
Oneida	222	42	31	3	—
Schoharie	60	7	2	10	7 (12%)
Seneca	60	6	7	3	7 (12%)
Kings	1,365	424	205	9	342 (25%)
New York City (single building)	1,220	1,500	597	135	257 (21%)
State Totals	7,619	3,255	1,644	424	1,385 (18%)

Source: "Report of Select Committee Appointed to Visit Charitable Institutions Supported by the State, and All City and County Poor and Work Houses and Jails. *New York Senate Documents, 1857,* no. 8 (Albany: 1859).

"average number of inmates" figure includes only the single building specifically designated as the almshouse, while all of the other numbers for the city apparently cover the entire welfare complex on several islands.

For the entire state, the average was 4.96 idiots in each of the 55 county almshouses (not including New York City and Kings County), compared with 15.2 lunatics. Overall, some 5.5 percent of almshouse residents were labeled idiots, and 16.8 percent were labeled lunatics. If New York City and Kings County are included, the percentage stays the same for idiots (probably because of an almost certain underreporting in Kings County) but climbs to 21.5 percent for lunatics. At the time of this survey, the Idiot Asylum at Syracuse had been open for about five years and had 104 children in residence. By comparison, there were 424 idiots reported in the almshouses, although most of those were more than 16 years of age and technically ineligible for admission to Syracuse. The death rates probably speak for themselves. They confirm what the figures here do not show, that large numbers of elderly and infirm poor people continued to come—or be left—to die in the almshouses. For the entire state, some 18 percent of almshouse inmates died in 1856. However, even granting an enfeebled clientele, places where frequently more than one-fifth of the residents died each year were little more than segregated warehouses for the inconveniently old and ill.

The bluntness of the New York City Charities commissioners bluntly stated the policy that almost flaunted a death rate as proof of a job well done. "Care has been taken not to diminish the terrors of this last resort of poverty because it has been deemed better that a few should test the minimum rate at which existence can be preserved, than that the many should find the poorhouse so comfortable a home that they would brave the shame of pauperism to gain admission to it" (New York City Board of Charities and Correction, 1876, pp. viii-ix).

The range of conditions

The death rate numbers fail to indicate the conditions (especially for lunatics and idiots) that contributed to so many deaths. The reformatory spirit of the Senate report in 1857 led to specific descriptions of the accommodations of every almshouse. In general, the committee found:

> The treatment of lunatics and idiots in these houses is frequently abusive. The cells and sheds where they are confined are wretched abodes, often wholly unprovided with bedding. In most cases, female lunatics had none but male attendants. Instances were testified to of the *whipping* of male and female idiots and lunatics, and of confining the latter in loathsome cells, and binding them with chains. . . . In some poor houses, the committee found lunatics, both male and female, in cells, in a state of nudity. The cells were intolerably offensive, littered with the long accumulated filth of the occupants, and with straw reduced to chaff by long use as bedding, portions of which, mingled with the filth, adhered to the persons of the inmates and formed the only covering they had. (Report of Select Committee, [1857] 1976, p. 4; emphasis in original)

Of course, situations differed, and some almshouses were better than others. The Albany City and County Poor House was apparently one of the better ones. Its four buildings, including a pesthouse and a separate insane asylum adjoined a 216-acre farm, and all able male inmates were apparently expected to work the farm. Among almshouses, farm work was seen as a way of cutting the costs of maintenance and also of teaching good habits of work to the able-bodied inmates; the farm colonies used on many of the large idiot asylums several decades later originated apparently in the almshouses. Such farms, however, failed in their cost-efficiency goal at both the almshouses and the asylums. Whether industrious habits were learned is unknown. The Albany house even had a school for the children, with a full-time teacher instructing them in speaking, reading, and writing English. A physician's daily visits were supplemented by visits from medical students at the local school. And although no treatment was given for the lunatics and idiots, seven cases of insanity were listed as cured.

At the other end of the spectrum were places like the Clinton County House, located outside Plattsburg. One "dilapidated" building housed an average of 65 inmates. There was no ventilation system, but there were so many cracks and crevices in the walls that in the winter "snow blowing through the crevices forms banks" (Report of Select Committee, p. 36). There was no attempt to separate inmates by age, disability, or sex. Indeed, men and women were allowed to "mingle promiscuously." There were no knives and forks but perhaps there was little need. Until just prior to the inspection, the diet reportedly consisted of "pea and bran soup; Indian pudding and sweetened water" (p. 37).

There were 6 lunatics and 10 idiots who apparently received especially gruesome treatment. Two lunatics never left their cells and were chained to the floor, with straw for a bed. Balls and chains on some were also used for restraint. Whipping was practiced. The committee summed up their feelings that "this house is a very poor one, indifferently kept, and a disgrace to the county in which it is located" (p. 38).

The New York City Almshouse

Special notice must be given to the Almshouse Department of New York City. In size and complexity, it was an entity unto itself. Prisons, workhouses, hospitals, orphanages, insane asylums, so-

called "colored houses," and even an almshouse proper were distributed throughout the city. Between 7,000 and 8,000 people were
confined at any given time in the 1850s. Many of the specialized
asylums were located on small islands in the East River (Blackwell's
and Randall's). Although it was not yet officially listed as a separate
facility, there was separate housing for 28 idiots on Randall's Island,
near the nursery. When H. B. Wilbur was opening the state asylum
for idiots in Albany (later Syracuse), he reported visiting Randall's
Island to pick out some severely retarded children for his school. The
committee was impressed, although there is no indication that
anything other than separate facilities was given to these 28 inmates.
Certainly the committee recognized the helplessness of idiocy that
they saw at Randall's Island. "The committee were gratified to find
that this unfortunate and generally neglected class here received that
particular care and attention which their helpless condition requires,
and that it is intended to secure for them all the benefit that they can
receive from such special efforts for their improvements as are
deemed practicable" (Report of Select Committee, [1857] 1976, p.
164). Over 100 other idiots, probably adults or multiply handicapped
people of any age, did not receive these "special efforts."

THE LEGACY OF THE ALMSHOUSE: CHRONICITY AND CUSTODIALISM

By the end of the nineteenth century, almshouses were largely
poorhouses for the elderly, the institutional precursors of today's
network of nursing homes (Katz, 1984, 1986). By 1900, very few
people labeled as insane were still living in county almshouses: 39 out
of 5,602 total population in September, 1901 (NYSBC, 1901, pp. 70,
74). Some 540 "feeble-minded or idiotic" people still lived in county
almshouses, amounting to almost 10 per cent of the total county
almshouse population (NYSBC, 1901, pp. 75, 80). Certainly the
early hopes and good intentions of the Jacksonian reformers in the
1820s had long since gone by the boards. Almshouses were never
really "workhouses": self-supporting havens for the helpless and
vocational training for the idle. In their failure to meet stated

objectives, the almshouses' story is only the first of many disappointments resulting from the institutional path taken in the antebellum years. The purpose of reviewing that failure is to establish the connection of the almshouse to the idiot asylum, which followed the very same path. There is one continuous line of concept and practice begun in the straw-covered cells of the almshouse and continuing through the back wards of the specialized prisons called asylums for the feebleminded.

Three main points emerge from this examination of the role of almshouses in the nineteenth century. They outline a legacy for the idiot asylums that has been largely ignored by historians of mental retardation in the nineteenth century.

Contradictory purposes

First, the almshouse failed because, as pointed out by Katz (1984), the contradictory purposes were never reconcilable. From their earliest colonial incarnations, almshouses were meant as homes for the helpless. With the reforms of the 1820s, following the Yates Report in New York, the almshouse was also meant to serve the new function of imposing discipline and control upon the labor market. The able-bodied poor were meant to be deterred from even wanting to enter the almshouse, but also, once inside, to be put to work. Certainly, the figures show that the number of disabled people supported by the almshouses as a percentage of the total inmate census did go down.

The story was the same or similar outside New York. The Pauper Abstracts in Massachusetts show that the number of idiots in that state's almshouses declined from 370 in 1837 to 306 in 1858 (reaching a low of 280 in 1856), while the total number of state paupers during 1837–58 almost tripled, 4,846 to 14,016 (Report of the Special Joint Committee, [1859] 1976, p. 131). Despite this increase in so-called able-bodied poor, the almshouses were never self-sufficient. Indeed, in Massachusetts, the value of inmate labor actually declined (Report of the Special Joint Committee, p. 131).

Some recent studies of almshouse history suggest that part of the reason for these numbers is that the working classes gradually came to use the almshouses for their own purposes in their struggle to survive in the new economy. One study of Seneca County in New York shows clearly that while county officials were trying to use the almshouse as a kind of clearinghouse for redistributing paupers elsewhere, the poor were equally keen on using the almshouse as temporary shelter in moving from summer to winter, or from town to town (Altschuler and Saltzgaber, 1984). It was not just paupers who were using the almshouse, but also temporarily unemployed members of the working class. Increasingly the almshouses became almost a network of hostels for temporary respite as the unemployed traveled the country looking for wage labor. Based on the results of his detailed analysis of the Erie County Almshouse, Katz concludes:

> Its occupants, in general, were not passive, degraded paupers who drifted into poorhouses, where they lived out their lives in dependent torpor. On the contrary, most remained only for a short period. Whatever the official purposes of the poorhouse, the poor themselves put it to their own uses: in its early years as a short-term residence for native families in distress; and in later years, as a place to stay for a while during harsh seasons of the year, unemployment, or family crisis; as a hospital in which unmarried women could have their children; and, of course, as a place of last resort for the sick, helpless, and elderly. (Katz, 1983, p. 87)

From a narrower perspective, this change in poorhouse population reveals a pattern that repeats throughout the history of institutionalizing mentally retarded people; the rate of idiots left at large in the community remained much higher than the rate for the insane, with whom they were so often paired in statistics and conception. Whether or not the census data is reliable, the important point is that those who collected and those who reported cases of insanity and idiocy "saw" much more madness than imbecility about them. And the madness seemed to be spreading. As we saw, 21.5 percent of the inmates in New York in 1857 were classed as insane, compared with 5.5 percent for idiots (Report of Select Committee, [1857] 1976). The Pauper Abstracts for Massachusetts showed a decrease in numbers of idiots from 1837 to 1858, but the number of insane for the same period rose almost 60 percent. By 1857 in Massachusetts, the three state insane asylums housed an additional 400 insane paupers (Report of the Special Joint Committee, [1859] 1976, pp. 131–32).

Perhaps most intriguing of all is what Edward Jarvis (a colleague of Howe's and an important statistician of insanity) found in Massachusetts in 1855: of 1,087 idiots identified, fully 60 percent were independent, compared with only 42 percent of the insane (Jarvis, [1855] 1971, p. 100). The reasons for the relatively low rates of institutionalization of idiots compared with lunatics (examined more carefully in Chapter 3) are not entirely clear, but the pattern of admission clearly is one more source of continuity between the almshouse and the asylum.

Chronicity and poverty

Perhaps the most important distinction in an entire century of increasingly specialized distinctions among segments of the poor was that between the deserving and nondeserving paupers. It is here that the conceptual connection between chronicity and the economics of "uselessness" became institutionalized.

Several writers have detailed the changes in economic and social structure and their effects on welfare policy during the nineteenth century (Braverman, 1974; Katz, 1978, 1986; Piven and Cloward, 1972; Scull, 1979). For purposes of this study, the rise of commercial capitalism, not industrialization or urbanization—which came, for the most part, after the Civil War—best explains the need to rationalize and discipline a workforce new to the requirements of wage labor. As labor itself became a market in the new republic, much more careful welfare policies were needed that did not indiscriminantly reward both the truly helpless and the merely lazy or intemperate. Outdoor relief was seen as incompatible with a productive workforce. Centralized, "indoor" relief models replaced the distribution of "outdoor" payments as more controllable and more rational ways to give out support. The point was to deter the pauper, first from entering the almshouse in the first place and, failing that, to make sure there was a separation of those who should be working from those legitimately excused. The latter were an inescapable burden, but the former were both a threat to be subdued and a challenge to be reformed. Both groups were defined by their relationship to productivity and "contribution." Jarvis was plain on the important elements of relief for the "truly needy."

In whatever way we look at them, these lunatics [including idiots] are a burden upon the Commonwealth. The curable during their limited period of disease, and the incurable during the remainder of their lives, not only cease to produce, but they must eat the bread they do not earn, and consume the substance they do not create, receiving their sustenance from the treasury of the Commonwealth or of some of its towns, or from the income or capital of some of its members. (Jarvis, [1855] 1971, p. 104)

There was no obligation to feed without compensation those who were not idiotic, insane, elderly, or orphaned. The new system demanded that "want" should serve as "the stimulus to the capable" (Scull, 1980, p. 41). The rigors of working for the county initially seemed both to promise instruction in the proper habits of industry for the pauper and to make it clear that custody did not imply comfort as well.

Simultaneous with the rise of the almshouse system, and continuing through the century, there was a spreading intensification and medicalization of relief to the poor in the form of institutions for specific categories of disease or disability, administered by medical doctors who specialized in mental disorders, and centralized in terms of control by the state rather than by cities or counties. Carried over from the almshouses, however, was the clear distinction between those who were potentially productive and those who were not.

Chronicity and custodialism

The almshouse clearly established the connection between chronicity and custodialism as well. The descriptions of inspectors, even allowing for some self-righteous hyperbole, paint a harsh and dismal picture even of relatively well-run facilities. Certainly, some of the almshouses were no worse than the best-run asylum, and they had the advantage of closer ties to inmates' communities. Nonetheless, the almshouses quickly devolved into a system notorious for the cruelty of its treatment of those least able to fend for themselves. For a victim unfortunate enough to combine the problems of idiocy or insanity with epilepsy, violent behavior, or severe physical disability, then the prospects of life in an almshouse must have been nightmarish.

An adequate interpretation must go beyond pervasive sadism or moral obtuseness of poorhouse administrators. Rather, the contradictions of the almshouse purposes seem to ordain the ultimate triumph of deterrence and neglect as the mode of life in the almshouse. For someone identified as helpless or chronic, the conclusion is that treatment regimens are pointless. Custody is all that is required if the condition is truly chronic. Benign maintenance and caregiving were hardly ever encountered in almshouse existence, where care was grudging, minimal, and often needlessly abusive. The purpose of the custody was to make it as unattractive as possible, to "test the minimum" required for survival.

At the heart of abusive custodialism was the individualistic ethic essential to the marketplace. The ideology of the new republic was the meritocratic one of social equality. If equality is guaranteed by the social system, then any inequality that persists must be part of the natural order or its violations. There must be an explanation for failure that faults the individual, not the system. Temporary failure must be explained as individual idleness or weakness of will. Chronic failure also must be individualized as nature's version of bankruptcy, with blame implicit at least for the parents, if not the afflicted themselves (Figlio, 1978).

The moral element in the approach toward chronicity is social in origin, naturalistic (medical) in content, and individualistic in focus.

Custodialism was not the only legacy of the almshouse, but it was the one with the most practical consequences in the lives of those people left abandoned to it in the name of progress. As will become clear in the next chapter, the legacy of custodialism was carried over intact and uninterrupted into the "enlightened" era of the earliest specialized asylums.

Chapter Three The Rise of the Idiot Asylums, 1850—1890

In 1848, Sylvanus Walker became one of the first admissions to the experimental school for idiots set up by Samuel Gridley Howe in one wing of his school for blind children in Boston. Howe wrote about the boy, as did the first teacher at Howe's School, James B. Richards, who saw Sylvanus's "redemption" from the darkness of idiocy as an excellent example of what a persistent teacher (i.e., Richards) and a developmental model could accomplish in the "education of the feeble-minded" (Richards, 1885). The story is important because it marks a transition point in the history of official American social policy toward retarded people. Sylvanus stood, literally as well as figuratively, thanks apparently to Howe and Richards, at the inception of public asylums specifically designated for pauper idiots. He also stood at the culmination of efforts of zealous reformers such as his benefactor, Howe, to improve the status of every class of "degradation" to be found in the new republic. Sylvanus became a star.

If seen as part of the optimism of the first half of the nineteenth century, Sylvanus's story is merely a particularly striking example of the litany of "miracles" common in the reformers' writings. Lunatics became sane, vagrants became industrious workers, deaf and blind children became articulate and educated adults, and children of the poor rose from their ignorance and delinquency under the care of public schools. As discussed in the last chapter, though, the zeal of the reformer, however sincere, was soon eroded by a steady tide of uncured, uneducated, unemployed, and stubbornly unrepentant poor.

If seen in the context of the last half of the 1800s, Sylvanus's story is noteworthy for its rarity in a 50-year saga of official custodialism and actual abandonment of people with severe disabilities. The miracles disappeared from the asylum anecdotes. The potential of curing society's ills was replaced with the promise of protection from society's failures. Sylvanus Walker is emblematic of all that preceded his presence in Howe's asylum, and of all that quickly disappeared in the decades following his achievement. He is emblematic, as well, of a transition in social policy toward state control and increasing centralization that contrasts sharply with unchanged social practices of continued neglect and exclusion.

Howe described Sylvanus's condition when the boy first entered the newly established school:

> He could not stand or even sit erect. He had no command of his limbs, not even so much as an infant of three months, . . . but laid [sic] almost like a jelly fish, as though his body were a mass of flesh without any bones in it. He could not even chew solid food, but had to be fed on milk, of which he consumed an inordinate quantity. . . . He drivelled at the mouth, and his habits were in all respects like those of an infant. He was speechless, neither using nor understanding language, though he made several sounds, which seemed a feeble imitation of words. (Howe, 1851, p. 116)

Howe quotes a newspaper account of the change in Sylvanus's abilities after just two and one-half years of schooling, then makes his own assessment:

> "The boy . . . now sits, stands up, shakes hands, is pleased, and smiles, asks you how you do, and reads readily any part of a little book which was put in his hands less than three months ago, points out any word you ask for on the page, and does all this with so much pleasure, that when you are about to turn away from him, he asks to be allowed to read more, and eagerly reads to you his favorite passages."
>
> *This boy is not now an idiot; nevertheless, he was in a state of idiocy, and, to all appearance, of hopeless idiocy, when we received him* [emphasis added]. He was considered one of the most unfavorable subjects that could be found, and

taken because it was desired to have some of the worst as well as some of the best cases. . . .

    May there not be scores of such cases among the hundreds of idiots in our Commonwealth, who are now left in their brutishness, because they seem incapable of receiving instruction? (Howe, 1851, pp. 116–17)

Writing almost 40 years after the work with Sylvanus, James B. Richards gave voice to the optimism of that earlier era in what must have seemed ironic words even in 1885. Richards quoted what he himself had said to Howe after witnessing the first smile of recognition on Sylvanus' face: "If we can redeem one, . . . we will redeem them all over the country. We will open the doors so wide that every State shall pass an act to found an institution for these unfortunates, and every intelligent being shall feel that it is a privilege to enter into this great work." (Richards, 1885, p. 176) Every state did indeed eventually found specialized institutions for the "unfortunates." Richards's vision failed, of course, in that few souls would be redeemed by these state-sponsored purgatories.

History does not tell us what ultimately happened to Sylvanus Walker, and even what is told is difficult to accept. It is hard to believe both sides of the before-and-after descriptions. Could the boy truly have been as low-functioning as Howe describes, and if so, could he indeed have made the progress that Howe affirms? Indeed, Howe undoubtedly made his case as impressive as possible for the legislators who could further fund his school if convinced of its worthiness. Yet, writing some years later, after Howe's death and in the midst of an era that was very pessimistic (about mentally retarded people, Richards gave much the same description as Howe, with some disagreement on Sylvanus's age. It is easiest to see this case as a fluke. Indeed, that is how most superintendents of Howe's era came to view such early successes. Nonetheless, it still amazes that any effort at all was expended on Sylvanus. The optimism of Howe's endeavor, whatever the results, is remarkable even today.

Where did such optimism come from? How did Sylvanus come to be under Howe's and Richards's tutelage? More important, why were there no more like Sylvanus? As significant as were the early educational efforts of a few people such as Howe, Richards, and H.

B. Wilbur in New York, their importance lay as much in the aberration of their work from the norms of society as in their undeniable achievements with a few feebleminded children. Most people like Sylvanus Walker, even if less severely disabled than he, had no help from anyone like Samuel Gridley Howe. Indeed, even the optimism of Howe and other reformers quickly narrowed its focus to much more mildly disabled youth. The claims of powerful new therapies and habilitative techniques quickly adopted a logic that accepted the unimprovability of most people like Sylvanus, so as to ensure the drama of the improvable few.

Most histories of mental retardation divide the period roughly from 1850 to 1890 in two, regarding 1875 as ending an era of unmitigated heroes and laudatory practice. The years following 1875, in the usual chronology, betrayed the promise of the earlier practices.

Viewed from the perspective of severely retarded people and their families, that characterization desperately needs revision. Within the grounds of the idiot asylums, the optimism of the reformers merely echoed that at the consolidation of the county almshouse system and then again at the establishment of the first insane asylums. The optimism, again, rested on some oddly contradictory perceptions. The new elements of institutional specialization and professionalization rationalized those contradictions, but contradictions they remained. Beyond the walls of the new asylums of this era, life for most idiots changed very little. As with insane asylums, small, private schools for idiots catered to wealthy clientele, while most poor idiots lived in poorhouses, in some of the emerging hospitals, or at home. The few state idiot asylums functioned apparently as a last resort for a small percentage of the moderately retarded population. The debate over whether to consign those idiots and lunatics designated as beyond hope of cure or remediation to special, separate asylums or to combine them with their more mildly disabled peers in congregate facilities, raised the issues of professionalism, state responsibility, and the hierarchical class system's way of dealing with its marginal members. What developed, then, in these four decades was three paths to abandonment. Each path had its own logic and direction, but all ended in a custodial cul-de-sac. The journey in each case is, nonetheless, instructive.

ABANDONMENT WITHIN THE NEW ASYLUM: THE FALLACY OF THE GOLDEN AGE

The first two residential schools for idiots both opened in Massachusetts in 1848. One was Howe's "experiment," housed in a wing of his school for the blind. The other was the private school opened in H. B. Wilbur's home in the town of Barre. Most accounts date the modern history of mental retardation in America from the beginning of these specialized institutions.

Most histories also describe this period as one of enlightened care and active treatment or education. Admittedly brief, this golden age of humane care is usually described as ending by 1870 (Graney, 1979; Wolfensberger, 1975) or 1875 (Adams, 1971; Tyor, 1972; Tyor and Bell, 1984), or at least by the beginning of the 1880s (Scheerenberger, 1983). After this innovative start, according to all these accounts, the overseers of custodialism took over the asylums and began the long dark age of incarceration and cruelty that came to characterize American institutions. Most of the descriptions of these early years in asylum history paint glowing pictures of idealism and good will combined with innovative techniques (Hollander, 1986). The founders of idiot asylums are variously depicted as "indomitable individuals" (Whitney, 1949–50, p. 359) whose "compassionate and well-informed concern" (Adams, 1971, p. 23), together with "perceptive and purposeful" (Graney, 1979, p. 95) administration, led to educational facilities where the progressive outlooks constituted a "fresh, noble experiment" (Scheerenberger, 1983; Tyor and Bell, 1984).

The celebratory tone of these accounts rests especially on the figures of Howe and Wilbur. Howe's writings are evaluated as "remarkable" for both their thoroughness and their "eloquent" combination of compassion and understanding (Baumeister, 1970, p. 6). Wilbur was a "remarkable person, physician, and pioneer" (Scheerenberger, p. 120). If one focuses on attitudes toward severely disabled people, however, such assessments are "remarkable" themselves in the apparent disregard of the moralistic contumely and self-serving distinctions that characterize the writings of these two leaders (as well as others).

One danger in attempting to revise historiographical excesses is giving too much weight to the evidence in the opposite direction. It is far too broad a brush that would paint everything Howe and Wilbur did as nothing more than upper-class efforts at social control of unwanted deviants. Most of the superintendents (Howe is a notable exception) were not upper class at all, but rather part of a growing professional upper middle class that became increasingly influential during these decades (Bledstein, 1976). Moreover, it is undeniable that Howe, Wilbur, and Richards—assisted by Jean-Marc-Gaspard Itard's protégé, Edouard Seguin, an 1848 émigré from France—did pursue innovative developments in educating those previously thought completely unteachable in academic subjects like reading and mathematics (Lane, 1976; Shattuck, 1980; Talbot, 1964). Finally, the sincerity and honor of Wilbur and Howe are not in question here. The social context which their beliefs and actions took shape affected Howe and Wilbur in both obvious and subtle ways, both directly and indirectly. In other words, they were effective spokesmen for their era, and not only for themselves.

My point is not to question the basic morality of the early reformers' intentions but to illustrate how an exclusive focus on stated intentions can obscure the reality of events. Intentions, in themselves, explain nothing if isolated from the practices that followed them. This period is not adequately described as a golden age of institutions. Nor is it simply an example of good intentions gone awry. It is closer to the truth, if less succinct, to describe it as an era of mixed motives combined with traditional distinctions and new locales, all under the subtle influence of an increasingly industrial, corporational, and "scientific" society.

The Issue of Curability

Most recent historians have explicitly denied that Howe, Wilbur, and the other "founders" ever espoused the position that idiocy could be cured (Graney, 1979; Scheerenberger, 1983; Tyor, 1972; Tyor and Bell, 1984, Wolfensberger, 1975). Unlike their predecessors in the establishment of insane asylums, the idiot asylum leaders never got caught up in the unreasonable expectations of totally curing the condition of idiocy, according to this view. Scheerenberger (1983) is firm about the point:

> It should be noted that one of the persistent historical myths about Howe and other early American institutional leaders is that they intended to "cure" mental retardation; yet, there is no historical evidence to support that contention. In fact, Howe talked of improvement only, not cure. (p. 104)

Unfortunately, the issue of belief in the curability of idiocy is much too murky for unqualified assertions. When Howe talked of his results with Sylvanus Walker, he sounded very much as though some form of idiocy had been cured. "This boy is not now an idiot; nevertheless, he was in a state of idiocy" (Howe, 1851, p. 117). Wilbur reported similar results. Two boys he brought to Syracuse from Randall's Island progressed from being apparently congenital idiots who had almost no language and were partially paralyzed, to a level where both showed "as much intelligence as ordinary children of their age" (Syracuse, 1857, p. 26).[1]

Certainly, Howe and Wilbur also made many statements cautioning against false hopes, and from the earliest point they made the distinction between those children who could and those who could not benefit from remedial instruction. The most often cited statement of Wilbur's begins: "We do not propose to create faculties absolutely wanting; nor to bring all grades of idiocy to the same standard of development or discipline." However, he concludes the paragraph by claiming that the faculties of intelligence in the idiot "are not absolutely wanting" but simply "dormant and undeveloped" (Syracuse, 1852, p. 15).

Quotations pulled from annual reports of idiot asylums, or from public pronouncements with specific and occasionally competing aims and audiences, are probably not the best way to answer the question of whether the founders of the first "experimental schools" believed in curing idiocy. Indeed, the question is a narrow and distracting version of the mixture of hope and fear running throughout the reform literature of the period. Rothman (1971) has captured this ambivalence marvelously, yet the complexity seems lost in much of the mental retardation historiography. The tenor of the times definitely was one of confidence that intractable problems could be solved through enlightened management and application of scientific principles.

The same superintendents, or alienists, as they were called, who were proclaiming their 90 percent cure rates for people admitted to their insane asylums were among the first to spark interest in the European efforts with idiot schools. The professional association for superintendents of the insane asylums, the Association of Medical Superintendents of American Institutions for the Insane, appointed a committee to study the feasibility of idiot asylums in 1844 at its very first meeting (Jones, 1963). Isaac Ray, the prominent superintendent of the Butler Asylum in Rhode Island, reported favorably on European efforts to educate "these unfortunates" (Ray, 1846). The accounts of Guggenbuhl "curing" cretins at his mountain retreat in Switzerland were published in the major medical journals in England (Twining, 1843) and America (Brown, 1847). News of his work and the work of Seguin, Falret, and Voisin in France and Saegert in Germany was more than enough to get the enthusiastic attention of crusaders such as Howe, Horace Mann, and Charles Sumner in Boston (Barr, 1910; Fernald, 1893; Kanner, 1964; Scheerenberger, 1983). From 1848 to 1858, institutions for idiots were opened in Massachusetts, New York, Pennsylvania, Ohio, and Connecticut. Although only the asylums in New York and Ohio were entirely public facilities, all of the states represented assumed some involvement and financial responsibility for the education of feebleminded children.

The prevailing optimism of the time clearly applied to the reformers' work with idiocy. The optimism mirrored and enlarged upon what was deemed possible during the Enlightenment in Europe. For its intellectual descendants in America, the consequences of human action became more consequential. The contingency of everything except logical necessity was the belief of the utilitarian advocates of the new scientific society. Seguin himself was a socialist activist in France. His mentor, Itard, and his colleagues Esquirol, Voisin, and Flourens, were all equally active in the reforms following the French Revolution. An ideological receptivity to Seguin's optimism and to "scientific" techniques among American reformers like Howe helps explain Seguin's influence in the New World. Saegert and Guggenbuhl were more influential in England (Haskell, 1944; Kanner, 1964; Talbot, 1967).

Chronicity and Curability: The Symbiotic Relationship

Perhaps the fairest description of Howe's and Wilbur's beliefs is that, at least early on, they seemed convinced that they could indeed cure some people who were mentally retarded. Others, perhaps, they could improve but not cure. A third category of retardation they declared to be beyond hope of any improvement. Current historical assessments that diminish or deny the import of the curative claims for the first category of retardation may serve to enhance the standing of Howe and Wilbur as the enlightened founders of the best traditions among today's professionals. Unfortunately, these efforts to make the "heroes" of this story more palatable for today's cynical audience must also disregard the various purposes for which Howe and Wilbur, and every other superintendent of their day, intended their reports. The New York legislature had twice turned down a proposal to fund an idiot asylum, essentially for reasons of cost effectiveness (Brockett, 1855). Wilbur had to walk a thin line in convincing the legislators of the dramatic benefits of the state's continued funding while lamenting the impressive possibilities left unrealized for lack of more funds. Howe discussed the problem explicitly in 1857 in a speech given at the Pennsylvania Training School for Feeble-Minded Children (still in existence today as the Elwyn Institute), and he made a strong statement of incurability.

> We are sure then of final success; but, in presenting to the public the claims of the idiot for a share of its beneficence, we cannot urge those economical considerations which enter into the account in the case of the insane, the blind, and deaf. We cannot remove idiocy; and we must be careful not to hurt our cause by promising too much in the way of lessening its evils. Idiocy is a terrible, —it is radical, —it is an incurable defect. (cited in Royfe, 1972, p. 48)

There were intricate connections between the early optimism of people such as Howe and Wilbur and their steady conviction that some idiots were beyond hope. Fairly quickly after the early stories of Sylvanus Walker and a few other successes, the continuum of improvement and cure most often defended by this first generation of asylum heads seems to have become a vague application of a much tighter definition of success. A developmental standard of individual improvement fell away in the face of what Christopher Lasch (1973) has called the "single standard of honor" in the last half of the nineteenth century: economic productivity. Under this standard, very few of Howe's or Wilbur's charges could succeed. In the late 1850s, the talk was not of how even the lowest-functioning individual could benefit from instruction, but of how no one should expect economic self-sufficiency from any but a few of the mildest cases.

The change in Wilbur's tone after his first reports to the New York legislature would almost be poignant if not so self-serving. Improvement was irrelevant if productivity was not guaranteed, yet Wilbur had to explain his own failure to "produce" more successes. In the idiot asylum's very first annual report (Syracuse, 1852), Wilbur claimed that his admissions policy knew "no restrictions as to the degree of idiocy" (p. 12).

> The range of development [among those admitted] is from one who is but little below the lower grades of ordinary human intelligence, and who could not be taught to read, or write, or count, by the ordinary educational efforts for that purpose, down to one who cannot walk, nor stand, nor even sit alone; who cannot feed herself, has no idea of language, no fear of falling, faint perceptions of the objects of sight, and who would have starved to death with food within her reach and before her eyes. (p. 13)

Improvement in the most extreme cases would be limited, but still apparently worthwhile. Success in these instances would see the low-grade idiots improved but not cured. Yet even here the standard of economic self-sufficiency arose along with an early reference to custodial asylums. Such low level cases, said Wilbur, would be "rendered decent in their habits, more obedient, furnished with more extended means of happiness, educated in some simple occupations and industry, capable of self-support under judicious management in their own families, or in well-conducted public industrial institutions for adult idiots" (p. 20).

Within six years, Wilbur was appealing to the legislators, for more realistic expectations. "Candor, however, compels me to confess that in a State charitable institution it is somewhat difficult to please all parties who avail themselves of its benefits. . . . I doubt not, then, that a feeling of partial and temporary disappointment may have existed at the results in individual cases" (Syracuse, 1857, p. 13). By the end of the Civil War (in which some of Wilbur's pupils fought), improvement alone was no longer enough. Usefulness was the single standard, and those without economic potential did not belong. The optimistic notion of curability changed over time in relation to those deemed on the edge between curable and chronic, though not for those securely located at either end of the success-failure continuum. Curability shrank; chronicity grew; the blame for failure was aimed at an ever bigger target.

> Observing then [the pupils] in classes, it must be confessed that there is always one class, constituting perhaps twenty percent of the whole number, whose improvement is mainly confined to a change in their habits. In a strict construction of our by-laws most of these would never have been admitted, or if admitted, retained only for a brief period of trial. But in the absence of any proper custodial institution they are suffered to remain year after year a serious clog upon the progress of others. (Syracuse, 1869, p. 9)

The complexity of "curability" is an essential part of its conceptual connection to chronicity. The idiot asylums began within the cultural ambience of success and cure that was part of the reformist spirit of the first half of the nineteenth century. Severely disabled people were both included in and excluded from that context of cure. Chronicity was the boundary concept that allowed a specific, "scientific" definition of cure and improvement. After a brief attempt to base their optimism in the potential for development, the early reformers quickly adopted the economic standard of honor applied so overtly in the almshouse model. Given that switch, the connection between chronicity and poverty was reaffirmed within the more specialized confines of the idiot asylums. As economic utility became the distinction between success and failure, the ranks of failures inevitably swelled. However, the failure itself remained the responsibility of the uncured individual.

Chronicity, Morality, and the Medical Perspective

In addition to pessimism about who could be helped within the idiot asylum, there was also present throughout this period an underlying belief in individual culpability for one's status in life. Although certainly more pronounced after 1860, a rather constant refrain of moral disdain for defect in the writings of Howe, Wilbur, and others was sounded from the beginning. They repeated it often, whether the overall tone of their remarks was modest or optimistic. That refrain continued the almshouse perception of chronicity and morality as ineluctably entwined in the case of the most severely disabled people, reaffirmed poverty and custody as the unavoidable concomitants to chronicity. The more medically oriented writings of Howe and, implicitly, the briefer comments of Wilbur invariably affirmed that certain portions of the deviant group (in this case, the idiotic) were beyond hope, even when hope was defined in the broad sense of any improvement at all. If Sylvanus Walker showed dramatic improvement, it was because his idiocy was superficial only, not because true idiocy had been overcome. Of course, the usually unstated premise was that the ultimate way of identifying those who could not be helped was by finding that they were not helped. "The aim has been, so far as is possible, to admit those whose age and condition gave chance for improvement. . . . On ascertaining the existence of confirmed insanity, or epilepsy, or other disorders which are beyond the reach of the curative means possessed by the Institution, such children have been discharged to make room for other and more improvable cases" (Howe, [1858] 1972, p. 71).

Wilbur made much the same point a few years later when he iterated a distinction emphasized by Seguin between superficial and profound or congenital idiocy. Seguin's version of French empiricism argued that the basic mental faculties could be stimulated and exercised just like muscles. He also acknowledged (although dismissed as rare) that if disease had damaged the nervous system, then such stimulation was futile. Education, said Seguin and Wilbur, could overcome atrophy of the nervous system, but not malformation. Of course, brain damage was an inference one made if education failed, because otherwise, in this circular logic, education worked. When discussing admissions to his Syracuse Asylum, Wilbur described (Syracuse, 1864, p. 10) the connection of organic disease to idiocy as unfortunately frequent, even though he had earlier believed it rare. He mentions cases of organic defect, the specific conditions of which "are so beyond the reach of one's observation, are oftentimes so subtle in their character and pathological symptoms, that they can only be inferred, . . . by a failure after a fair trial of the most approved means to obviate them" (p. 11).

The overt explanation for chronicity was medical: a matter of lesions or brain damage. Unfortunately, except for cases with obvious behavioral or physical signs such as epilepsy or hydrocephalus, the presence of lesions was discoverable only retroactively. If therapy failed, that was simple proof that lesions existed. The connection of organicity with morality is implicit. Wilbur repeatedly stressed that the central defect of idiots was one of the "will," thus proclaiming the criminal tendencies of idiots some 30 years before Isaac Kerlin (a prominent superintendent from Pennsylvania) talked of "moral imbeciles" (Kerlin, 1884; Syracuse, 1852). As Wilbur described it, "the want of intelligence in the class we have to deal with, leads to the commission of crimes often of a serious character. The annals of crime furnish abundant and forcible illustrations upon this point" (p. 18).

Of course, the most severely disabled people did not usually commit crimes. They were the result of immorality, not the perpetrators of it. For this reason, Wilbur claimed there was no urgency in removing them from society. In the terms of the modern sociologist, Steven Spitzer, severely retarded people were merely "social junk," while more mildly retarded people were "social dynamite" (Spitzer, 1975). The latter, said Wilbur, needed to be removed before they exploded, while the former required disposal, but merely as a burden, not a threat.

It is not the drivelling idiot, utterly bereft of sense and helpless, who lingers out the few years of almost unconscious existence, that a very defective or enfeebled nervous system has but half vitalized; but it is the one comparatively healthy and active—the nerves or organic life not much impaired —

but yet deficient in intelligence, reason and judgment and with no moral
power to direct activity or resist temptation, whose animal nature, always
predominant, at last becomes imperious, that society should most concern
itself about, in anticipating the future, by precautionary measures. (Syracuse,
1863, p. 18)

From the time of his first attention to the matter in 1846, Howe
seems very clear about the connection of morality to defect. And the
worse the defect, the greater the iniquity that caused it. Through
idiocy, Howe argued, the sins of the parents were visited on their
children. Still, idiocy was the result of sin, the violation of natural
laws. Heredity for Howe included the inheritance of acquired
characteristics. Therefore, the drunkenness of the father, or lust
of the mother, was passed on to the children as the defective constitution characteristic of severe idiocy. In his report to the Massachusetts legislature about the causes of idiocy, Howe ([1858] 1972)
was adamant. "It may be assumed as certain," he said, that in all
cases of idiocy (as well as deafness and blindness), "the fault lies
with the progenitors. Whether they sinned in ignorance or in
wilfulness matters not as to the effect of the sin upon the offspring"
(pp. 4–5).

Howe elaborated the "medical" side of idiocy, whereas Wilbur
focused on the developmental or "educational" elements of the defect.
Indeed, Howe went on at some length about how morality and
physical structure were combined. Howe's biology combined a
somewhat revised version of the medieval doctrine of "humoral"
determination of basic personality traits with the more controversial
claims of phrenology—a then popular theory that he endorsed
without naming (Howe, [1858] 1972, p. 12–37). People tended to
possess temperaments based on the dominance of one of four
biological systems. A lymphatic constitution showed the dominance
of the glandular system and evinced itself in people who were lazy
and who slept and ate a lot. Obviously, some of the most severely
disabled people fell into this category for Howe. He describes (in
terms strikingly similar to those he had earlier applied to Sylvanus
Walker) one such case as "a wretched being . . . so deficient in
nervous energy that he lies almost as powerless as though he were a

mass of jelly, without a bone or a muscle in his composition" (p. 8). A fibrous constitution was muscular and bony. A nervous person, dominated by the brain and nervous system, could be unstable and subject to bouts of insanity. Finally, the sanguine person showed the dominance of the arterial system and usually had the most balanced and desirable temperament of the four.

Thus Howe found external signs of internal structure (in behavior and cranial bumps or head size). The moral connection was that passion and mentality were direct causes of internal structure. The five causes of idiocy show the moral reductionism of Howe, as well as the obsession with sexual behavior:

1. Low condition of physical organization of one or both parents;
2. Intemperance;
3. Self-abuse (i.e., masturbation);
4. Intermarriage;
5. Attempted abortion (pp. 25–37).

Poverty only exacerbated the problems of immorality. Indeed, Howe and his peers viewed poverty as but one more sign of individual weakness. Poverty worsened the chronicity of the idiocy, but it was poverty as a character flaw, not as a social injustice. Edward Jarvis, a close friend of Howe, described the connection well:

> Poverty is an inward principle, inrooted deeply within the man, and running through all his elements; it reaches his body, his health, his intellect, and his moral powers, as well as his estate. . . . Hence we find that, among those whom the world calls poor, there is less vital force, a lower tone of life, more ill health, more weakness, more early death, a diminished longevity. There are also less self-respect, ambition and hope, more idiocy and insanity, and more crime, than among the independent. (Jarvis, [1855] 1971, p. 52)

Here we have the medical and educational versions of individual moral responsibility described earlier as part of the almshouse legacy. In the case of the almshouse, social equality was guaranteed; therefore, any instances of inequality must be part of the natural order or violations of its laws. In the idiot asylums, the new regimen of specialized training improved the idiot's ability to function in society. Therefore, lack of improvement must stem from the organic, diseased, incurable status of the individuals. Once that determination was made, of course, their presence in a curative facility was unfair and distracting. By the early 1860s, Wilbur reported his reasons for dismissing people with little elaboration.

> An idiot of low grade, unable to walk, feeble in health; dismissed as incurable after eight month trial. . . . An idiot of low grade, filthy in his habits, helpless and sickly, with no idea of language, not even knowing his own name. . . . A boy whose head was exceedingly small; in fact smaller than any on record except those of Aztec [i.e., microcephalic] children. (Syracuse, 1862, pp. 11–12)

In Wilbur's explanation of his reasons for expelling those recalcitrant enough not to improve while under his tutelage, the irony is thick: There were more than enough proper candidates for admission to his school to justify abandonment of the unteachable low grades.

> It seems to me very desirable that all those of the present number in this asylum who have proved to be unteachable, or who have made all the improvement that can reasonably be anticipated in their case, should be at once dismissed, and, for the future, that whenever, after a fair trial, a pupil is found, from disease or otherwise, insusceptible of improvement, he should be removed to make room for better subjects. (Syracuse, 1864, p. 13)

Later historians have echoed a eulogy describing Wilbur as one for whom "no human being was too lowly or degraded for his notice" (Brown, 1884, p. 295), but such assessments neglect to point out that eviction was the only "notice" Wilbur gave to the most severely disabled people who found their way to his facility at Syracuse. At best, Wilbur approached these chronic inmates with a reluctant endurance of their continued presence in the asylum. For Howe, the moral essence of idiocy was always prominent and indissolubly connected with the presence of chronicity. For both of these early founders, the Sylvanus Walkers became the exception that proved the rule: idiocy is as idiocy does. If it does not do well enough, then abandonment is justified.

ABANDONMENT BEYOND THE ASYLUM

The Limits of Significance for the Idiot Asylum

Even if the efforts of Howe and Wilbur had, in fact, constituted a golden age, that age would have affected very few people. The single, overwhelming feature of the changes in policy toward retarded people between 1850 and 1875 is that they led to very little change in the daily lives of most of those individuals. Most mentally retarded people, especially those with severe retardation, continued to live in almshouses, with their families, or elsewhere in the community.

One of the few historical reviews to discuss this issue mentions the consistent gap between professional opinion and actual public practice toward retarded people (Lakin, Bruininks, and Sigford, 1981). What the authors say specifically about the eugenics panic in the twentieth century applies even more to the third quarter of the nineteenth century: "Despite the highly publicized comments of the 'leaders in the field,' which reviews of literature often present as dominating social policy in regard to the mentally retarded, never were policies implemented which attempted to remove systematically persons from the community solely because they were considered to be mentally deficient. Indeed, at times one must infer the posture of society from the degree to which the publicized proposals of experts were not acted upon" (p. 32).

The easiest way to demonstrate the persistence of living patterns is by using the demographics of this era. The relationship between the perception of social problems and the inclination to measure quantitatively the extent of those problems is something sociologists, as well as historians, have long noted (Katz, 1983; Kitsuse and Cicourel, 1963; Marks, 1974) It is not surprising, then, that coinciding with the rise in reformatory zeal in the first half of the nineteenth century was a growing enthusiasm of government officials ("statists") to collect numbers about aspects of government ("statistics"). It is more than coincidental that the 1840 census was the first to try to tabulate the number of insane and idiotic citizens in the country. In 1850, just as the first separate asylums for idiots were opening, so was the census keeping separate counts of idiotic and insane people for the first time. From the crude counts of the Yates Report in 1824 to the comparatively exhaustive efforts of Frederick Wines for the 1880 census, the numerical tracking of deviant populations is a mathematical mirror of contemporaneous social anxieties (Cohen, 1981).

The numbers are a reminder that relatively few people lived in the idiot asylums between 1850 and 1880. Wilbur's New York asylum opened its doors in 1851, the second such facility in the country. Wilbur was still the superintendent for the asylum when its 25th annual report was filed. The average population of the asylum for 1875 was 210, of whom 180 were "state pupils," or nonpaying residents (Syracuse, 1876, p. 2). Yet even in the earliest reports, the trustees of the Syracuse Asylum estimated that more than 700 idiots of "school age" (between 7 and 14 years old) needed institutional services in New York (Syracuse, 1853, p. 6). By comparison, for 1875 the average was more than 1,700 inmates in the three main state insane asylums (Utica, Hudson River, and Willard), not to mention the 300 or so in private asylums (Grob, 1973, pp. 384–87; NYSBC, 1873, p. 95). Howe's asylum in Boston was even smaller. Even by 1883, only 140 pupils were there, 55 of them state-supported, the others private (Raymond, 1948). In the 35 years after its opening, the Boston asylum authorization for poor idiot children went from 10 to 55 — hardly an overwhelming mandate. Sylvanus Walker was indeed the exception to the rule.

The imbalance between idiocy and insanity in the population continued in both the state and federal censuses. The federal census showed an increase in idiocy in New York State of almost 49 percent from 1850 to 1870. For the entire nation, the increase was about 55 percent. The corresponding figures for insanity were 151 percent and 139 percent (Table 3.1). Clearly, even allowing for the gross inaccuracies, which presumably affected idiocy and insanity rates similarly, the nation and New York State were much more attuned to examples of insanity than of idiocy. Idiots at large in the community were apparently not particularly threatening.

In 1873, Charles Hoyt, the secretary of the 6-year-old New York State Board of Commissioners of Public Charities, published the results of a year-long survey of upstate New York (NYSBC, 1873).

Table 3.1 PREVALENCE OF INSANITY AND IDIOCY IN UNITED STATES AND NEW YORK STATE, 1845–1880

Year	U.S. Census		New York State Census	
	No. of Idiots	No. of Insane	No. of Idiots	No. of Insane
1845	—	—	1,610	2,521*
1850	15,787	15,610	1,665	2,521
1855	—	—	1,812	2,742
1860	18,930	24,042	2,314	4,317
1865	—	—	1,451	3,114
1870	24,527	37,432	2,486	6,353
1875	—	—	2,392	8,091
1880	76,895	91,959	6,084	14,055

*Number from 1850.

Once again, the focus of concern was the number of lunatics and idiots left at large in the various communities (Table 3.2). City and county almshouses continued to dominate in the institutionalization of idiots. Some 27 percent of the total number of idiots resided in the almshouses, while only 6 percent were at the idiot asylum in Syracuse. The rate of insane people in city and county almshouses was even higher, 52 percent. However, several of the larger cities and a few of the counties (e.g., New York City and Kings, Monroe, and Oneida counties) had facilities specifically designated as insane asylums and were approved by the state to maintain adult paupers who were chronically insane. In the Hoyt figures, the number of identified idiots in the "custody" of friends or family far exceeded the number of those in institutions of whatever type. According to Hoyt, some 67 percent of the idiots in New York continued to reside in the various communities some 60 years after the Yates report first called for their removal to almshouses, and 20 years after the first state provisions for their control. By contrast only 23 percent of the insane remained in the community.

This survey, of course, long preceded the term "moron," or mildly retarded person, that was to account for three-fourths of all feeble-minded people in the twentieth century. The survey even preceded the obsession with the "moral imbeciles" that sprang up in the 1880s

Table 3.2 Hoyt Report: Custody of Idiots in Upstate New York, 1873

Place of Residence	No. of Males	No. of Females	Total No. (%)
Homes of family or friends	959	597	1,556 (67%)
State asylum (Syracuse)	74	63	137 (6%)
City almshouses	109	76	185 (8%)
County almshouses	213	221	434 (19%)
Total	1,355	957	2,312 (100%)

(Kerlin, 1884). In other words, most of the people Hoyt reported as idiots were probably at least moderately retarded. In functional terms, only those who were noticeably deficient drew the attention of neighbors and local physicians, who in turn reported them to Hoyt. The numbers in Hoyt's report are similar to the results for New York State obtained by the 1870 federal census. Hoyt found 2,312 idiots, while the federal census found 2,486. The common-sense approach to identifying idiocy that was used in both surveys is succinctly presented in the instructions to enumerators for the federal census: "The fact of idiocy will be better determined by the common consent of the neighborhood than by attempting to supply any scientific measure to the weakness of the mind or will" (cited in Gorwitz, 1974, p. 181).

There are other indications in the data of the State Board of Charities of where severely retarded people were living and how they were treated in this supposed golden age of service reform. Many counties and private charities during this period were developing hospitals to go along with their almshouses. Even in the 1880s, hospitals were still places where mainly poor people went (Rosenberg, 1981; Vogel, 1979). Wealthy people and the new middle class regarded the home as the proper environment for medical treatment. One of the groups starting to find the way into county and city hospitals were multiply handicapped children. Indeed, the largest concentration of "crippled and deformed" pauper children in October 1873 was the 146 distributed among the 46 hospitals in the state, mainly in the new orthopedic hospital for the "ruptured and crippled" in Manhattan (NYSBC, 1874, p. 41). It is not clear how many of these children were also considered idiotic or feebleminded. Nonetheless, it seems likely that some of them were mentally retarded, at least functionally. Some of the 146 severely physically disabled children (mild physical disability was classified under "paralytic") must have also been included in the 93 cases of idiocy reported by the hospitals. Unlike many of the specialized orthopedic hospitals and convalescent homes that sprang up around the larger cities after 1875, the New York City Hospital for the Ruptured and Crippled apparently had no formal restrictions that excluded feebleminded children from care (Reeves, 1914).

The Continuing Dominance of the Almshouse

The almshouses continued to hold more idiots than any other congregate setting in New York State (Table 3.3). By 1876, a total of 471 idiots was reported living in county almshouses and 186 in the city facilities. By 1882, the State Board of Charities was concerned that the state almshouses had become too comfortable for the chronic inmates:

> It is gratifying to observe that a gradual improvement in most of the poorhouses throughout the State is being effected. With few exceptions, accommodations and care for the chronic and incurable paupers, often such from inclination and choice, are all, and in some instances even more than their condition requires; thus stimulating the growth of pauperism by rendering dependence pleasing and attractive. For the curable or hopeful class, however, the hospital accommodations in most counties are greatly deficient, and in some of them wholly inadequate. The greatest evils appear to be: the congregating of the curable with the incurable; . . . and the absence of a proper system of registration of the sick. (NYSBC, 1882, p. 32)

Whether a pauper's condition is chronic through "inclination" or true infirmity—through moral laxity or natural defect—the state's response is now seen as extravagant. Even though the provisions for the incurable are said to be too nice, they become inadequate when viewed as the receptacle of the curable. The curable are mixed with the incurable, and that is seen as a problem. The facilities shared by the two groups are too nice for one and inadequate for the other.

Table 3.3   Distribution of Selected Disability Categories
among Almshouses in New York State, 1872–1878

Category	County Almshouses				City Almshouses			
	1872	1874	1876	1878	1872	1874	1876	1878
Idiots	339	395	471	323	189	200	186	257
Lunatics	1,239	1,394	1,456	1,615	2,168	2,396	2,667	3,335
Blind	150	174	149	149	–	105	109	133
Deaf	47	65	37	34	–	8	9	10
Total population*	6,338	6,774	6,548	6,841	8,500	8,557	8,686	9,203

*Total for all residents, with or without disabilities.

The biggest, and in many respects the worst, facility for idiots in
New York State was undoubtedly the buildings on Randall's Island
under the aegis of the New York City almshouse. It is not clear when,
exactly, the variety of children's buildings on this island in the East
River began to separate out idiots into segregated housing. When
Wilbur was selecting his first students for the new idiot asylum in
1851, he reported going to Randall's Island to bring back two of the
lowest-functioning children there. Together with the insane asylums
on Blackwell's and Ward's Islands, the orphanage, infant hospital,
and idiot buildings on Randall's Island had a terrible reputation
(Grob, 1973, pp. 118–123). Many of the attendants were inmates
from the prison, workhouse, or almshouse. The woman who came to
dominate New York City welfare reform, Josephine Shaw Lowell,
reported on a visit to Randall's Island.

> This [the building for "incurable idiot boys"] is the most discouraging place
> on Randall's Island, both for officials and visitors. The boys are helpless and
> often younger ones, and two men have charge of those who are nearly or quite
> grown up. They sleep in one large dormitory on straw beds, or on cots
> without sheets or pillow-cases, lying on rubber sheets with blankets over
> them. Two work-house women take care of the room and wash the beds, etc.
> It is a painful place. (Lowell, 1882, p. 312)

All told, Lowell found 212 people among the various idiot classes
on Randall's Island, out of a total of 1,181 (Lowell, p. 309). For those
who were poor, severely retarded, and also epileptic or physically

handicapped in New York City in 1875, the possibility of ending up on Randall's Island was much more real than being sent upstate to Syracuse. The idealism and innovation that supposedly characterized this era of reform in mental retardation drowned in the East River as far as the New York City poor were concerned. Although most mentally retarded people remained at home, those ending up in the almshouse or the new hospitals were confirmed in their chronicity by their very residence. The abandonment continued during this supposed golden age of care, both within and beyond the walls of the new asylums.

ABANDONED IN SEPARATE ASYLUMS: THE DEBATE OVER SEPARATE OR CONGREGATE FACILITIES

Beginning in 1867 the New York State Board of Charities, along with various reform and professional groups, became entangled in a 25-year argument with the superintendents of insane asylums. Wilbur, the superintendent of the only idiot asylum in the state aside from Randall's Island and a couple of small private homes, sided with the Board of Charities in this debate. The nature and interpretation of that debate has been ably told by several recent studies (Dwyer, 1987; Gitlin, 1982; Grob, 1983; Tomes, 1984). The relationship of that policy debate to the somewhat later arguments over asylums for the feebleminded has not been adequately explored, however. Beginning with the Willard Report in 1865 (Willard, 1865) and ending with the State Care Act of 1890, the state policy toward separate asylums for the chronically insane — indeed, for chronicity in general — was an exercise in saying one thing while doing another. But it also shows the early antagonisms of professionalization toward a generalist monitoring system.

The State Board of Charities

One of the keys to understanding this debate is the rise of the State Board of Charities. Following the example of Massachusetts in 1863,

New York established an eight-member board of commissioners in 1867. The positions were unsalaried and nonprofessional. The idea was basically to create a citizens' monitoring group to inspect state institutions and make recommendations to the legislature. Well-known figures of philanthropy and social reform such as William Letchworth and Josephine Shaw Lowell were appointed early on and quickly established the activist tone that the board maintained for its first 15 or 20 years (Grob, 1973; Schneider and Deutsch, 1941).

As early as 1869, the board was calling for the "abandonment" of both the chronically insane and the chronically idiotic to segregated asylums (NYSBC, 1869, p. xxxv). They wanted to empty the almshouses and state asylums of all those deemed beyond hope and to reserve the existing state hospitals and schools for acute, educable patients. Such a two-tier system of confinement was seen as more efficient and less expensive. Generosity was to be shown to the curable class, with "a greater outlay for buildings securing extended classification and hospital conveniences," and whatever other "remedial and corrective agencies as are designed to effect recovery" (NYSBC, 1879, p. 41). However, the chronic class of people

> require custodial accommodations only, and the buildings for these should be designed at the lowest possible cost consistent with their proper oversight and care. These buildings should be plain, comfortable and durable, and properly adapted to their purposes, but without ornamentation or embellishment. . . . Any expenditure for this purpose, beyond these simple requirements, becomes burdensome, and by rendering dependence too attractive, serves to encourage a desire for continuous residence and constant support on the part who accept public aid, and thereby extends pauperism. (NYSBC, 1879, pp. 41–42)

Initially, the board used an 1865 study of the terrible conditions of insane paupers in the county almshouses (Willard, 1865) as the basis of its call for a system of separate chronic asylums. The first such asylum in the nation, the Willard State Asylum for the Chronic Insane, opened in Ovid, New York, in 1869, despite the strong opposition of John Gray, superintendent of the Utica insane asylum (Dwyer, 1987). There followed a fairly busy period of asylum building in the state. By 1881, there were six state insane asylums. Two were for chronic cases (Willard and Binghamton), and four were assigned acute cases (Utica, Buffalo, Hudson River/ Poughkeepsie, and Middletown). In addition, the custodial asylum for feebleminded women had opened in 1878 in Newark, New York, near Rochester, although not officially distinct from the Syracuse Asylum until 1885.

Wilbur's Support of Separate Asylums

Separate custodial institutions like Willard Asylum were strongly opposed by most insane asylum superintendents. Their professional organization, the Association of Medical Superintendents of American Institutions for the Insane (now the American Psychiatric Association), passed numerous resolutions against such separation (Gitlin, 1982; Grob, 1983; Tomes, 1984). Gray, the head of the Utica Asylum and editor of the *American Journal of Insanity*, editorialized at one point that the Willard Asylum must have resulted from the legislators being distracted by the Civil War (Willard Asylum, 1865). What Gray wanted instead was what came to be called the cottage, or congregate, arrangement, under which new hospitals would accept a whole range of patients other than acute cases. Of course, all of the less desirable cases would be carefully confined in "cottages" separated from the other buildings. Each hospital should have an adjacent farm. Thus, the financial savings could still be had.

As superintendent at Syracuse, H. B. Wilbur was at odds with most of his peers in other states in his response to this debate. Wilbur was a bitter critic of Gray's administration at Utica (Graney, 1979; Grob, 1983; Wilbur, 1876). Together with Edouard Seguin's son, Edward, several other members of the burgeoning profession of neurology, and some lay charity workers, Wilbur was active in the brief but notable asylum reform efforts of the National Association for the Protection of the Insane and the Prevention of Insanity, formally organized in 1880.

Wilbur's main criticisms of the existing state insane asylums were that the superintendents of these facilities overused restraints on their inmates, were unscientific in their approaches, and allowed their asylums to become grossly overcrowded (Blustein, 1981; Spitzka, 1878a, 1878b). Wilbur was vigorously in favor of establishing a facility of 1,000 beds or more, such as the Willard Asylum. Gray's opposition was but one more example of his opposition to asylum reform, according to Wilbur.

Wilbur proposed sending the inmates of his idiot asylum to Willard also, using the facility as a sort of all-purpose chronic asylum. In his annual reports for 1869 and 1870, Wilbur endorsed the Willard plan and mentioned an existing building on the Ovid site that could be used for unteachable idiots. "It would seem," he argued, "as if the mere presentation of the facts would suffice to ensure the necessary legislation" (Syracuse, 1870, p. 12). Wilbur said the accumulation of unteachable inmates at his idiot asylum "embarrasses the general management" (p. 11). The Board of Charities endorsed Wilbur's proposal and reported that the superintendent at Willard also approved (NYSBC, 1869). Although no transfer of inmates from Wilbur's asylum to Willard took place, later admissions to the asylum at Rome, New York, indicate that a significant number of idiots and imbeciles somehow made their way into Willard.

The striking feature of Wilbur's approval of the Willard plan is his clear endorsement of the State Board of Charities view that a horizontal classification across diagnostic categories into acute and chronic classes was more important than the vertical classification by disability groups such as insanity, feeblemindedness, and epilepsy. Nor was his view on this issue limited to the Willard asylum.

The Newark Custodial Asylum, begun as an adjunct of Syracuse in 1878, was endorsed by Wilbur after Josephine Shaw Lowell called for such a facility as a necessity (Stewart, 1911; Tyor, 1972). In a report to the newly formed association for superintendents of asylums for feebleminded persons, Wilbur stated that he knew from the beginning of his asylum that some form of custodial care would be needed. As contended earlier in the chapter, custodialism never disappeared for severely handicapped people. The report also shows Wilbur disingenuously distancing himself from the decision not to build separate cottages for custodial care on the grounds at Syracuse. Wilbur ruled the Syracuse facility firmly, and to suppose the trustees would have set organizational policy without clear direction from their superintendent stretches credulity. Wilbur's report just after Newark had been approved also shows the dual components of custodial care: the helpless, or those judged chronically unteachable, and the homeless, or those who could not be released despite a mild disability because of moral weakness and poverty.

> Our board of trustees have from time to time suggested the idea of a custodial institution or asylum, or the establishment of such an institution to take those who graduate from this institution, and who have no homes, and to also receive unteachable idiots. There would have been no difficulty in obtaining an appropriation, in my judgment, for adding a custodial department to this institution [i.e., Syracuse]. The board of trustees felt that it would not be desirable to have such an institution so near the educational establishment . . . . Suitable provision for the life care of the homeless and helpless members of the class of idiots was contemplated as a future necessity by the original founders of the educational institution for their benefit. (Wilbur, 1878, pp. 96–97)

The Triumph of the Congregate Asylum

Whatever his reasons, Wilbur was in the minority among asylum superintendents. The consensus among the heads of asylums for the feebleminded, led by Isaac Kerlin in Pennsylvania, was identical to that of the heads of insane asylums. Instead of separate institutions, the cottage, or congregate, plan was put forth as the best of both worlds. The unteachable elements, housed in low-cost, separate buildings, would still have the advantages of the large, scientific training school. "Those buildings devoted to the asylum department [i.e., low-grade inmates] should be planned to secure an abundance of sunlight and air without obstructive partitions, with great liberality of floor space, and be located at some distance from the other departments, — say from one-half to three quarters of a mile" (Kerlin, 1884, p. 260). He goes on to add that these buildings should be separated not only by distance but also by ravines and woods if possible (p. 261). In 1871, the board at Elwyn Training School, headed by Kerlin, endorsed the establishment of a "custodial department," and the Pennsylvania legislature removed all age restrictions for admission (Hurd, 1916, p. 506). This was the model that was endorsed by most states, with New York a noticeable exception. By 1883 the Massachusetts School for the Feeble-Minded, headed by Howe until he died in 1876, had separate departments for education and custody. Indeed, they were even funded independently, with money for the education department coming from the State Department of Education (Kerlin, 1886; Tyor, 1972). By 1880, the idiot asylums in Ohio, Illinois, and Iowa were clearly committed to serving as large, congregate facilities for their states (Wines, 1888).

The debate over separate facilities continued for several years after Wilbur's death in 1882. The arguments were still swirling around institutions like the Rome Asylum for Unteachable Idiots in New York well into the twentieth century. For the most part, however, by the 1880s there was not so much a debate as a rather one-sided defense of a position no longer under serious attack. The proponents of the congregate asylum spent the rest of the nineteenth century in the public policy equivalent of running up the score on a hopelessly defeated opponent. Indeed, Kerlin even tried to "rehabilitate" Wilbur by arguing after Wilbur's death that this founding father of idiot asylums had not really meant to support specialized custodial facilities such as Willard or Newark (see Fish, 1892, p. 217).

The arguments in favor of the congregate asylum are remarkably revealing of the social context at the time. The debate over asylum organization is the most extensive discussion of "low-grade" inmates by the superintendents who were much more eager to focus on those people they could claim to change. At least three main reasons were commonly offered in support of the large, multipurpose, congregate facility.

Economy

Free labor would be available through reliance on higher-functioning inmates to do basic maintenance and other jobs necessary for the smooth operation of the asylum. Kerlin estimated the worth of inmate labor at Elwyn to be around $400 per month, or the equivalent of 20 attendants at a $20-per-month salary (Kerlin, 1884, p. 252). Usually, such peonage was vigorously defended as turning social burdens into productive citizens, the argument used by poorhouse reformers earlier in the century. Nonetheless, the cost efficiency of the practice was clearly crucial to the superintendents. Kerlin offered a "striking example" of economy accomplished at Elwyn. "Our baker, to whom we paid thirty-five dollars per month, eloped; our boys are now running the bakery for eleven people. They are baking four to six barrels of flour daily at no expense for wages" (Fish, 1892, p. 217).

Training

Inmate labor, of course, was not only cheap but it was supposedly also wonderful therapy for those doing the work. Perhaps the favorite illustration of this advantage was the high-grade imbecile caring for the low-grade resident. Alexander Johnson of Indiana found the arrangement inspiring:

> Most touching of all the touching sights in the institution is to see the tenderness and patience exercised by a great, big, overgrown man-baby toward a tiny child-baby, when put into his care. Here is a place which the imbecile can fill often as well as and certainly more willingly than a hired helper. . . . The very need of someone to love, which in the outside world so often betrays the poor feeble-minded girl, in the institution may make her chief usefulness. (A. Johnson, 1896, pp. 216–17)

Organization

The third main argument was that large collections of inmates functioning on many levels made for efficient classification and diagnosis. What better way to prove scientific expertise than to oversee a diverse asylum population that could be dissected into any number of clinical subdivisions and resorted as individual therapy goals indicated? Those who held this view bemoaned the stultifying effect of creating a homogeneous asylum population that was, by definition, incapable of much change. It would be difficult to demonstrate one's professionalism with uniformly unteachable clientele. Kerlin described his vision of the ideal congregate facility as large, heterogeneous "villages of the simple." Compared with the "hospitalism" of the small, purely custodial asylum, "the large, diffuse, and thoroughly classified institution is another affair, and can be to its wards and employes as cosmopolitan as a city" (Kerlin, 1884, p. 262). Indeed, the organizational and therapeutic advantages often were viewed as two sides of the same coin. In a speech before an association of Wisconsin teachers in 1890, Albert Salisbury described the multipurpose institution as a healthy, organic maturation of the original, purely educational facilities.

> If the school and the custodial department exist side by side under the same management, the transfer of inmates, complete or partial, final or temporary, can be effected with the least difficulty; and even that minority of cases who are not subjects for educational effort are, nevertheless, susceptible of the habit-forming processes and require expert supervision. The State institution should be inaugurated as a school, with the legal sanction and provision for the natural and inevitable growth of the custodial feature. (cited in Fish, 1891, p. 105)

In New York, the triumph of the congregate insane asylum was completed officially by 1890. By then, the State Care Act had been passed, removing any legal distinctions between chronic and acute insanity. The new policy was to establish all-purpose, regional hospitals for insanity throughout the state. Each hospital, including Willard and Binghamton, that had been designated for incurable cases, was now to receive insane of any type or degree. The vertical division of dependency triumphed in terms of state practice and policy. Within each of the institutions, of course, the functional assignment of inmates to the chronic or acute departments remained rigid. Chronicity was firmly rooted within the disability categories created, defined, and applied almost exclusively by the increasingly dominant medical perspective of the superintendents. It was a triumph for "professionalism" and "expertise."

However, it was an incomplete triumph in New York until after the turn of the century. At least officially, New York's idiot asylums maintained the specialized facilities that Wilbur had argued for during his life. Newark remained designated for mildly and moderately retarded women. A facility specifically for epileptic and retarded people (Craig Asylum) began in the 1890s. Syracuse tried to maintain its reputation as a school; the Rome asylum for "unteachable idiots" opened in New York. This resistance to the congregate bandwagon is probably attributable, in roughly equal parts, to Wilbur's continuing influence and to the inertia of a policy once in place. However, New York's idiot asylums were not immune to the social and administrative forces that had led to the triumph of the congregate asylum in other states. It is precisely the interaction of those congregative forces with the separatist official policy that makes the Rome asylum such an important institutional case study.

THE GEOGRAPHY OF ABANDONMENT

The eventual triumph of a policy of custodialism for mildly and moderately retarded people was, in reality, merely an expansion of the custodial approach that long applied to the most severely retarded population. There were some new settings, but abandonment is abandonment no matter what the local scenery is like. Three historical landmarks are crucial to understanding the evolution of 19th century policy and practice toward chronically retarded people.

The Emergence of "Scientific" Abandonment

Howe's and Wilbur's early attempts to exclude "chronically helpless" people from their new facilities were simply a specialized version of the more general distinction between the able-bodied poor and the "truly needy" that was first institutionalized in the almshouses (see Chapter 2). Specialization in the care of retarded people was reinforced by the medical judgment applied to insanity. What was new about the first idiot asylums was the claim that professional, "scientific" attention to this segment of the almshouse population could save, or at least help, some idiots and imbeciles. Prior to this, people with mental retardation were a subset of the hopeless. Howe and Wilbur (and Seguin and others) had made the claim that idiocy and incurability merely overlapped. There was hope for some.

Ironically, the claims that some could be cured through medical diagnosis and proper education left those who were still judged incurable even more bereft of hope than before. Their chronicity had been established "scientifically," rather than by the best judgment of amateurs. The emergence of clinical cure entailed the clinical failure. This organic dimension of chronicity, in both its medical and educational versions, quickly came to function as the officially sanctioned explanation of the other three dimensions: economics, morality, and aesthetics. It represented the ascendancy of professionalism as a therapeutic mirror of the increased efficiency with which an ever more impatient corporate society dissected and controlled its labor force.

Abandonment Outside the Asylums

Perhaps the single overwhelming feature of the changes in institutional policy toward idiocy between 1850 and 1890 was that the vast majority of people labeled idiots and imbeciles were unaffected by those changes in any measurable way. Most retarded people, from the simple-minded to the idiotic, continued to live in communities, with their families, or in the county or city almshouses. Why was the rate of institutionalization so much greater for the insane than for idiots? Why were idiots allowed to remain in the almshouses or at home some 40 years after the first state asylums specifically designated for their care had opened, around 1850?

The simple explanation is that society identified many more insane people than feebleminded in its midst. Thus, insanity received more official attention. Once the problem gained the attention of the state, the institutional solutions of the asylum experts were inevitable in government response. There are, however, at least three additional considerations.

Idiocy as social afterthought

As this chapter has discussed, the true social pressure at this time was for a clear definition of chronic disability in terms of a group of "surplus people" (Farber, 1968), excluded from the ever stronger expectations of productivity. The increasingly utilitarian definition of cure, or even improvement, meant that severely retarded people, along with the elderly poor and dependent children, were simply beyond potential participation in society. Because idiots (and the elderly, and children) were not expected to be productive, their presence in the marketplace was not particularly threatening to the maintenance of a cooperative workforce. At most, the threat was indirect: feebleminded children could be a drain on the family life of workers. The early superintendents often used just such a rationale to call for more diligent institutionalization (Kerlin, 1884; Knight, 1891).

Even such a burden as an "imbecile" child might not have seemed to require special facilities. The local almshouse was more convenient and, for all its cruelty and neglect, accessible for the parents. The physical segregation of idiots could be less aggressively pursued because they were, in effect, already segregated by physiology and fate.

By the same token, institutionalization of insane adults and criminals was reasonable precisely because they belonged to the class of potentially productive workers. The one group of retarded people who moved in perception from "social junk" to "social dynamite" (Spitzer, 1975), and thus were the target of more aggressive incarceration in this period, were the high-grade "imbeciles" whom Howe and Wilbur said they could cure. Perhaps the least noticed "contribution" of these two founding fathers was to begin the change in the official (and, to a degree, popular) perception of mildly retarded people from a family burden to a social threat.

Idiocy as social symbol

Not only was the social presence of severely retarded people no threat to the work ethic, but there were also positive reasons to leave them in the community. Severely retarded people were part of the surplus group that served as an economic example, showing those who did produce and did behave what they were thereby avoiding. If the working classes needed an object lesson in the benefits of social compliance, then the status of severely retarded people was readily observable. They did not so much lose the game of social participation as not even get to play. The game was clearly wage-earning utility and productivity, imbued with a moral imperative that made winning a purely individual responsibility. Incurability and unproductiveness combined in a group on whom no expectations were placed and to whom no opportunities were given. They remained in the community for their symbolic value.

According to at least one historian of the Middle Ages (Midelfort, 1987), such social symbolism in idiocy would be merely a secular evolution of the religious function of the "court fool" tradition in medieval Europe. According to Midelfort, one of the main reasons that aristocracy liked to keep "fatuous" simpletons or "natural fools" around was the theological conviction that their example fostered humility and fear before God. After all, even a king needs to be reminded that it is by God's grace that he is so high in the great "chain of being." Daily dealings with a fool were thought to serve as such reminders. For the post-Enlightenment world of nineteenth-century capitalism, the need for reminders was more democratic, less divine. Daily dealings with the feebleminded taught the masses what a privilege it was simply to participate in the economy, even if the rewards seemed meager.

Idiocy and family resistance

It seems clear that there was a continuing undercurrent of family resistance to pressure to commit children to institutions unless absolutely necessary. Poor people were not passive recipients of whatever instructions the social engineers and asylum advocates were giving during this era, and they adapted to the rise of the almshouses by using them as convenient hostels during winter or spells of unemployment (see Chapter 2). Similarly, the pressure to "give up" children to the new asylums was apparently resisted by many families, and even the idiot asylum case records reveal pleas from numerous families for the return of their institutionalized children (see Chapter 6).

If family resistance is considered also as an explanation of differential rates of institutionalization, it fits with the higher rates for insanity than for retardation. Insane asylums focused on adults, who were more likely to be totally without support if they themselves became dependent. The institutions of Howe and Wilbur, and even the later generations of idiot asylums, focused on children as the foremost candidates for their "schools." Despite public remarks of the two founders, "putting away" a child in a distant institution was then—as now—perceived as a dreadful step to take (Friedberger, 1981). One of the factors that countered parental resistance was the severity of the child's disability, as indicated by statistics from the admission records of the era. As part of a larger study, Tyor (1977) found that admissions to the Faribault Asylum in Minnesota for the years 1879–1919 showed an overrepresentation of severely retarded children whose parents were both living. The age of admission for such children was also younger on average. One surmises that without the greater care demands and health problems of more severe levels of retardation, intact families tended to keep their disabled children at home as long as possible. Irony, therefore, enters the story once again. The one child that Howe and Wilbur did not want in their asylums—the severely retarded, multiply handicapped child—was precisely the one whose parents were most likely to seek early admission.

The Triumph of Professional Monopoly

What triumphed in this era was not the eventual domination of the custodial approach to asylum management. Nor was there a triumph of social persuasion to remove all retarded people from society. Custody was from the beginning the official policy, and the working classes of society continued to frustrate its efficient implementation. What triumphed, rather, was the argument of asylum professionals that only they could properly provide all the levels of service available to retarded people, and that they could do it efficiently only in large congregate facilities. Whether the purpose was care of the burdensome, confinement of the dangerous, or cure of the few, this new class of professionals claimed jurisdiction. Their arguments failed to convince society to clean communities of all retarded people, but within the institutional structure and the professional system, their triumph was almost total. It was a triumph of both consolidation and expertise, and it still influences the course of decision making in mental retardation policy.

The More Things Change . . .

In 1855, the secretary of state for New York printed the contents of a letter he had received from someone who thought that Providence, Rhode Island, had a notably better almshouse than those in New York. The inmates in Providence were at least kept busy, commented the observer, even if the task was a mockery of useful labor. The correspondent described how, on his last visit, he had seen "a party of men carrying wood from one corner of the yard to another and piling it there; when it was all removed it was brought back again and piled in the old place" (cited in Katz, 1984, p. 120).

In 1892, the superintendent of the Massachusetts Idiot Asylum, Walter Fernald, described a strikingly similar practice as a therapeutic activity for the "low-grade" inmates of his institution.

> The exercise consists in carrying these stones, one at a time, from one circle to the other until all are transferred. Children learn to do this who are mentally incapable of understanding or performing the most simple formal gymnastic exercise. It is work reduced to its lowest terms. They really enjoy this exercise and will keep at it for a long time. The materials employed are indestructible and this is a very great advantage. . . . While performing these simple exercises the child ceases his destructive actions or vicious habits and perhaps for the first time realizes the luxury of normal muscular fatigue. (Fernald, 1892, p. 454)

The developments in social policy and practice in the last half of the 19th century toward severely retarded people are aptly characterized by these two examples of institutional life some 37 years apart. Everything changed and nothing changed. Between 1850 and 1890, the institutional model that survives to this day grew to maturity. A new professionalism and specialization flourished within the walls of the asylums for idiots. Without really changing the basic social division between productive people and chronic dependents, a new professionalism emerged in the idiot asylums that was eager to consolidate its position in the service system. When educational results seemed too little, then plain old custodialism got transformed into various versions of "rock therapy." The asylum quit speaking of itself as a school and instead focused attention on the varieties of work and the "luxury of fatigue" experienced by the inmates while contributing to their own keep. Finally it implies that the question about the appropriateness of congregate facilities was a moot point by 1890.

Increasingly, the state asylums and their private counterparts became microcosmic reproductions of the larger society: hierarchical systems that promised productivity and efficiency, with an increasingly strong element of state intervention. The metaphors of the era changed, but remained as far from the truth as ever. The earliest almshouses supposedly modeled themselves after the "one big happy family" ideal. They quickly turned into warehouses for the poor and incapacitated. Later, the first idiot asylums proclaimed themselves as "schools" for defective students. However, the large state asylums of the 1870s and 1880s wanted nothing more than to be efficient "factories of the feebleminded." (To this day, when a visitor travels to the small towns where many of this era's asylums were built, the simplest strategy for locating the facilities is to look for a smokestack towering over the landscape.) Whether the asylums were portrayed as home, school, or factory, though, the institutional practice toward those judged beyond help remained brutal and stultifying.

Chapter Four Policy
and Productivity
in Rome's
Early Years

One risk of specialized historical studies is an unintended suggestion that the events so important to the field being studied were also
among the most important events for the entire country. Perhaps I
should reaffirm, then, that public policy toward severely retarded
people in the nineteenth century was never at the cutting edge of
American social reform. The triumph of the large, custodial, congregate asylum over smaller, specialized facilities as the accepted model
for state policy toward feebleminded citizens must be kept in
perspective. The 1890 federal census identified only 20 public and 4
private asylums for idiots, housing a total of 5,254 inmates (Billings,
1895), out of a growing nation of more than 62 million people.

Mental retardation history is reflective, rather than formative, of
the larger course of events in American society. What happened to
mentally retarded people at the hands of the state during any specific
era had usually been tried before, on other, larger groups of people,
and with much more public attention. Even if one argues, as I do, that
mental retardation history offers important, and occasionally singu-
lar, insights into the true character of those larger processes, the
relative size and sequence of events must still be kept in mind.

The 30 years or so from the end of the Civil War to the opening of
the Rome Custodial Asylum for Unteachable Idiots in 1894 were
truly momentous ones in the nation's history. From 1865 to 1900 the
population more than doubled, from 36 million to 77.5 million. By

1900 there were 20 millionnaires in the United States Senate alone, compared with only a dozen in the entire country at the time of the Civil War (Ehrenreich, 1985). The number of people engaged in manufacturing doubled between 1870 and 1890, and the same was true for mining, transportation, public utilities, and construction (Cashman, 1984). "Iron replaced wood; steel replaced iron; and electricity and steam replaced horsepower" (Cashman, 1984, p. 13). One percent of the population owned 47% of the country's assets (Ehrenreich, 1985, p. 23). In short, this so-called gilded age saw the emergence of the now familiar national profile: urban, industrial, corporate, with the juxtaposition of enormous wealth and widespread poverty.

The boom-and-bust economic cycle left factory workers and miners newly educated in the law of supply and demand as applied to the workplace. Labor organizing came in with a struggle in infamous episodes such as the Haymarket affair in Chicago, and the Homestead Steel strike outside of Pittsburgh. By 1893, a depression second in severity only to that of the 1930s gripped the industrial cities. The best estimates are that between 18 and 20 percent of the workforce (some 3 million people) were left unemployed and unprotected by 1894 (U.S. Bureau of the Census, 1976, p. 135; Zinn, 1980, pp. 271–73). The contradictions in the new system were becoming a challenge to American political and economic order. The working classes confronted the fact that their society "obliges able-bodied adults to be self-supporting, yet it does not, either by law or through its institutions, guarantee jobs to those who are expected to support themselves" (Keyssar, 1986, p. 6).

In New York especially, the worker facing that challenge was likely to be a recent immigrant and a city resident. By 1890, 10 percent of all the people in America lived in New York State, and 60 percent of those lived in urban settings (Schneider and Deutsch, 1941, p. 13). The nation as a whole did not pass the 50 percent urban mark until 1920 (Larson, 1977, p. 248). It was in the city that the rigidity of the class structure was most apparent, of course.

The last decade of the nineteenth century saw the maturation of the newly professional middle class. Cadres of experts seemed deployed in every segment of society: teachers, engineers, professors, doctors, dentists, journalists, and midlevel managers and administrators (Bledstein, 1976; Ehrenreich, 1985; Larson, 1977). Between 1870 and 1910, this new class (including clerical and sales workers) grew from 750,000 to 5.5 million (Hofstadter, 1955, p. 216). The "knowledge monopolies" promised to produce an America that was more efficient, more productive, healthier, and more humane, as well.

Within this swirl of economic and cultural change, the Rome Custodial Asylum is illustrative of how the various dimensions of chronicity melded together with the larger forces of the Progressive era within institutional settings. In many ways, Rome represents the culmination of a century of social policy and practice toward severely retarded people.

What changed in the nineteenth century was professional opinion about where the custody of severely retarded people should occur, and about how many of the feebleminded population (the preferred generic term for all levels of mental retardation by 1890: Powell, 1887; Warner, [1894] 1971) should be included in that custodial policy. Rome was simultaneously an exception to and a confirmation of this institutional trend. State policy makers seem variously to have regarded Rome as an intentional experiment or a simple afterthought, in much the same way that mental retardation itself was. In the early years of its existence, Rome was the location of impressive innovations, stark neglect and punishment, and fairly typical exploitation. Depending on the viewpoint, the early Rome Asylum ranged from a self-sufficient factory and farm to a personal proving ground of professional competence; from a haven of relief where reluctant families could place their children, to a state-funded custodial warehouse where eager county officials could dump their most troublesome charges.

This chapter will examine the earliest years of Rome: its haphazard beginning and the struggles of the facility's first superintendent. Chapter 5 will examine the role of the central figure in Rome's history, Charles Bernstein, and Chapter 6 will conclude the case study by examining the files of the first 1,000 people admitted to Rome.

THE OPENING OF ROME, 1890—1902

The Policy Background

The Rome Custodial Asylum for Unteachable Idiots was something of an oddity from the day it opened its doors on October 1,
1894. As described in Chapter 3, the clear move among asylum
professionals was to large, congregate facilities divided by disability
type but not by degree. Whether mild or severe cases, feebleminded
people belonged in one place, insane people in another, physically
disabled people in another, deaf, blind, and so on down the list of
"defective" populations.

Craig Colony, a special facility for epileptics—up to 98 percent of
whom were supposedly also retarded (Hebberd, 1912)—went
through an arduous three-year process of planning and committee
work, from 1892 to 1895, before opening with some notice (e.g., the
State Board of Charities published the facility's annual reports
together with its own report, the only facility so favored). For
Letchworth Village, the next state asylum for the feebleminded after
Rome, planning took five years, from 1906 to 1911, for site selection,
population identification, and architectural designs for the first 10
years of expansion. In contrast, it took a mere 13 months after
legislative authorization before Rome began operations as a state
facility. Rome's beginnings were unusual also because the location
was redundant. Both of the two existing state idiot asylums were in
the same general upstate region as Rome (one in Syracuse and the
other in the small town of Newark, near Rochester), none closer than
250 miles to New York City, where well over half of the state's 6.5
million people lived.

The somewhat idiosyncratic development of New York State idiot
asylums shows the continuing power of individuals in the midst of
larger movements of social control. As the last chapter described
developments, the call for custodial provision of idiots was fairly
constant from 1851 on. Wilbur and his board of managers defended
the identity of the Syracuse Asylum as a "school" for high-grade
("teachable") feebleminded youngsters. New York officially resisted
the congregate plan of other states, at least for idiot asylums, that

is—probably because of the influence of Wilbur at Syracuse, and of Josephine Shaw Lowell at Newark. Wilbur wanted a separate custodial asylum. Recall from Chapter 3 that after advocating strongly in the 1860s the opening of the Willard Asylum for the chronically insane, Wilbur even proposed that facility as a suitable place for the transfer of his lower functioning inmates. Lowell, appointed by Governor Samuel Tilden to the State Board of Charities in 1876, was promptly shocked in her first tour of county almshouses at the number of pregnant women she encountered. She initiated the move for Newark, demanding that it be designated exclusively for feebleminded women of child-bearing age. As such, it was seen by legislators and the Board of Charities as a specialized part of the women's reform schools and "houses of refuge" that New York, Massachusetts, and other states encouraged as the first blow in what became the battle of eugenics (Brenzel, 1983). Wilbur and Lowell each used the influence of the other to accomplish their own ends at Newark. Wilbur got at least a partial outlet for his older, "custodial" inmates; Lowell got a place to segregate the most "vulnerable" and supposedly most promiscuous segment of wayward women.

By 1893, there still was no designated facility for custodial adult males and unteachable idiots of whatever age. Rome began, then, as an extemporaneous answer to a 40-year-old question. The location was the unplanned result of other legislation targeting the insane, combined with a need to smooth some ruffled county feathers and a desire to shore up a remnant of power for a decimated Board of Charities. The approach to Rome, while hasty, inconsistent, and largely irrelevant to quality care, had stout defenders in the State Board of Charities, the County Commissioners of the Poor, and the officials of the Syracuse Asylum (NYSBC, 1895).

The State Care Act

Rome was not the product of abstract discussions of policy disputes or professionalization in the field of mental retardation, but an immediate result of reform in state policy toward insane people. In 1890, New York passed the State Care Act, culminating an eight-year struggle to remove responsibility for the insane from county officials to the state. Prior to this, up to 52 counties maintained insane patients in their local almshouses, although only 14 were authorized to do so (Schneider and Deutsch, 1941, p. 92). The State Care Act established, for the first time, the principle of state responsibility for the care of all insane residents of New York. It officially abandoned the policy of separate facilities for acute and chronic insanity. The state was divided into districts, each of them the location of a state hospital (the names of all the state facilities were also legally changed in 1890, doing away with "asylum"). The hospital was to receive as rapidly as possible all insane inmates within the district. With the establishment of a State Commission in Lunacy, New York officially removed responsibility for the insane from the province of charity to the province of medicine. Asylums became hospitals. The State Board of Charities no longer had jurisdiction over any "State Hospital for the Insane." County welfare systems were removed from the process except as referral sources. The cost of care was covered by the state, not referred back to the counties as had been the practice. Only New York City, Brooklyn, and Buffalo were allowed to operate their own separate facilities because of the numbers of people involved (Schneider and Deutsch, 1941, p. 97), and even these counties voluntarily ceded control to the state by 1896, in the face of powerful financial incentives (Grob, 1983).

For years, the State Care Act had been strongly opposed by Commissioners of the Poor in those counties with official exemptions to operate their own insane asylums (Fitzgerald, 1900). Once the financial component of state responsibility was added, however, the local resistance disintegrated, although some commissioners feared a loss of power and of professionalism. Since 1878, the state had mandated the removal of all children between 3 and 16 years of age, disabled or not, from the county almshouses. In 1890 the State Care Act took away the second largest group of clients from poorhouse superintendents in the larger counties. Loss of money was the overwhelming consideration, but resentment among the county commissioners and some municipal leaders apparently arose also over the loss of local discretion in placement decisions. The State Board of Charities was left with control of only 10 state institutions (Rome and

Craig made 12) and the county almshouses. A decrease in the importance of the almshouses in state policy diminished the influence of the Board.

Oneida was one of the counties caught up in this new massive assertion of state control and responsibility. A separate building for the insane erected in 1876 as part of the poorhouse complex some two miles south of Rome became expendable. The county sold the entire poorhouse complex to the state, as mandated by law for the insane asylum part of the facilities, and built a new facility elsewhere. For a little over $200,000, the state gained ownership of 350 acres with four residential buildings and assorted barns and outbuildings. After a few months of being designated a Temporary State Hospital, the facility was officially established as the Oneida State Custodial Asylum. A year later, the name "Oneida" was changed to "Rome". The law establishing the Rome Custodial Asylum was permissive, rather than mandatory as with the State Care Act, about the counties' use of the new custodial facility. "Each county in the state is entitled, if vacancies exist, to send such unteachable idiots as are a charge upon said county to this institution" (chap. 348, Laws of New York, 1893).

This account of events is not, of course, what one finds in the histories of the Rome facility later included in various annual reports and general narratives of institutional development. In most accounts, the Rome facility was the considered result of careful planning, addressing a pressing need for state care. Only a few suggestions of alternative explanations can be found in anything approaching official testimony. Some 40 years after the fact, Homer Folks, head of the Charity Aid Society and a major state and national figure in social welfare for decades, spoke at an anniversary celebration for Letchworth Village in downstate New York. He praised the organization and planning of the facility by contrasting it with the happenstance nature of Rome's creation.

> The Rome institution came into existence at that location for no better reason than that Oneida County had a building on its hands, when the State assumed care for the insane. It was not well located for an additional State institution for the feebleminded, but having been built, it had to be used, and the State, having caused the removal of the insane from it, took it over for the benefit of the feebleminded. (cited in Winslow, 1937, p. 9)

An unplanned birth in the state's family of institutions, Rome risked organizational abandonment from its earliest days. Its institutional managers soon discovered that abandonment might have been preferable.

THE EVOLUTION OF ROME, 1894–1902

When the Rome asylum opened in May of 1894, nearly half of the 400 or so inmates from the old Oneida County Insane Asylum had not yet been relocated to the various state hospitals. Additional buildings of the almshouse complex were still being used by Oneida County as well. It was four months before the buildings were completely turned over to the state. On October 1, 1894, the Rome Temporary State Hospital officially became the Rome Custodial Asylum. Over 170 of the former county insane asylum inmates were officially admitted to the new idiot asylum, although most seem to have been sent elsewhere later (the case records of the early admissions to Rome are very sketchy). At the end of the first year of operation, there were 199 inmates under the new superintendent, John Fitzgerald, and his medical assistant—fresh out of medical school—Charles Bernstein (Rome, 1896). Despite the 50 percent reduction in population from the almshouse era, some basic problems in the standard of care in the facility were immediately apparent.

Confronted with horrendous maintenance problems and organizational inadequacies and quickly overshadowed by the activism of his successor, Fitzgerald as superintendent nonetheless clearly announced some of the basic themes developed by Bernstein. Three themes in particular that emerge from Fitzgerald's annual reports to the legislature were prominent concerns of his, as well as predictive of Bernstein's efforts: the dilapidated physical plant, constant—and related—claims of underfunding, and the changing depiction of the asylum population.

The Dilapidated Physical Plant

Even those calling for basic abandonment in the care of unteachable idiots could not have envisioned the squalor endured by the new inmates, as described by an official inspection report (Rome, 1896). The single overwhelming sensation of the place must have been an unbearable stench. The drainage system under the buildings was "nothing more or less than elongated cesspools in which sewage water remains and decomposes, and from which the gases are drawn into the building" (Rome, 1896, p. 48). All of the pipes leaked. The toilets were barely usable: the wood seats saturated with 20 years of urine, the floors rotting, the pipes corroded. The corridors, day rooms, and sleeping rooms were said to "reek with the noisome odors of the sewer" (Rome, 1896, p. 49). On top of this, the piggery, cow yard, and slaughterhouse were directly upwind of the residences. There was no electricity and no ventilation system, and in the winter, when windows had to remain closed, the smell became stifling. The basement of one building contained the kitchen and dining facilities, partially under a first floor water closet (as the bathrooms were called), and the basement ceiling often dripped with urine-soaked condensation. The dirt floors of the basement were saturated from the leaky underground pipes. Even when the dirt became soggy, the basement had to be used by both staff and inmates.

In 1897, inspectors for the State Board of Charities—not a group known for its extravagant expectations when it came to standards of care for unteachable idiots—still found the eating facility repulsive:

> The dining-rooms are in the basement of the old county house and are only fit for cellar purposes, to which they should be abandoned. The whole place needs grouting to make it even desirable for such use. It seems like the refinement of cruelty to compel human beings to eat in a place where no merciful man would think fit for his cattle. It is uncomfortable enough at all seasons, but when the steam is on, the patients receive the drippings from the pipes down their backs as they sit at the table. (NYSBC, 1898, p. 183)

Of course, a few paragraphs later, when the same inspectors summarized their impressions of Rome, they found that "the institution seems to be under the best of care and management, and the inmates were as well and contented as one could expect from such an unfortunate class" (p. 184).

It was not until his fourth annual report, for 1898, that Fitzgerald felt able to claim that the initial inadequacies of the buildings had been fully addressed. "The asylum has reached the point where instead of rectifying the conditions left us by our predecessors, we look forward to the future with bright hopes for its success. Hereafter the policy will be expansion commensurate with the needs of the helpless class for whom a generous public dedicated it" (Rome, 1899, p. 39).

By 1900, in the context of a speech to county superintendents of the poor, Fitzgerald portrayed the life of his inmates as almost idyllic. Compared with life at home or in an ill-prepared almshouse, who could question the idiot's preference for the wonderful care the state provided free of charge at Rome.

> His physical wants are supplied; he is among his equals and those who sympathize with him in his childish troubles. He has an interest in community life. His dormant faculties are aroused by healthful employment and school exercises.
>
> During his leisure moments, he is provided with sports and entertainment within his comprehension. The satisfaction of the imbeciles with their existence in an institution has been impressed upon me during the last few years by the pleasure shown on innumerable occasions when they have returned from their homes after a short visit. The love, kindness and thoughtfulness of their parents cannot compensate them for the joy of again being with their similarly afflicted fellow-beings. In fact, the institution has become their natural home to the exclusion of any other. (Fitzgerald, 1900, pp. 177–78)

Not surprisingly, Fitzgerald concluded that such a joyful place could only be created and maintained within large state facilities such as those at Rome. Private charities and county provisions would never be up to the task of creating this "natural home." The reason, according to Fitzgerald, was simple: "The work of caring for these afflicted ones has no attractiveness in itself, as they have, beyond question, the most repulsive types of humanity among them" (Fitzgerald, 1900, p. 175).

Despite his professions of satisfaction, living among such "repulsive types of humanity" must have worn down Fitzgerald's tolerance. He resigned within two years of his speech to the superintendents. In fact, throughout his eight-year tenure at Rome, 1894 to 1902, Fitzgerald's complaints of inadequate support always overwhelmed his claims of achievement. When he left in December 1902 to head the charity services for Brooklyn, it seems likely that his departure was a relief for everyone concerned. The board of managers made some gracious comments about how much Fitzgerald would be missed, but clearly his interests were more in efficient administration than in the programmatic aspects that were coming to the fore. To mark the transition, the board, together with the new superintendent, Charles Bernstein, wrote a 129-page report that was double the length of any of the eight previous ones, and described, in detail never approached by Fitzgerald, the goals and activities of the various asylum departments.

The Issue of Appropriations

Fitzgerald's concern about the dilapidated state of his institution certainly seems to have been justified. In the calls for increased capital appropriations each year, though, the reports gradually assumed an almost stridently critical tone toward the legislators who held the purse strings. The result in many cases was a curious mélange of cajole and attack, promise and frustration. The legislative penury, however, was not quite as extreme as Fitzgerald claimed.

Allegations of underfunding

By 1902, Fitzgerald bitterly complained of the "mistaken policy of the authorities at Albany in cutting down appropriations which experience warranted the management of this institution in asking" (Rome, 1902, p. 28). The annual report of 1901 is blunt in its criticism:

> We have reason to believe that an appropriation bill for this institution . . . died in committee from sheer neglect. One of the results of this failure to secure the appropriation so badly needed and urgently requested, has been that one of our new buildings stands vacant . . . Another result was, that where we expected to take in 150 patients for whom quarters were available, we are enabled to receive only 90. . . . We could enumerate a number of similar results, but it is useless. (Rome, 1901, p. 19)

Some of the circumstances provoking these complaints do, indeed, seem oddly wasteful and ill-planned. For three years, two new dormitories and an administration building, the residence for the superintendent and his family, were delayed because of inadequate appropriations (Rome, 1899, 1900). Even when construction began, the process seems often to have wasted time and money. For example, in more than one instance after the physical structure of a building was completed, installation of plumbing, heating vents, and wiring was left undone until the following year and then required tearing up part of the walls and flooring. Even after construction, the haphazard appropriations blocked the use of new facilities. Entire buildings were left partially unoccupied because there was not enough money to buy furniture. One did not have enough chairs for all of the inmates to sit down at one time. Fitzgerald had great difficulty getting money to build an adequate cold storage room. For years, staff had to buy meat daily because they could not store it. All of these problems had to do with the expansion of the Rome facility, not the quality of what was already there.

Some of the other financial complaints concerned the provisions for the staff. During the early years, the ratio of attendants to inmates at Rome hovered around 1:12 (based on information in the annual reports), inferior to the 1:10 average for northeastern asylums (Grob, 1983, p. 19). Attendants at Rome earned from $14 to $30 a month, depending on responsibility and on sex (the maximum pay for women, $20, was the minimum for men). By way of comparison, the maximum salary, paid to only two or three of the male Rome attendants, was 25 percent below the $40-per-month average non-farm income in 1890 (U.S. Bureau of the Census, 1976). Perhaps more telling, the starting salaries at Rome were almost 15 percent lower than the national average starting salary for insane asylum attendants in 1890 (Grob, 1983, p. 328). The attendants worked from 5:00 A.M. until 8:00 or 10:00 P.M. They did get every Sunday off—at least, they had free time if they could not sing. Fitzgerald, in his first annual report, expresses his regrets that the "employees are so few in number that, up to the present time, we have been unable to organize an orchestra or band, though we have succeeded in forming a good choir who assist during religious services, and at other times sing on the wards to the evident enjoyment of the patients" (Rome 1895, p. 22).

Other complaints about support for staff indirectly comment on the quality of life for inmates as well. The wards and food that Fitzgerald seemed satisfied with for inmates became totally inadequate for attendants and other staff. In 1899, the state passed a law prohibiting the use of institutional funds to purchase special provisions just for institutional employees. Fitzgerald's reaction reveals more than he intended about his standards of judgment for institutional affairs. The legislation, he said, "directly affects the maintenance of every officer and employe, and practically places them on a par with the inmates as regards their food supplies. We cannot help but consider this an injustice here. In many of the institutions the inmates require a more varied diet than we would feel justified in furnishing our inmates, and as a result, the officers and employes are limited to a less variety than prevails in other institutions" (Rome, 1900, p. 43).

At the end of his tenure, Fitzgerald made a similar argument regarding the need for a separate "cottage" for the attendants. The language reminds one of his remark, cited earlier, about how unattractive working among such "repulsive" types of humanity really was. Of course, such a cottage would free beds in the wards for more inmates. That was not the primary consideration, however. "It is not only repugnant to the natural inclinations of employees to sleep in the wards with patients, but it is, in addition, injurious to their health and dispositions. It is assuredly sufficiently hazardous to their health to be compelled to be associated with the patients from twelve to fifteen hours per day, without insisting on their remaining in such close proximity with patients during their sleeping hours" (Rome, 1902, p. 11).

Funding comparisons with other institutions

Despite these protestations of financial abandonment when it came to appropriations for Rome, a comparison of per capita expenditures for Fitzgerald's years of leadership yields a much less straightforward picture (see Table 4.1). Compared with the other two state asylums for feebleminded people, Rome fared much better than Newark and better than Syracuse in many years. A comparison with all of the state hospitals shows Rome consistently coming out slightly better in average annual maintenance expenditures.

Table 4.1 Maintenance Expenditures, New York State Asylums
for the Feebleminded and the Insane, 1896–1902

Year	Maintenance Expenditures	Average No. of Residents	Per Capita Expenditures
Rome State Custodial Asylum (Feebleminded)			
1896	$ 48,856	193	$253.14
1898	63,470	339	187.22
1900	67,184	354	189.79
1902	86,236	524	165.57
Syracuse State Asylum for Feebleminded Children			
1896	$ 93,243	517	$180.35
1898	94,766	511	185.45
1900	99,943	515	194.06
1902	92,883	519	178.96
Newark State Custodial Asylum (Feebleminded)			
1896	$ 48,401	368	$131.52
1898	47,945	392	122.31
1900	47,331	413	114.60
1902	55,295	450	122.88
Total, State Asylums for the Feebleminded			
1896	$ 190,500	1,078	$176.72
1898	206,181	1,242	166.01
1900	214,458	1,282	167.28
1902	234,414	1,493	157.01
Total, State Insane Asylums			
1896	$2,266,897	19,478	$116.38
1898	3,638,431	20,845	174.55
1900	4,028,354	22,088	182.38
1902	3,776,068	23,269	162.28

Sources: State Board of Charities, annual reports, 1896, 1898, 1900, 1902; New York State Department of Mental Hygiene, annual report, 1930.

It is difficult to compare the numbers of the State Lunacy Commission and those of the State Board of Charities as to what constitutes "ordinary" or "maintenance" expenditures. The first year or two of institutional expenditures are usually very high and not comparable to those of well-established facilities (e. g., the figures for Rome in 1896). To some extent, economies of scale enter in, so that the larger facilities in general have lower per capita costs than smaller ones. However, comparison of Newark and Syracuse shows that this is not an absolute. Facilities such as the Hudson River State Hospital (Poughkeepsie) or the Rochester State Hospital certainly fared much better on average than Rome. On the other hand, the Willard facility shared with Newark the dubious honor of regularly being two of the lowest three state institutions in terms of per capita support (the third was the State Soldiers and Sailors Hospital in Bath).

At least in its first decade, Rome was supported at a rate comparable to Syracuse despite being officially designated as a purely custodial facility, while Syracuse was viewed as an "educational" facility. Also, these figures do not include capital expenditures for new construction, which, despite its slowness, was occurring at Rome but not at Syracuse. The comparisons can only be suggestive. The different populations at the three idiot asylums, for instance, no doubt affected the maintenance rates. To some extent, however, the variables seem to cancel each other out. Syracuse, for example, had more able inmates who could perform money-saving work. On the other hand, its population included a high percentage of children under the age of 15, and those children were taught by a larger number of higher-paid teachers. The limited acreage at Syracuse (even including the farm colony at nearby Fairmount) greatly restricted the farming the inmates could do as well. For its part, Newark's all-female inmates were much higher-functioning, on the whole, than Rome's population, and perhaps more self-sufficient. On the other hand, they were presumably less productive in farming than men.

The funding levels also give some weight to professionalization in medical facilities of idiot asylums. Certainly Fitzgerald and Bernstein of Rome could not have missed the lesson of Newark, which was tied more closely to the Charity Aid movement than it was to the legacy of Wilbur and Howe. Legislators and Board of Charities commissioners viewed Newark more as a house of refuge than as a specialized state asylum, which were run by doctors, as required by law. It was not until well into the twentieth century that Newark had its first M.D. as superintendent, despite several changes in administration. The point is not that the medical superintendents at the other asylums served any legitimately medical functions. As illustrated by Fitzgerald at Rome, or even Wilbur in an earlier era, their concerns were administrative and organizational, not medical. The point, however, is the power of perception. For a variety of reasons, facilities operated by doctors were better funded than those general-purpose charity facilities with no claim to true "professional expertise" in management.

Rome was essentially ordinary in terms of the state's support for its various specialized asylums. It generally fell somewhere in the middle on a per capita basis. Despite the complaints of Fitzgerald and his managers, Rome's financial resources were lavish compared to those of Newark or Willard, and more or less average compared to other asylums in New York. Even on a national basis, Rome did well during these years. In 1895, the National Conference on Charities and Correction reported that the median per capita expenditure for state institutions for the feebleminded was $168.50. Rome's was consistently higher than this during Fitzgerald's tenure. The problems Rome faced, then, were not unique to Rome because of marked lack of funds. The patterns that emerge from the case study of Rome cannot be dismissed as predictable results of its abnormal poverty.

The Changing Depiction of the Rome Inmates

The third theme that repeatedly occurs in the annual reports of Fitzgerald, which overlaps with funding, is a deemphasis on the chronicity of the Rome inmates in an effort to escape the fate of Newark. Fitzgerald focused on the improvable side of the two dimensions of trainability and productivity (immorality was still a chronic threat). Fitzgerald made increasing claims of the capacity for improvement of the inmates in the institution, seeking to change the purely custodial profile with which his institution had begun. It was an effort that Bernstein continued and dramatically expanded (even into the dimension of morality) when he took over in 1903. How much Bernstein, as the first assistant medical officer, was responsible for Fitzgerald's change in perspective is difficult to establish.

For the first three years after opening as a state idiot asylum, Rome apparently kept its inmates locked in their wards most of the time. In their first report, the managers said this was because a "highway" (a road leading to the farm community of Lowell south of the institution, now State Route 26) was too close to the asylum buildings for safety. They proposed an ingenious plan that would get the inmates outside, give them work to do, and reroute the highway farther from the asylum: let the inmates move the roadbed. "The inmates may then have the privacy which their condition demands, and not be subject to the jest or ridicule of the passerby, and at the same time, have all the liberty consistent with their unfortunate condition" (Rome, 1896, p. 9).

By the second annual report, Fitzgerald was cautiously proclaiming the value of the work done by "our permanent population," although most of it was done indoors on the wards, in the laundry, the kitchen, and dining room. He seemed careful not to oversell the potential of his clients, adding that few inmates were "capable of doing a full day's labor, nevertheless, a little done by each one employed will produce surprising results in the aggregate" (Rome, 1897, p. 31). To exploit the potential of the inmates fully, Fitzgerald began to ask for more money for equipment, shops, teachers, and trainers. This was the initial move at Rome to deemphasize the passive, low-cost, custodial implications of the original mandate establishing the facility for unteachable idiots. Fitzgerald recognized that his request represented a departure and initially tried to make his case on humanitarian grounds.

> It is an absolute necessity that we should establish some industries that will furnish physical, mental and moral training to our inmates. Classes should be formed in cabinet work, carpentry work, brush broom and matmaking, shoemaking and tailoring, as well as classes in calisthenics, gymnastics and kindergarden [*sic*] work. . . . To neglect to furnish means for such employment, with competent instructors for our inmates, is to permit them to become more depraved than they are. It is true this is a custodial institution, but the object of that custody should be to benefit, elevate and improve, as well as to care for, not demoralize, degrade and render hopeless by inaction and lack of training. To establish such industries money is required. (Rome, 1897, p. 37)

If the inmates could not work, at least they could be exercised. As Fitzgerald explained the following year, "Patients who cannot be employed otherwise at present are being drilled in marching" (Rome, 1898, p. 35).

The humanitarian commitment to realizing the inmates' potential was quickly balanced with claims of the economic savings derived from the free labor of inmates. The annual reports go to great lengths to record the amount and type of labor provided by inmates each year. Inmates worked as attendants, made clothing and furniture for the asylum, grew produce, livestock, and poultry for the asylum, did extensive landscaping, and worked on maintenance, laundry, dining room, and kitchen crews. There was no service (except administration) required for their incarceration that the inmates themselves were not forced to provide in some measure, for free. Indeed, even when special construction jobs were contracted out, the private contractors were also required to use as much inmate labor as possible and to deduct the value of the labor from their bill.

Yearly statistics detailed the total number of days that inmates worked, the items made, produce grown, and livestock slaughtered. During Fitzgerald's tenure, up to 45 percent of the inmates were reported as employed, although not apparently full-time. The annual norm was around 30–35 percent. Such free labor became less an opportunity for growth for the individual resident than a simple obligation to keep the cost of his or her care as low as possible. In a statement that could easily have been uttered unchanged some 70 years earlier by an almshouse caretaker, Fitzgerald proclaimed his intention to get all the free labor he could from the able-bodied inmates by focusing on jobs that normally would be paid work. "It is our purpose, as much as their mental and physical capacity will permit, to engage our inmates in remunerative employment, so that the State will obtain, so far as may be, compensation for its generous contributions for their support" (Rome, 1901, p. 36).

The obsession with work and "habits of industry" (Rome, 1896, p. 21)—that favorite catchphrase of the nineteenth century—that began in the first management of almshouses thus continued down to Rome. Even in this asylum specifically designated for the "lowest" class of idiots, one sees the rapid move to distinguish between the relatively able-bodied and the "truly" incapacitated. The implications of this basic distinction appeared in almost every subsequent discussion of the inmates at Rome.

Thus, the logic behind the calls to expand the population as rapidly as possible may be interpreted as a recruitment of labor to run the place. As labor was valuable to the inmate's character and the state's pocketbook, very old and very young admissions had to be kept to a minimum, as they were the least able to work. In 1901, some 55 percent (66/119) of new admissions to Rome were between 15 and 25 years of age, compared with the overall rate of 37 percent (230/625) for the previous six years (Rome, 1902, p. 46; 1901, p. 56). As Chapter 6 will discuss, the mean age at admission to Rome during 1896–1902 was much higher than the national average. If inmates were to do the work required, there was also a need for expertise and professionalism in training some of those previously thought unteachable.

A brief examination of the characteristics of the population during Fitzgerald's years as superintendent shows that from the very first the Rome Custodial Asylum had some very high-functioning inmates. Indeed, given the basic twofold diagnostic division of imbeciles and idiots still in use at the time, the idiot class never represented more than 5.3 percent of the total population (see Table 4.2). Even including the vague transition category of "idio-imbecile," the percentage during the first eight years never rose above 21 percent. In part, the explanation is that two out of three idiots died within a few years of admission (see Table 4.3). Indeed, the differential in death rates from the lowest-functioning to the highest-functioning guaran-

Table 4.2 Distribution of Rome Population by Functional Level, 1896–1902

Level	1896 (%)	1897 (%)	1898 (%)	1899 (%)	1900 (%)	1901 (%)	1902 (%)
Idiots	8 (3.3)	18 (5.3)	12 (3.5)	13 (3.6)	11 (3.1)	13 (2.9)	12 (2.2)
"Idio-Imbecile"	34 (14.0)	50 (15.7)	47 (13.7)	52 (14.6)	50 (14.2)	70 (15.8)	79 (14.4)
Low Imbecile	95 (39.0)	138 (40.5)	139 (40.6)	144 (40.4)	143 (40.6)	180 (40.5)	211 (38.4)
Medium Imbecile	60 (24.6)	77 (22.6)	85 (24.8)	97 (27.2)	97 (27.5)	121 (27.3)	175 (31.8)
High Imbecile	12 (5.0)	23 (6.7)	26 (7.6)	31 (8.7)	34 (9.6)	49 (11.0)	61 (11.1)
Insane	21 (8.6)	22 (6.5)	21 (6.1)	9 (2.5)	9 (2.6)	7 (1.6)	6 (1.1)
Epileptic	14 (5.7)	13 (3.8)	12 (3.5)	10 (2.8)	8 (2.3)	4 (0.9)	6 (1.1)

Table 4.3 Death Rates at Rome by Functional Level, 1896–1902 (Cumulative)

Level	No. of Admissions	No. of Deaths	As % of Admissions	Rate of Death As % of Total Deaths
Idiots	34	22	64.7	12.7
"Idio-Imbecile"	102	22	21.6	12.7
Low Imbecile	273	62	22.7	35.8
Medium Imbecile	213	28	13.1	16.2
High Imbecile	68	1	1.5	0.6
Insane	163	20	12.3	11.6
Epileptic	29	18	62.1	10.4
Total	882	173	19.6	100.0

teed that even if admission rates remained fairly constant in terms of functional levels (Table 4.4), the overall proportion of high- and medium-grade imbeciles would grow. (In interpreting the admission data from Tables 4.4 and 4.5, it makes some sense to discard the three middle years, 1898–1900, because admissions were relatively few due to delays in ward construction. For example, the nine admissions in 1900 make percentages fairly meaningless. A better procedure would be to compare 1896–97 and 1901–2.)

Though the process became much more pronounced in the decade after Fitzgerald, the tendency of admissions to concentrate in the 10- to 20-year old age range shows up in Table 4.5 when comparing the first two years to the last two. By 1902, a crossover lasting at least through the 1930s had occurred, and more than 50 percent of the admissions were under 21 years of age (not counting the atypical middle years). There was a relationship between age at admission and functional level. Most children under 10 years old who were admitted tended to be lower-functioning or physically impaired; less serious conditions would not have been likely to be officially noticed or to lead to institutionalization before school age. Any feebleminded child of 7–14 years who was thought educable was either referred to Syracuse or, in the larger cities, placed in one of growing number of special education classes of the school systems. The "natural" infirmi-

Table 4.4 Distribution of Rome Admissions by Functional Level, 1896–1902

Level	1896 (%)	1897 (%)	1898 (%)	1899 (%)	1900 (%)	1901 (%)	1902 (%)
Idiots	5 (5.1)	18 (14.1)	—	1 (2.2)	—	5 (4.2)	—
"Idio-Imbecile"	13 (13.1)	22 (17.2)	2 (5.7)	5 (11.1)	—	23 (19.3)	15 (10.9)
Low Imbecile	45 (45.5)	49 (38.3)	11 (31.4)	15 (33.3)	2 (22.2)	44 (37.0)	44 (31.9)
Medium Imbecile	25 (25.3)	21 (16.4)	16 (45.7)	17 (37.8)	4 (44.4)	29 (24.4)	61 (44.2)
High Imbecile	4 (4.0)	13 (10.6)	5 (14.3)	7 (15.5)	3 (33.3)	15 (12.6)	13 (9.4)
Insane/Epileptic	7 (7.1)	5 (3.9)	1 (2.9)	—	—	3 (2.5)	5 (3.6)

ties of old age made elderly admissions less capable of productive labor as a group, regardless of functional level. In 1902 Rome had 415 men to only 135 women, rounding out the profile of the person Rome was admitting when Bernstein took over.

Rome became the not unwillingly receptacle for able-bodied young men of mild or moderate levels of retardation from poor families—some of them troublesome teenagers rejected by the Syracuse Asylum, some shipped upstate from New York City, some from other counties throughout the state. The Custodial Asylum for Unteachable Idiots was changing its image and its purpose as rapidly as possible, resembling nothing so much as the typical congregate

Table 4.5 Age at Admission to Rome, 1896–1902

Age in Years	1896 (%)	1897 (%)	1898 (%)	1899 (%)	1900 (%)	1901 (%)	1902 (%)
0–5	—	—	—	—	—	—	1 (0.7)
5–10	—	3 (2.3)	2 (5.7)	—	—	2 (1.7)	12 (8.7)
10–15	3 (3.0)	9 (7.0)	—	3 (6.7)	1 (11.0)	19 (16.0)	29 (21.0)
15–20	29 (29.3)	26 (20.3)	14 (40.0)	21 (46.7)	5 (55.5)	38 (31.9)	44 (31.9)
20 +	67 (67.7)	90 (70.3)	19 (54.3)	21 (46.7)	3 (33.3)	60 (50.4)	52 (37.7)
Total	99	128	35	45	9	119	138

Source: Rome State Custodial Asylum, annual reports.

asylum encouraged by most other states and asylum professionals but supposedly rejected by New York.

THE FIRST EIGHT YEARS: FITZGERALD'S LEGACY

Throughout the first eight years of Rome, then, the overlapping themes of money and professionalism accompanied de facto alterations in the official mandate of the growing asylum. To some extent, the constant clamor of the officials at Rome for capital expansion was a response to pressure for admissions from the various county supervisors of the poor. It also was an alternative way to increase power when confined to a relatively low-status clientele. By contrast, Syracuse dealt with a higher-functioning, educable population, and it strenuously resisted any large-scale growth. For Rome, an increase in admissions meant opportunities to admit higher-functioning inmates to bear out the claims of industrial potential among its residents by Rome officials. The circular process, then, allowed a move to increase professional status by illustrating the great strides made by institutional expertise in training a population thought to be untrainable. The focus on productiveness and training allowed officials to "attract" the higher-functioning clients needed to substantiate claims of professionalism, yet the unteachable category remained officially available as an explanation for those who failed. In short, the organizational, professional, and economic forces that led to the triumph of the congregate asylum elsewhere also worked in Rome despite its purely custodial origins. The process became even clearer after Bernstein took over as superintendent.

Chapter Five Institutional Innovation and the Uses of Failure

Charles Bernstein is an interesting historical figure whose undeniable accomplishments and reforms have been somewhat overlooked in both the shadows of his more famous contemporaries (e.g., Fernald, Barr, and Goddard), and the glaring light of his ultimate failure to establish a stable model of alternative care. In many ways he was a provincial man, occasionally gruff, and with only a mediocre formal education (Riggs, 1936). He never worked professionally anywhere other than Rome, starting as a medical assistant in 1894 at the age of 22, taking over as superintendent in 1902, and remaining in that post until his death in 1942. He married one of the early teachers of young children at Rome, had no children of his own, and, upon assuming the superintendency, took up permanent residence in the superintendent's house on the grounds of the Rome asylum.

Bernstein was not the "careful" scientist or psychometrician to match the reputation of people such as Henry H. Goddard and Edgar A. Doll at the Vineland Training School in New Jersey, or Frederick Kuhlman at Faribault in Minnesota. He was a medical doctor, as was Fitzgerald (indeed, as required by law for superintendents of most mental asylums), yet his administration at Rome had more to do with agriculture and economics that with disease processes. He was not the prolific writer and asylum proselytizer that Kerlin and Barr were in Pennsylvania and Fernald in Massachusetts. Even Bernstein's long-time associate at Rome, Ward Millias, indirectly conceded as much in his eulogy by way of praising Bernstein's dedication. "His was not the coldly intellectual approach, but rather the warm vivid appreciation of these ineffective people and a desire to help them improve their way of life" (Millias, 1942–43, p. 17).

Certainly, Bernstein was responsible for many of the programmatic changes that began even before Fitzgerald left and expanded rapidly after Bernstein took over. In a discussion section at a meeting of the New York State Conference of Charities and Correction, Bernstein implied as much without mentioning any names. Bernstein began his remarks with an indirect rebuff of a paper just delivered by an officer of the Syracuse facility. The paper had once again proclaimed the need to get all of the custodial cases out of Syracuse, where they got much more training than they needed or deserved. It was a position that Fitzgerald, on his own, had not actively contested. Bernstein disagreed and struggled to establish the benefits that professionalism and expertise could bring to even those that Syracuse regarded as unteachable.

> Anyone who has spent any time with the custodial class of feeble-minded and observed them closely would soon be impressed with the fact that housing, clothing and feeding them, and that alone, was surely a short-sighted policy, as, under such treatment, they are bound to grow more dull, stupid, destructive, filthy or violent (this depending on treatment) and require a constantly increasing amount of personal attention from the attendants (Bernstein, 1903, p. 201).

Bernstein continued with a mildly worded rejection of Fitzgerald's former policy, taking indirect credit for the program reforms already begun by the "assistant physician" (that is, Bernstein himself).

> After having observed this [custodial] class of cases here for three years with no efforts being made toward their training, I was convinced that something must needs be done for them, and the line of work herein outlined was instituted. . . . The work has been under the immediate direction of the assistant physician here with two trained teachers, one in manual training thereat, and has so raised the grade of mentality and improved personal appearance of the inmates, that frequent visitors to the institution note and comment thereon. (Bernstein, 1903, p. 201)

BERNSTEIN'S PROGRESSIVISM

Bernstein's innovations were definitely selective. What recognition Bernstein had among his colleagues was based not on the programs he began within the walls of Rome for the lower-functioning inmates, but on the residential and vocational options he began outside the institution for the inmates with the mildest levels of retardation. With this population of "morons," "defective delinquents," "moral imbeciles," and other high-functioning individuals supposedly never intended for the Rome institution, Bernstein was in many ways the most progressive and daring asylum superintendent in America from 1905 to 1925.

Perhaps the most succinct way to demonstrate this aspect of Bernstein's administration is to compare his positions on a number of issues with those of his contemporary, Walter Fernald. Fernald was the long-time superintendent of the Massachusetts institution started by Howe, who appeared at the end of Chapter 3 defending the "luxury of fatigue" available by moving rocks from one circle to another. From 1887 until his death in 1924, Fernald was a prominent spokesman for the field of mental retardation. In a famous paper delivered before a meeting of his fellow superintendents in 1912, entitled "The Burden of the Feeble-Minded" (Fernald, 1912), he summarized the perceived problems posed by mentally retarded people and discussed his solutions. Fernald's positions were broadly endorsed by his institutional colleagues in the discussion that followed the presentation of the paper. Indeed, despite Fernald's intemperate language, the solutions proposed in the paper were fairly moderate within asylum circles. For example, in contrast to H. H. Goddard, Charles Davenport and others, Fernald did not think sterilization was a good solution. He did not oppose it so much as believe it to be impracticable and dangerous as a substitute for institutionalization. For Fernald, the proper response to the menace of feeblemindedness was segregation, not surgery.[1]

Fernald's paper and the ensuing discussion, however, not only adumbrate the mainstream position of asylum superintendents in this era of eugenics. The unanimously negative response to Bernstein's

mild dissent from Fernald also illustrates the professional courage
Bernstein demonstrated in defending his vision of community placements and parole. It is only fair to note that Fernald himself recanted
or moderated many of his positions before his death, advocating
many of the policies initiated by Bernstein (Fernald, 1924).

In 1912, however, Fernald was fearful that the exploding numbers
of feebleminded people—"a parasitic, predatory class" (Fernald,
1912, p. 90)—would soon plague the country with crimes, prostitu-
tion, defective offspring, and countless other social disasters. In
response to this threat, Fernald advocated:

1. Permanent, lifelong segregation of all feebleminded people, especially
   women of child-bearing age.
2. More and larger institutions.
3. No extrainstitutional placements of males with farmers (this did not
   exclude large, self-contained institutional farm "colonies" of 100 or
   more inmates such as Fernald had at Templeton, and Wilbur,
   Bernstein, and many other superintendents had near their own
   insitutions).
4. No extrainstitutional placement or parole of morons except as a
   compromise with families who want discharge of a relative to return
   home.[2]
5. A massive public education campaign about the dangers of feeble-
   minded people and the necessity to prevent them from procreating.
   (Fernald, 1912)

Bernstein disagreed with all of these points except the call for
public education, and discussed his positions openly in his annual
reports and in professional publications. However, as with his
criticism of Fitzgerald, some of Bernstein's most revealing exchanges
of views with his colleagues survive in the transcripts of discussion
sections at the annual meetings of professional organizations such as
the New York State Conference of Charities and Correction (Bernstein, 1912a) or the main national organization for mental retardation
professionals (Bernstein, 1912b), known at that time as the American
Association for the Study of the Feeble-Minded (formerly the
Association of Medical Officers of American Institutions for Idiotic

and Feeble-Minded Persons, and now the American Association on Mental Retardation).

During the pre–World War I years 1912 to 1917, Bernstein's position developed in exactly the opposite direction taken by most of his peers. For example, in the 1912 meeting of the New York State Conference of Charities and Correction, Bernstein responded to a presentation by Charles C. Davenport, a leading advocate of sterilization for social control of feebleminded people. In his comments, Bernstein made the suggestion that feebleminded people were, in fact, capable of becoming self-supporting. However, at this point he seems to have seen this capacity mainly in terms of self-sufficient institutions making full use of the inmates' free labor. It was, in essence, a continuation of the mainstream rejection of specialized facilities such as Rome.

> I know well enough that if we were given sufficient farm land for the males — I don't know but that I might say for the females, too; but I am sure of the males — that we could make them almost, if not quite, self-supporting. We cannot do it, though, . . . by supporting high-grade and low-grade feeble-minded in different institutions; for if the feebleminded of the higher-grades are of any worth at all, and if it is worthwhile to make them happy, they will never be worth more to the community and they will never be happier than they will be in helping to care for their less fortunate sisters and brothers. For I know that in many instances a feebleminded woman will mother a lower-grade feebleminded child, and thus cater to mother-instinct, making the woman happy, and she takes the place of a paid employee, partly or wholly, in caring for that case. (Bernstein, 1912c, p.146)

Even in 1912, however, the inklings of Bernstein's later position can be found. In another example of Bernstein responding to a presentation rather than making one himself, he gave the invited response to Fernald's 1912 diatribe against feebleminded people. His comments seem mild, and his criticism of Fernald indirect. Nonetheless, his disagreement is clear and in the minority. After complimenting Fernald's presentation, he illustrates his own very different approach: "I have been interested in the matter of placing out boys and I have been trying to convince our managers of the advantage of that" (Bernstein, 1912a, p. 100). Even more daring is Bernstein's suggestion that such a practice of outplacements be extended to women: "I don't know but what I would like to see some of the girls sent out if the families could be well picked and we could have a supervision over them" (p. 101).

The response to Bernstein was dramatic. Charles Little, the newly appointed head of the Letchworth Village Asylum in New York, complains obliquely that Bernstein was undermining the efforts of others: "I think we are defeating our own purposes to some extent when some of us take the position that the feebleminded and the defective delinquent and that higher group should be permanently placed in an institution, and some of us even think that they ought to be placed out in homes" (Bernstein, 1912b, p. 103). Little's opposition to Bernstein's proposal is echoed by superintendents from Minnesota and Ohio, as well as by Fernald of Massachusetts.

Despite this chilly reception, Bernstein's opinions continued to change in this direction, and he followed up with actions. By 1914, in addition to the relatively small farm colonies for men that he had started, Bernstein started opening fairly small "domestic colonies" for young women—what would now be called large group homes. He rented houses in the middle of communities such as the city of Rome and trained mildly retarded women to live there and work during the day as domestics in the homes of the wealthier families. In some cases, the women worked during the day in nearby factories or knitting mills, in what sounds like an "enclave" (Rhodes and Valenta, 1985) employment model.

> While the patients were employed in the mill, they had their own forelady, who acted as liaison officer between them, the management and other employees. Organized labor was not entirely happy over the arrangement, but accepted it because local labor supply was insufficient to keep the mill operating to capacity. On a production basis our girls were found to be 75 per cent efficient as compared to the usual run of labor. . . . The mental defectives were required to live in a healthy manner. Physical hygiene was enforced. Our girls were not out late nights. A steady reservoir of workers was set up which was not subject to the ordinary vicissitudes of free labor. Twenty-five girls reported for duty every day. (Millias, 1942–43, p. 420)

Most such residents, including the males who worked on farms, were eventually paroled or discharged from Rome entirely (Riggs,

1936; Rome, 1915; Wilber, 1969). Bernstein opposed the opening of any more asylums in New York State and, instead, advocated the rapid expansion of domestic, industrial, and farm colonies and supervised parole (Bernstein, 1920). He thought that most mildly retarded adults, or morons, should not be institutionalized at all (Rome, 1917), and complained of the debilitating effect of such incarceration upon the inmates (Rome, 1917; Scheerenberger, 1983).

Many of these policies were fairly common in other human service fields such as juvenile delinquency, mental illness, and criminology (Rothman, 1980). Indeed, "small" farm colonies, of fewer than 40 residents, had been successfully tried by several insane asylum superintendents in upstate New York before Bernstein's tenure at Rome. As usual, however, mental retardation as a field was far from the cutting edge of social welfare reform. Among his peers, Bernstein's policies on parole and small colonies, together with his opposition to sterilization and blanket institutionalization, were considered experimental at best, and flagrant irresponsibility at worst.

By 1917, Bernstein's policies and his vigorous defense of them were well known among his institutional colleagues. Indeed, his policies were gaining some acceptance within the American Association for the Study of the Feeble-Minded. Bernstein was secure enough, and his colonies widespread enough, to respond with some sarcasm to Fernald's grudging admission that perhaps some modest parole and outplacement would not be disastrous. Behind the sarcasm, though, one senses a deeper resentment in Bernstein. Despite having been elected president of the association twice by 1917, Bernstein never felt totally accepted or, perhaps, adequately appreciated by his peers (Riggs, 1936). The edge of bitterness seems especially cutting in Bernstein's response to a comment of Fernald's that, in fact, there probably were some morons capable of telling the truth, but as a rule they should not be left at large in the community: "I am glad that Dr. Fernald believes that not every fool is a liar or a thief. If I send a boy or a girl out, there is a cry that the boys burn buildings and the girls are immoral. It is not so. I say there are many of the feebleminded who are better citizens than I am" (Bernstein, 1917, p. 29).

By the time of America's involvement in World War I, Bernstein's innovations were well established and the worst years of professional isolation were over. He had firmly changed the image and legacy of the Rome institution. Only in the last few years before his death in 1942 did the facility start to regain its original reputation as a massive, purely custodial institution; the Bernstein network of over 60 domestic, industrial, and farm colonies gradually withered away.

By 1915, Bernstein was completing his second term as president of the American Association for the Study of the Feeble-Minded. Letchworth Village, in downstate New York, was taking over as the state's newest and supposedly most exemplary institution for the feebleminded; it embodied many of Bernstein's programs for colonies and parole despite Superintendent Little's early opposition. And in large cities throughout the state, special classes and schools for mildly handicapped children and adolescents such as Bernstein used for his outplacement programs were rapidly expanding (New York State Commission, 1915). In 1919, authority over all of the institutions was consolidated at the state level under a separate Commission for Mental Defectives. It began a gradual dissolution of the asylum tradition that had produced generations of leaders such as Wilbur, Bernstein, and Little. It had been a loosely coupled system where one of the superintendents (all men) could, over decades of relatively autonomous administration, stamp an institution with his own personality and programs. Increasingly after 1920, the entire mental health system was bureaucratized and more tightly coordinated programmatically, as well as financially, in Albany.

THE THEMES OF LEADERSHIP

In the first 10 to 15 years of his new administration Bernstein inaugurated his policies of deinstitutionalization and community colonies, with vigorous defenses at state and national conferences, but there were limits to Bernstein's progressivism. They emerged especially in the treatment of the most severely disabled inmates who remained at Rome. As already noted, from the very first year of his leadership, Bernstein was eager to differentiate himself from Fitzgerald's administration and Rome's original mandate, while building upon some of the trends begun (perhaps at Bernstein's instigation as head physician) under Fitzgerald's tenure. Accompanying Bernstein's colony and parole policies, four additional themes run through the annual reports for the years from 1903 to 1918 or so: the official disappearance of idiots and low-grade imbeciles; the use of chronicity for internal discipline and administrative control; the pervasive endorsement of vocationalism and economic utility, both institutionally and individually, as the continuing standard of institutional success; and the growth of professionalism.

Bernstein and the Vanishing Idiots

By 1915, Bernstein was backing up his often-made claim that the population at Rome was dramatically changing. Supposedly, there had been a complete reversal in admission patterns within the first decade of his superintendency that left only 20 percent of new inmates in the idiot or imbecile range (Rome, 1916, p. 19). Such admission rates would eventually make Rome's inmates look very similar to those at other institutions in New York and elsewhere. According to Wallin (1917), the residents at Vineland, a training school in New Jersey, had all been tested on the Binet Intelligence Test by 1910, and 19 percent scored in the idiot range, 54 percent in the imbecile range (p. 115). Fernald reported that 18.8 percent of the Waverly residents scored in the idiot range (Massachusetts School for the Feeble-Minded, 1914, p. 27). According to the Federal Census of Institutions in 1923, almost 16 percent of the inmates nationally were classified as idiots (6,642 out of 42,336) (U.S. Bureau of the Census, 1923). Even Kuhlman's important 1916 survey of institutional populations in six large congregate facilities outside the Northeast (in California, Illinois, Indiana, Kansas, Minnesota, and Wisconsin) found a self-reported rate of only 26 percent for idiots in institutions (Kuhlman 1916).

Continuing a trend

It was important to Bernstein that Rome should come to resemble this national profile, and that it not be viewed as a custodial depository for unteachable idiots. In actuality, Bernstein needed to do very little to achieve this end, as the inmate distribution for Rome in 1902 presented in Chapter 4 clearly showed (see Table 4.2). Bernstein's characterization, then, of an institutional transformation at Rome tends to overstate the discontinuity between his and Fitzgerald's admissions profiles.

There were no "morons" then at Rome because this category did not exist until Goddard popularized the term in 1910, after widespread adoption of his 1908 translation of the Binet Intelligence Test had established the notion of "mental age" (Zenderland, 1986). Before then, purely functional criteria were used to assign people to one level or another of retardation. Of course, the new category included many people who would not previously have been labeled feebleminded—all those who scored as high as a supposed mental age of 12 years. However, it is equally true that some people described as morons by Goddard (and Bernstein) had previously been labeled high-grade imbeciles or borderline cases (in my judgment, based on behavioral descriptions in the case records of the reading, writing, and math skills of these individuals).

While Fitzgerald's Rome had no morons, it did have a growing number of high- and moderate-grade imbeciles. By the time Fitzgerald left Rome in 1902, his own figures indicate that some 409 idiots and low-grade imbeciles had been admitted; some 281 admissions had been moderate- or high-grade imbeciles, not counting those individuals not labeled feebleminded at all (Rome, 1903). At least by internal classification, then, the transformation described by Bernstein had begun long before 1910.

The struggle for a new image

Bernstein's active public stance before the legislators, his professional peers, and the general public was intended to force a change of image as well as substance for Rome. He commented on this "image" problem in one of his earliest annual reports.

It is surprising to observe the erroneous impression existing in the minds of the various people who visit this asylum, and even many who do not, regarding the mental condition of the cases cared for here, and these erroneous impressions are very often found to exist with those who have official connection with the institution. Nearly every visitor is surprised to learn either through observation or by being told that we have others here than the very lowest grades of humanity. (Rome, 1906, p. 41)

Bernstein systematically set about to remove almost all references to the presence of unteachable idiots among the inmates at Rome. In his very first annual report to the New York legislature, Bernstein notably dispensed with Fitzgerald's practice of breaking down admission statistics according to functional level. Without access to case files or other information, the legislators (as well as later historians) had only Bernstein's comments to indicate the functional level of the new admissions. Until the 1930s, Bernstein rarely discussed the status of the lower-functioning portion of the inmates at Rome. Instead, Bernstein's attention was aggressively focused on the need for increased programming and colonization for a much higher-functioning "clientele." Despite his disagreements with Fernald and the other superintendents over how to deal with the suddenly burgeoning population of morons, Bernstein was in complete agreement with his colleagues that it was this segment of the feebleminded population that required the urgent attention of the experts. In words that echo Wilbur's and Howe's expression of preference for mildly retarded inmates, Frederick Kuhlman, a prominent superintendent and psychometrician from Minnesota, summarized the reasons for dismissal of the low-grade segment as an object of professional concern:

Pauperism, delinquency and crime in their association with feeblemindedness are for the most part connected with the higher grades only. Secondly, the majority of feebleminded children have feebleminded parents, and these feebleminded parents are invariably the high grade. Thirdly, the high grade cases alone can be trained to useful activities to such a degree as to yield practical returns. For each of these three reasons it is more important to provide special institutional care for the high grade than for the low grade. To provide for the lower grades only does little more than relieve the individual homes from which they come which, though it means much to these homes, does but relatively little that is of interest to society in general. (Kuhlman, 1916, pp. 9–10)

In his first complete year as superintendent, Bernstein had his board of managers recommend to the legislature an official change in name and mandate for the Rome facility. From hereon, the petition read, the Rome institution should be designated simply as an "asylum for the care of the custodial classes of feebleminded." The reasoning was simple:

> The time has now arrived when it is a fully demonstrated fact that the term "unteachable idiots" should no longer be used in connection with this asylum, or in fact any other, it being surely an unwarranted stigma on the lives of these poor unfortunates to so characterize them, when as a matter of fact not one percent, if any, of our inmates are truly unteachable, many of them being able to read and write, and over 50 percent of them have been taught to be useful. (Rome, 1904, p. 23)

By 1919, any connotation of custodialism in the name was dropped, as Rome's name was changed to the Rome State School.

Bernstein got both the name change and an expanded official mandate. By 1910, Bernstein had begun to focus his attention on the expansion of his extrainstitutional programs for mildly retarded young adults.

Bernstein and the Use of Chronicity As Punishment

The people who had previously been viewed as unteachable idiots did not vanish, of course; Bernstein would not have wanted them to. The category of chronicity could serve several useful institutional functions, as the earlier institutional history discussed in Chapter 4 illustrated. As with Wilbur and Howe before him, and so many reformers to follow, Bernstein's progressivism stopped at the door to the back ward, which housed those with the most severe and multiple disabilities. The few public comments Bernstein made about these residents of Rome reveal a much more conventional and custodial spirit.

Soon after Bernstein took over at Rome, he proudly reported to the legislature that only three wards in the whole asylum remained locked (Rome, 1905), those containing the lowest-grade inmates and the disciplinary cases, mixed with the "crippled idiots." Bernstein used the wards housing the most severely retarded inmates as punishment cells for any mildly retarded malcontents. Needless to say, these wards were not meant to be pleasant. Bernstein even used distinctive types of clothing as both a stigmatic identification of the "failures" and an additional disciplinary humiliation.

> Uniforms have been adopted for all inmates male and female two grades for each, one for low grade cases who destroy and soil their clothing and another for those who are brighter and more cleanly. This serves as a good disciplinary measure within the asylum and also serves to mark the patient if one leaves the grounds of the institution and they are then almost invariably quickly returned to us especially in view of the standing reward of two dollars. (Rome, 1916, p. 25)

Bernstein's description of his disciplinary measures shows a perception of low-grade inmates more as a disembodied category than as a distinct group of individuals. The people were apparently something of a nuisance, but the category was useful as a means of control for the higher-functioning people.

> Our means of discipline are to curtail privileges, placing the erring ones on other than open or unlocked wards; placing them on a low-grade ward and compelling them to work there; removing them from the specially set and served tables for the higher grade cases and seating them among the low-grade cases; not allowing them at entertainments; taking their dress-up suits of clothes away from them, etc. No form of physically-inflicted punishment is allowed, those forms appealing to the mind through curtailed privileges being entirely effectual. (Rome, 1903, p. 59)

One is left to imagine what life was like for those who were not the objects of Bernstein's punishment but the living definition of that punishment. To be punished was to become low-grade.

Bernstein and the Standard of Economic Utility

In a discussion in 1917, Bernstein gave a short critique of those who wanted to segregate all feebleminded people for life. He meant his statement as a defense of his extrainstitutional programs. "We have heard so much of segregating the feebleminded and piling them up in masses because they were dangerous, or because we could not make use of them. . . . We see now what a large percentage can be made use of—over half of them. What industry would shut up business because a small percentage of the output is a failure? Are we going to pile them up in a mass in custody much longer because some of them are failures?" (Bernstein, 1917, pp. 32–33).

This quotation is striking because it combines both Bernstein's relatively reformist posture toward mildly retarded people—so-called morons and high-grade imbeciles—with an implicit endorsement of the custodial abandonment approach to more severely retarded people, especially those labeled as idiots. In either case, the principle of economic utility is the deciding factor. The inmates are the commodities, the asylum the factory. Continued isolation in the asylum was unquestioned for those who were inefficient "failures." As Bernstein bluntly phrased it, the institution was meant for those whom the marketplace "could not make use of."

Increasingly, the economic utility of inmates was discussed in terms of both individual's productivity in the marketplace and the individual's productivity for the institution itself. Economic utility not only made the retarded individual a valuable commodity to be "sold" back to the community, but it was also the standard for movement within the institution itself. There is no challenge to the sincerity of Bernstein's motives for colony expansion in recognizing the enormous economic utility those colonies possessed for the Rome institution, or the larger cultural context of the marketplace metaphors.

Institutional utility

Capital outlays for new institutional buildings were always difficult for Rome to acquire, as Fitzgerald and Bernstein both discovered. Bernstein's domestic and farm colonies, however, relied upon relatively inexpensive rentals or purchases of existing farms and houses that each provided residence for between 20 and 40 "boys and girls." Bernstein explained that he referred to his inmates as "boys" and "girls" regardless of their ages because "thus speaking of them in their presence tends to incite in them subjection, as they, if called boys and girls, they hearing it, never learn to think of themselves as anything but children" (Rome, 1903, p. 55). Most of Bernstein's annual reports sound more like a combination of real estate speculation and agricultural science than summaries of mental institutions. His proposals for land acquisition, in particular, became more and more detailed. Beyond the initial savings over building costs, the farms and domestic colonies became money-makers for Bernstein after an average of one year of operation (Bernstein, 1920). The farms returned around two dollars' worth of crops, meat, and dairy products for every dollar of maintenance and rental spent. For the women's domestic colonies, the return rate was reportedly even higher (Bernstein, 1920). As a result, Bernstein was able to sell his colony programs as fiscally prudent as well as programmatically progressive, and do it all in language that sounds familiar to current arguments for deinstitutionalization.

> We must do other than make the support of the defective and dependent classes a dead load or burden on the State, but must on the other hand add leaven to the load, and instead of asking the State to go on providing beds at $500 to $1000 each . . . we must provide other means of care wherein $50 to $100 beds, as in colonies, may be provided and the trained inmates thereon require little or no direct appropriation for their maintenance. . . . Where custodial care is required something more economical and many times more humane than brick and stone walls and iron fences may meet the need, such for instance, as for the feebleminded or delinquent the kindly fostering care of a good man and wife on a farm colony, who through their loving care and thoughtful foresight will have no trouble whatever in holding at home boys and girls of these classes. (Rome, 1916, pp. 17–18)

Bernstein's fervor led to some extravagant suggestions for state approval. At one point, Bernstein wanted the state to assume possession of all abandoned farm property and allow Rome to use it as colonies (Rome, 1916). He was willing to take untillable land, have his inmates clear the acreage to make it arable, rehabilitate the farm buildings, and then sell the property to private farmers while his "boys" moved on to other reclamation projects (pp. 21–22). He proposed taking over all the unused state property bordering all of the barge canals (p. 21). Perhaps the most bizarre plan proposed by Bernstein was taking over the New York State Fair Grounds in Syracuse as a "colony" for up to 1,000 men, instead of the "good new concrete buildings with good toilet facilities" (p. 21) going to waste for 355 days a year. Bernstein's inmates would do the year-round upkeep at no charge, and during the 10 days of the fair each year they could be moved to tents on the outskirts of the fairgrounds, where they would not bother the visitors.

Individual training

The economic utility of the inmates' labor to the institution could be fully exploited only if efficiently organized. To that end, Bernstein quickly established a diagnostic and instructional program that focused on the vocational potential of each new admission. Instead of labeling inmates according to the traditional categories of medical pathology—idiot, idio-imbecile, imbecile, and, later, moron— Bernstein classed them by "ability to work" (1903, p. 114). He identified five levels of inmates' vocational utility: "Class 1: Unable to do any work; Class 2: Capable of self care only; Class 3: Can assist others in some work; Class 4: Usefulness in industrial departments; Class 5: Good workers" (1903, p. 114).

A new inmate was to receive either training or employment based on the vocational classification. Training was intended exclusively to raise vocational ability from one level to the next. The "school" department was totally given over to manual training and industrial classes. Bernstein's explanation could serve for many of today's special educators as an adequate justification of a "functional" curriculum: "We do appreciate the need of some primary school work for a few of the younger and brighter boys and girls. However, . . . for the great majority it only serves to render them conscious of their limitation and dissatisfied with their surroundings. . . . habits of industry and manual and industrial occupation . . . are of much more worth than intellectual training, both to the individual and to the State in rendering the individual able to give to the State in labor, some compensation in return for all the State has done" (Rome, 1908, p. 21).

Of 200 cases admitted between 1900 and 1902, Bernstein reported that only 38 were "unamenable" to such training. Of the 162 remaining cases, some 87 percent reportedly improved by at least one classification level by 1903 (1903, p. 118). It must be noted, of course, that despite the colonies, the work of most of the inmates was either attendant care on the wards or basic landscaping and road grading. In

1903, for example, out of 600 inmates reported as being "in training," one-fourth (150) were on the "wards" and more than 30 percent (187 males) were assigned to "grading." The others' assignments were domestic occupations in the laundry, kitchen, dining room, and such, farming, and crafts (tailoring, carpentry, sewing, etc.). Even such work, Bernstein said, was eminently more valuable to the low-functioning inmate than the futility of classwork. "I am convinced that I can do more for a low grade feebleminded boy, who soils himself and is destructive, through one summer's work for such boy with a pile of earth to be moved with pick, shovel and barrow, and a good attendant direct him, than could any teacher working with him in the schoolroom for the same length of time" (Rome, 1908, p. 21).

One final benefit of useful labor that Bernstein, as well as most other superintendents, cited harks back to Fernald's praise of the "luxury of fatigue." Tired inmates might or might not have been happy inmates, but it seems clear that they were less troublesome. As in much of the discussion of this era, this factor was almost always described with nuances of sexual euphemism. Hard work made the inmate too exhausted to practice sexual perversions such as masturbation, or "self abuse." (Rome, 1904, p. 58) As Bernstein put it in one discussion: "You can't work those boys too hard" (Bernstein, 1912c, p. 194).

Value to the state in terms of labor performed; value to the inmate in terms of personal utility and self-support; and value to the superintendents in terms of easier behavior management; for all these reasons, Bernstein emphasized vocational training and employment of feebleminded inmates as the responsibility of the well-run institution. "One-half the happiness in life is in having our minds occupied and in knowing that we are doing useful work, and the feebleminded are no exception to this rule" (Rome, 1904, p. 58).

Bernstein and the Quest for Professional Status

Bernstein's annual reports and other writing during the period from 1903 through 1918 or so show a steady concern with the public perception of his occupation as a legitimate profession requiring expertise and deserving of respect. This theme is certainly not as overt as, say, Bernstein's concern with vocationalism. It occurs, however, as an unstated subtext.

The field as a whole was not well established as a legitimate subcategory of medical or educational expertise. In 1896, two years after Bernstein began at Rome, the 20th annual meeting of the Association of Medical Officers of American Institutions for Idiotic and Feeble-Minded Persons was attended by only nine active members (Sloan and Stevens, 1976, p. 35). There were 58 active and 95 honorary members that year. By 1919, the number of active members of what was then called the American Association for the Study of the Feeble-Minded had grown to only 76 (Sloan and Stevens, 1976, p. 99). In 1917, there was a strong move within the association to discontinue its professional journal, the *Journal of Psycho-Asthenics*, because there were thought not to be enough papers of sufficient quality to support the publication. Moreover, during that same time the growth of "ungraded" classes in the public school systems created an expanding group of "special educators" who represented potential competition for the institutional superintendents as a professional class of experts in the training of feebleminded people. By 1915, there were reportedly 116 such classes in New York State, 76 of them in New York City under the leadership of Elizabeth Farrell (New York State Commission, 1915, p. 62). In contrast, only one new institution for the feebleminded, (Letchworth) was started in New York between 1900 and 1920.

Between 1910 and 1920, the proportion of feebleminded people in institutions grew from 37.5 to 55.5 inmates per 100,000 general population in New York (Pollack and Furbush, 1921). However, New York slid from 6th to 10th among all the states in the rate of institutionalization of feebleminded people. During the same decade, the state moved from second to first in the rate of institutionalization of mentally ill people (343.2 to 374.6 per 100,000) (Pollack and Furbush, 1921). Nationally, by 1920, there were still only 43 public institutions for feebleminded people in the entire country, compared with 158 state and federal hospitals for people labeled mentally ill, thus severely limiting the professional peer group of asylum superintendents (Pollack and Furbush, 1921, p. 140). Despite the eugenics scare, despite more than 60 years of asylum tradition in the Northeast, and despite such professional developments as the congregate asylum and intelligence testing, asylum superintendents were far from an established professional group in the first two decades of Bernstein's administration. They certainly lagged far behind their administrative rivals in mental hospitals (Gitlin, 1982).

The fragility of professional status was a factor in the ultimate triumph of the congregate asylum. Purely custodial responsibility could not lead to a high occupational stature for asylum superintendency. Aside from the justifications of economy, efficiency, and better treatment and training, the congregate asylum as an institutional arrangement presented opportunities for the elaboration and demonstration of professional expertise.

The problem of professional respectability that Bernstein, as head of a nominally custodial facility, faced was ironically verified when the planning committee for Letchworth Village in Rockland County had to decide what kind of institution the newest asylum for the feebleminded should be. Originally, the facility was to be a purely custodial facility for the New York City population, the Eastern State Custodial Asylum. The three-member planning commission appointed by the legislature to research the structure and location of the new asylum (a marked departure from the manner in which the Rome asylum began), however, firmly recommended that the new facility not be custodial in nature. The recommendation's backhanded reference to how "even" Rome had trainable inmates showed the reputation of custodialism that Bernstein faced.

In his efforts to establish a professional reputation, as well as pursue his relatively progressive inclinations, Bernstein took several steps to reinforce the image of expertise and excellence that he sought for Rome and for his profession as a whole. Those specific steps were the product of two basic strategies of rising professionalism: claiming a monopoly on knowledge, and asserting administrative discretion, or professional autonomy.

Bernstein and the monopoly on knowledge

One ingredient in any successful claim to professionalism is a distinct area of special expertise. With the rise of occupational professionalism in the last half of the nineteenth century, the fastest way to establish such expertise was through creation and control of a training and licensing process. The 1910 Flexner Report on medical school education in America is the best-known argument in favor of specialized knowledge as the basis for formal membership in a specific professional class (Starr, 1982). At the turn of the century, there was little, if any, formalized training in asylum management. Bernstein was one of the first to begin specialized training "schools" at the institution.

In only his second year of leadership at Rome, Bernstein initiated a two-year training program for apprentice attendants. Bernstein hoped not only to establish a standardized curriculum for introductory knowledge about the care and treatment of mental deficiency, but also to create a steady supply of trained attendants for Rome. Not incidentally, the attendants-in-training at Rome were also a source of institutional labor at rock-bottom prices. Bernstein also advocated a minimal training level for attendants statewide.

Bernstein started a summer school for teachers in 1915. Throughout his career, he gave frequent lectures to sociology and psychology classes at area colleges (Syracuse, Colgate, Hamilton, Skidmore, and the Oswego Normal School). Through the summer school, Bernstein was able to influence the knowledge and perspective of an entire generation of teachers. The Rome annual reports during this period often printed the entire schedule of classes and the specific lecture series led by Bernstein each summer. The school gave Bernstein a context in which to push his emphasis on industrial training, over more traditional efforts at reading and writing, as the key to effective and efficient institution management. The desired effect of the training was perfectly illustrated in one teacher's recollection of his first year at Rome. The observations are very similar to what many of today's advocates of functional curricula for students with severe disabilities are promoting. The target population has changed but the arguments have remained the same.

> As I looked about me I was frankly confused. Boys were taught to cobble shoes, read, sew, make bird houses, write and polish floors. Girls were taught to sew, clean house, read, write, cook and serve meals. Whatever tasks were at hand boys and girls were taught to tackle. I was confused because I had

never in my then short professional experience seen a teacher of cobbling nor a teacher of potato peeling. There was a question in my mind: Is peeling potatoes education? The answer soon became obvious. It *is* education, and will be as long as mentally handicapped boys and girls are to be fitted to live among their normal neighbors with the least amount of friction and dependence. (cited in Riggs, 1936, p. 54)

The school lasted only until 1935 (why it ceased is unclear). Moreover, it was never officially licensed by the State Department of Education as a recognized course of study, although students from the Oswego Normal School received credit for attending. Still, according to one report, Bernstein's stature was high enough in New York State that "a certificate from Rome was a certificate from him and its holder was acknowledged as a licentiate in this department of knowledge" (Millias, 1942–43, p. 18). In Bernstein's vision, the institution was no longer to be simply the custodial home of large numbers of feebleminded people; it was to be the repository of knowledge about those people as well.

Bernstein and professional autonomy

As mentioned repeatedly, most of Bernstein's more progressive measures affected mildly retarded admissions to Rome. This focus on the more able class was important in removing the custodial stigma from Rome. Professionally, however, the initiatives that Bernstein took also had the effect of drastically increasing the degree of discretion required in administering those programs, an indication of expertise and professional autonomy. The expert makes precise judgments about who among the inmates can make it on a farm colony, not to mention parole. If the continuum of program options is lengthened, then the number of decisions about any individual's particular program is comparably increased. Only someone who is thoroughly familiar with both those options and the problems of the individual, and who is adept at making fine diagnostic distinctions, could be entrusted with such heightened discretion.

The programs also relied on a detailed classification system for the inmates, no longer limited to idiots and imbeciles, and maybe idio-imbeciles if you wanted to get technical. The power of the new intelligence tests allowed the superintendent unimagined levels of detail in assigning mental ages to inmates. As discussed earlier, Bernstein also pushed a parallel system of functional (vocational) classification that further determined the training and residence of admissions to Rome. The more elaborate the taxonomy of mental defect, the more credible the claims to expertise by those who used the taxonomic structure to organize their institutions.

Bernstein was apparently concerned that his status among his employees at Rome also be regularly reinforced. In the "Rules and Regulations for Employees" reprinted in the annual report for 1907, there are many requirements for cleanliness, kindness, and professional deportment. Rule 43, however, concerns a detail of social hierarchy that is simultaneously indicative of both how fragile and how important professional stature was to Bernstein; "Whenever a physician enters the ward all the attendants shall rise and the senior attendant shall accompany him through the ward, and be prepared to give all necessary information concerning the patients in his or her charge" (Rome, 1907, p. 87). Only the superintendent and his two medical assistants had medical degrees.

THE OFFICIAL RECORD OF CHANGE BY 1920

When the official name of the Rome institution was changed again in 1919, — at the request of Bernstein — to the Rome State School, it represented, at least symbolically, the triumph of 15 years of effort by Bernstein to reform the image (and the substance) of his institution. The official designation as an asylum for "unteachable idiots" had been dropped earlier. At last, the reference to a "custodial" function had also vanished. At least nominally, Bernstein had banished the identification of Rome with chronicity. His activist programs of parole and colonization, his expansion of manual and industrial instruction, a dramatic growth in admissions from the population of newly discovered morons, and his specific assumption of professional training responsibilities all served Bernstein well if one of his aims was to escape the professionally limiting and culturally isolating association with those people deemed beyond help or reform. Regardless of his aims, the result of his efforts was to change what people (at least, officials and other superintendents) thought of when they thought of Rome. Chronicity hovered now in the background as a continuing but minor category of Rome's function. That, in any case, was the official story of the Rome State School. The more informal reality of the case records is that chronicity—in all its dimensions—remained a very major category. The next chapter will examine this perspective as the final part of the story of Rome.

Chapter Six Profiles of Chronicity

From the very first days of Rome, the people admitted had a wide range of ability. Dennis K. (case no.68)[1] was one of the earliest admissions, arriving in 1894, yet was typical of the high-functioning, mildly handicapped sort of inmate that Bernstein would emphasize after he officially took over as superintendent in 1902. When given an intelligence test in 1919, at the age of 67 (after 25 years of residency at Rome), Dennis K.'s score gave him a mental age of seven years, placing him at the bottom of the so-called "moron" range of mild retardation. His case record says he could read and write. In the summer and fall, Bernstein would include K. among the male inmates hired out to local farmers for hop picking. (Hop berries were then a common crop in upstate New York for use in making beer and ale). K. was typical for other reasons as well. Like many other inmates admitted in the first decade, he was a transfer from another state institution (in this case, Utica), rather than coming directly from the community where the pressure for admissions supposedly originated. At 42 years of age, Dennis K. was older than the average admission, yet not at all unusual for Rome (much to Bernstein's chagrin). Indeed, K.'s age is the only discernible reason why Bernstein did not placed him in one of the farm colonies. K. died at Rome in 1930, at the age of 78, having lived there for 36 years.

Also admitted to Rome in 1894 was George G. (case no.118). G. was at the opposite end of the spectrum from Dennis K. in terms of skills and behavior. According to G.'s case record, he could not talk and had a "very poor understanding of language; practically nothing." George G.'s daily life at Rome was the kind that did not make it into the annual reports, and can be only partially inferred from the skimpy notes in the files. G. did not work on farms or participate in the vocational training on the grounds at Rome. He did not leave the asylum for seasonal work. Indeed, the records suggest that he seldom left E-8, the notorious ward for the lowest-functioning inmates and for disciplinary cases. In the words of one staff member at Rome, near the end of George's life, he was simply "one of the filthy cases from E-8."

One other feature of George G.'s institutional history at Rome is interesting (although not unusual, as I will discuss later). In 1907, a brother of G. asked in a letter to Bernstein whether George could come to live with him on his farm in Nebraska. In the labored hand of someone who did not write often or easily, the brother asked Bernstein for permission that he did not technically need. "Please let me know how long [George] has to stay in the Asylum. Can we get him if the contition [*sic*] warrant for him to come out of the Asylum? There is plenty of work if you think he can do any light work. (no.118) Bernstein replied to the brother with the standard denial to family requests for custody, relying on his "professional authority" to make his medical opinion sound like a legal barrier to discharge.

> George can never be entirely cured of his condition. Friends of inmates are allowed to take them out *when their condition is such as to warrant it* [emphasis added]. However, George can never be cured and will always have to remain in the Asylum as a home. He can only do a little work and that under close supervision and it would be impossible for him to work outside. George is not insane, but he is feeble-minded. We assure you he is kindly treated and all in our power done for him. (no.118)

George died four years after this exchange of letters. Even his corpse could not leave Rome. He was buried on the grounds in an inmate cemetery, which was later destroyed.

The examples of Dennis K. and George G. illustrate both the value and the limitations of case records as evidence. The records offer a chance at personalizing the account with names, events, and individual descriptions. At least with the Rome case records, however, much of the evidence remains frustrating, especially for severely retarded people. For the most part, one must inevitably rely on what the caretakers and social agents have to say about severely retarded people, evidence that is indirect. We have Itard's notebooks of his struggle to teach Victor but no diary of Victor's struggle to learn. The superintendents wrote the annual reports, not the inmates.

Given this major evidentiary limitation, however, there remains the importance of the distinction between public and private commentary. Did Bernstein say the same things in his correspondence to families that he said in his reports to the legislature? How did the staff at Rome perceive their jobs? How did they portray the inmates with whom they worked? Do the descriptive statistics presented for the public record agree with whatever numbers can be independently compiled from the files? Any account, then, of the early years of the Rome Asylum would be incomplete without some effort to go beyond the published pronouncements of Fitzgerald and Bernstein, no matter how revealing those public comments are. This chapter will examine the case records of the inmates at Rome in seeking an additional glimpse of what life in the institution must have been like in the early years of its existence.

EXAMINING THE FILES

Bernstein officially took over as superintendent at Rome in 1902, although circumstantial evidence suggests that he had much of the operational responsibility for administration even before then. By that time, some 900 people had been admitted to the asylum and approximately 550 of them still resided at Rome. With this base population, Bernstein began his efforts to reform both the practice and the perception of the Rome facility. Even after 1902, the inmates who had been admitted under Fitzgerald's tenure continued to be the largest influence on what Bernstein could and could not do to change the image of his institution's purpose.

What the Files Contained

I examined the files of 418 of the original 900 admissions. By the 1980s, records of only 64 of the first 200 admissions remained in the

archives[2] at Rome. Many of these 200 were holdovers from the
Oneida County Almshouse who had lived in the insane asylum part
of the county facility before the state purchased the facility under the
State Care Act. Presumably many of the missing records among the
200 were of people who were fairly quickly redistributed from Rome
to various state insane asylums. Of the next 300 admissions (case
no.201 through no.500), case records exist for 282, and all of these
were examined. Of the final 400 admissions for the period covered
(case no.501 through no.900), I randomly selected some 72 cases
(18%) for full examination.

The contents of the records themselves varied greatly from case to
case. Some contained only a name on an otherwise blank sheet of
paper. Other files were several inches thick with the institutional
records of over 60 years of life at Rome. Of the many ways that the
data could have been grouped and sorted, one of the most straightforward procedures was simply to categorize the information according
to who wrote it. This approach led to three basic divisions. First,
there were those records written by various agents of the social
welfare system not employed by Rome, usually as part of the
admission process. Second, there were those records created by the
staff at Rome, including Bernstein. Finally, there were those records
created by the inmates themselves or their family members, usually in
the form of letters.

Official External Attention

The most common form of information contained in most of the
files, though not in all, related to the initial referral for admission.
Legally, every person referred for admission to Rome had to be
certified by two medical doctors as appropriately impaired. For
purposes of the Rome State Custodial Asylum, the doctors simply
substituted the form normally used for insane asylum referrals. This
form, called a medical certificate of lunacy, was sometimes little more
than a handwritten (or occasionally typed) statement that the person
was "insane" and "a proper person for care and treatment" in a state
asylum, together with a sentence or two giving reasons for the
doctor's opinion. In other cases, especially those from the larger

counties, the certification form was typically about three pages, with specific questions about family history, personal habits, observed behavior, communication, and other topics. In all cases, the forms spoke of lunacy and insanity, not idiocy or feeblemindedness. However, in many cases the doctor filling out the form did make that distinction.

A second form present in most of the case files, the "Form of Request for Admission to the Rome State Custodial Asylum," was similar in many respects to the longest version of the certificate of lunacy. Instead of a private medical doctor, however, these forms were usually filled out by the county poorhouse superintendent or staff of the referring institution. (An example of this form is contained in the Appendix.)

Other types of information that would fall into this category would include patient histories written by the referring institution, correspondence from almshouse officials, or legal documents (regarding inheritances, criminal activity, lawsuits, and so on). These were comparatively rare in the files that I examined.

Official Internal Attention

Internal documents produced about residents at Rome once they had been admitted concerned health, discipline, IQ tests, and external inquiries. Whenever an inmate was moved from one ward to another, a transfer sheet supposed to be completed. If illness or injury caused someone to be transferred to the institutional hospital, this sheet would briefly describe the reason. If behavior problems sent an inmate to E-8 (a particularly gruesome ward), the accompanying sheet would explain the problem. Death produced a transfer sheet to the morgue. These sheets were filled out by the ward attendants or doctors and often contained varied — even contradictory — descriptions of a single inmate.

Beginning about 1915, Bernstein started giving all of his inmates IQ tests (usually the Binet, occasionally the Kuhlman). The actual test forms with the comments of the examiner are occasionally included in an inmate's file. For 67-year-old Dennis K., for example, the examiner wrote a complaint on the IQ form file that K. was not particularly cooperative and "cares little whether he scores high or not" (case no.68).

One of the most revealing types of information in the files was the letters written by Bernstein about specific cases to inquiring family members or local almshouse officials. There were also standardized pieces of correspondence (mostly pleas for Christmas contributions) that Bernstein annually sent out to relatives.

Discharge (including transfer to other institutions) or death forms were in most of the files. Together with the admission forms, they allowed direct compilation of descriptive data about such things as length of stay and reason for discharge. A few of the files had photographs of the inmates.

Personal and Family Correspondence

In a surprising number of the files that I examined (about 20 percent), there were letters from a family member to an inmate or to Bernstein. In almost every case, Bernstein responded to each letter. (Of course, it may also be true that only those letters to which Bernstein replied were saved in the first place.) The letters gave a limited but fascinating glimpse into how some families at the turn of the century reacted to having a mentally retarded child or sibling.

In a few of the files of higher-functioning inmates were letters written by the inmates themselves to Bernstein while they were on parole, or after they had moved to one of the colonies. Many more such letters were published in *The Herald*, an institutional newsletter published "by and for the pupils of the Rome State School."

CASE RECORDS AND THE WORTH OF KNOWLEDGE

In Chapters 4 and 5 I argued that the institutional character of the Rome Asylum emerged out of a programmatic paradox. On the one hand, Rome was founded explicitly to serve the most severely disabled segment of the feebleminded population. On the other hand, institutional status and professional image required a higher-functioning clientele with whom innovative programs could be expected to succeed. Charles Bernstein, especially, struggled in his annual reports and professional publications to establish the notion that Rome did indeed have some remediable inmates.

The quantity and quality of information kept in the case files at Rome are one way to gauge the strength of Rome's "warehouse" reputation. The records themselves indicate the haphazard and ill-planned beginning of the Rome facility, and they allow some revealing comparisons with other institutions of the era. They show, too, how Bernstein himself struggled with the two versions of Rome in a combination of public reformism and private resignation.

What Is Missing from the Files

The overwhelming impression one gets from looking at these early case records at Rome is how frustratingly skimpy they are. As mentioned earlier, for 136 of the first 200 admissions there are no records at all: no names, no ages, no gender. Only the gaps in assigned file numbers remain to remind one of the undeniable existence of these anonymous individuals. Of course, in these instances of total absence, there is always the possibility that records were once kept but were lost at some later date. Files for 13 of the original 200 admissions, however, suggest that the missing records are not the result of archival accidents. The 13 files contain only a name and a case number on an otherwise totally blank admission form. Out of the 418 total files examined, only 270 had information in four basic categories: age at admission, level of retardation, length of stay, and reason for discharge.

The most obvious explanation for the sketchy records is that information may not have been available for many of the early admissions. Coming from a county almshouse with no accompanying information, no identified family, and limited or nonexistent communication skills, an early admission to Rome may have been unavoidably anonymous no matter how much personal history Fitzgerald or Bernstein tried to discover. A second possibility is that the amount of information collected at Rome was no different from that at other institutions of the era—a general casualty of institutional attitudes.

Neither of these explanations seems adequate. Various circumstances may certainly have attenuated the personal history available
about the early admissions, for example. Once these individuals were
admitted, though, information could have been recorded about what
they were like, how they functioned, and what happened to them at
Rome. At the very minimum, it seems that the staff could have
recorded the date and the reason (death or transfer) for every
inmate's discharge from the Rome Asylum. A comparison of Rome's
record keeping with that of other contemporary asylums also fails to
satisfy. Many of the existing files at Rome have narratives of
individual history compiled by the referring institutions, including
Willard, Binghamton, and Syracuse, yet information ceases upon
transfer to Rome.

The conclusion emerges that Fitzgerald and Bernstein decided
that information about many of the early inmates at Rome was simply
not worth gathering, or if gathered, not worth saving. In a custodial
atmosphere, all one "needed" to know was whether an individual
belonged there or not. Once admitted, the official pessimism must
have made further information seem pointless. Just as the expertise
and professionalism needed to run an asylum for custodial idiots was
perceived as less than that required for a facility such as Syracuse, so
was information about the inmates themselves less valuable. In the
presence of chronicity, knowledge of the keepers about the kept is
worth less than in other cases.

The Forms Used at Rome

Beyond the quantity of information collected at Rome, a look at
the forms themselves shows an apparent lack of concern on the part
of the state about separating feeblemindedness from lunacy in the
medical certificates required for commitment to Rome, as was
apparently true for Newark and Syracuse as well. A single certificate
of lunacy served for Rome, Willard, or Utica. The form asked about
the "attacks" of insanity suffered by the subject, and concluded with
a certification by the doctor that the subject "is insane and a proper
person for care and treatment in some institution for the insane." On
such forms at Rome, many doctors scratched out wording in many of

the questions to make it appropriate for feeblemindedness. Doctors distinguished between idiocy and insanity, but the certificates did not. In terms of state attention to procedural safeguards, mental retardation had secondary status. Not only was the establishment of an idiot asylum at Rome, New York, a largely unplanned occurrence, but the identification of appropriate candidates for admission was also an ad hoc procedure as far as the state was concerned.

Even among the three state idiot asylums existing in New York at the turn of the century, at Syracuse, Newark, and Rome, there was an interesting contrast in admission forms. The application for admission to Syracuse was a model of diagnostic detail and patient history compared to the document used at Rome (see Appendix). The Syracuse form asks almost 80 questions, from how many colors the prospective candidate could identify, to any known "peculiarities" of aunts and uncles. The attention to functional description is impressive, and clearly framed in terms that would be meaningful to most parents. The tenor of the questions is largely positive: tell us what this child can do. "Can he do an errand?" "Is he fond of music?" "Can he tie shoestrings in a regular knot?" "Does he count? How many?"

By contrast, the Rome form seeks little information not already covered by the certificate of lunacy. The focus is clearly on adults, although Rome admitted children (younger than 7 or older than 14) as well. The tenor of the questions is overwhelmingly negative, and not intended for parents. Instead of an interest in self-care skills, the Rome form focuses on the use of tobacco or any other "morbid" habits. The clear focus is on all of the problem behaviors, bad habits, or unfortunate heritage that the individual might possess. "Is the patient violent, dangerous, destructive, irritable or passionate? (If so, give instances.)" "Is there any defect of the special senses? (If so, describe it.)" The Rome form has only 17 questions. Syracuse asked similar questions, of course, but in the context of some 80 others, they seem much less pessimistic and judgmental.

Even within the category of feeblemindedness, the value of knowledge about individuals was inversely proportional to the level of feeblemindedness: the more feebleminded the individual, the less useful any personal information.

Another Look at Rome Admissions Patterns

Even with all of the limitations that characterize the information contained in the case files, some useful descriptive statistics can still be generated for a comparison with the profile of Rome residents set forth by Fitzgerald and Bernstein in their annual reports. Moreover, some statistics presented here (length of stay, reason for discharge) were either not available in the annual reports or not in the same detail.

Given the great variation from file to file in the information that was available, even simple descriptive statistics might be misleading. For example, that portion of the 418 files that had "age at admission" data might be very different from the portion of the files with information about "assigned level of retardation." As a way of stabilizing the sample population for this statistical profile, then, I used only the 270 case records that contained information on at least four of the following five variables: sex, age at admission, length of stay, reason for discharge, and assigned level of retardation.

Age at admission

The figures on admission age drawn directly from the case files are generally very close to the figures contained in the annual reports (see Tables 4.2 through 4.5 in Chapter 4). From the numbers presented by Fitzgerald and Bernstein (see Table 4.5), one can determine that 54.5 percent of the admissions between 1896 and 1902 were more than 20 years of age. In the sample of the case records, the corresponding number was 67.7%. Fitzgerald appears not to have counted some of the earliest admissions to Rome in compiling his admission age data (although the inmates are included in other categories such as asylum population). Almost all of the omitted individuals would have been over 20 years old. The sample of case files itself somewhat underrepresents the admissions in 1901 and 1902. Following the trend discussed in Chapters 4 and 5, many of these individuals would have fallen in the 10- to 20-year age range. Whether one goes by the sample data or the percentages in the annual reports, the Rome inmates were older than average in the early years. As mentioned in Chapter 4, Tyor's examination (1977) of case files from 12 asylums showed an average age at admission of slightly over 15 years for the period from 1890 to 1909. The average for the Rome sample was almost 12 years older ($\bar{x}$ = 26.99).

Length of stay and reason for discharge

Two of the categories not contained in the annual report data are the length of stay at Rome and the reasons for eventual discharge. Information in these two categories extends beyond 1902 and covers Bernstein's tenure. Again the data from the sample are consistent with the earlier analysis. Once admitted to the asylum, Rome inmates tended to stay longer than the national average.

Tyor (1977) reports that the average length of institutional stay across the country from 1851 to 1919 was 11.6 years. The comparable figure for Rome in its first eight years was 15.9. Despite Bernstein's progressivism and experiments with parole, more than one of every four inmates in the sample (25.56 percent) stayed at Rome for more than 20 years. To be fair, Bernstein's aggressive establishment of farm and domestic colonies may actually have hidden some of the movement of residents, since a colony resident officially remained an inmate at Rome. On the other hand, Bernstein admitted publicly that one of the reasons not to discharge the colony residents was to hold the threat of relocation back to the Rome Asylum proper over their heads as a disciplinary strategy (a common rationale for the burgeoning parole movement of the Progressive era throughout the penal and mental health systems). In any case, together with the older age of admission to begin with, the lengthier retention at Rome shows that Bernstein had the problem of a much older than average institutional population. Even if Bernstein's charges had been as high-functioning as those of other asylum superintendents, the age factor alone would have decreased the productive utility of his inmates. As discussed in Chapter 5, Bernstein tackled the problem after the turn of the century by pushing for the admission of younger people and the transfer of older ones back to the poorhouses.

Most people in the sample left Rome not through transfer, however, but through death. More than 77 percent of the sample remained in Rome until they died or 1 1/2 times the percentage for the same period in Tyor's national study. In terms of death rate, Rome was erratic during the early years but the frequency was almost always at least three times higher than the New York State death rate. Between 1903 and 1918, for example, the deaths per 1,000 inmates at Rome ranged from 31.3 in 1916 to 91.7 in 1908. During the same years, the deaths per 1,000 population in New York State ranged from 15.0 to 19.9. The death rates at Rome were also consistently *higher* than at the other idiot asylums in New York, but *lower* than those for the state insane asylums. Rome had an older population to begin with, of course, than the other idiot asylums. And its residents were lower-functioning, in general, with the accompanying array of serious health problems.

When a Rome inmate died during this period, regardless of age at death, it was common practice if there was no next of kin to send the corpse to the Syracuse Medical School for use as a cadaver. If there were relatives, Rome would send a body to them via train for a fee of $25. Many, families could not raise this kind of money within the few days allowed after the death. Some of the most anguished letters from families concerned this dilemma, although Bernstein did not refer to the possible use of the body as a cadaver in his correspondence with a family about burial arrangements. Instead, if the family could not retrieve the body, the stated procedure was burial in the asylum cemetery. (The cemetery no longer exists, having been destroyed for construction projects. What remains today is a chained-off section of lawn with one symbolic tombstone and the names of people who had been buried on the grounds. In addition, several individuals were apparently buried in cemeteries in the city of Rome or surrounding communities.)

Assigned level of retardation

Trying to compare the distribution of inmates according to functional level as given in the annual reports and as found in the case records is both a frustrating and intriguing task. The distinct categories of feeblemindedness presented in the tables of the annual reports quickly become rather inapplicable abstractions when one looks at what evidence of individual ability remains in the records. This is not to imply that Fitzgerald or Bernstein "cooked" the data to fit some desired distribution pattern. It is simply that, for the most part, the records have no evidence of official classification. The comparison gets messier with the files of people who lived long enough to receive several "official" designations. Thus the "feeble-minded" person admitted in 1896 might have become a "moron" by 1915, but neither label fits the "high grade imbecile" tag used in annual reports. In many of the sample files, the only indication of functional level came not from Rome staff, but from the referring almshouse or institution on the request for admission, or from a local doctor on the certificate of lunacy. These functional descriptions, while interesting individually, hindered comparisons even more. Is someone described as "foolish" and "unhelpful" to be taken as an idiot, an imbecile, or simply someone with a well developed sense of the absurd?

Despite these frustrations, the profile of functional levels drawn from the case file sample was still useful, first of all as cumulative evidence of the number of multiply handicapped people among the early admissions. This information was not collected in any form in the annual reports. Second, it provides some insight into how the classifications of "specialists" such as Fitzgerald and Bernstein compared to the more informal descriptions of the referring officials of various stripes.

In any case, the construction of categories became an admittedly interpretive—and even somewhat arbitrary—task. I generally took words such as "simpleton" and "backward" to refer to the mildest level of retardation, or feeblemindedness. In many cases, there was additional information about conversations, literacy, or other abilities of the person that would indicate fairly high level skills. In some instances, of course, there were intelligence test results done many years after admission. The use of the modifiers such as "total" or "absolute" in front of a word like "idiot" or "imbecile" usually led me to place someone in the "idiocy" category, especially if there was additional behavioral description. "Idio-imbecile" was a phrase used only in idiot asylums, and the numbers for that category came from Rome assessments. The middle category of "imbecile" was probably the fuzziest grouping. The word itself was used fairly frequently. The problem was whether the word was being used colloquially, to mean feeblemindedness in general; in the "pre-moron" sense, to mean anything above idiocy but below normal, or in the narrower, twentieth century usage of something akin to moderate retardation. Whenever possible, I relied on other descriptive information for inferences, but if there was none and if the word occurred in several places, then I assigned the person to the imbecile category.

The results of this interpretation are consistent with much of what Fitzgerald and Bernstein officially reported. A significant number of people who were judged to be fairly mildly retarded were admitted to the institution from the very first days. Bernstein's claim of a 20 percent admission rate for morons (high-grade imbeciles) in the Fitzgerald years was matched almost exactly by the 19.5 percent of the sample classed as feebleminded. The percentage of people classed as idiots or idio-imbeciles in the annual reports (15.4 percent; see Table 4.3) was less than half of that derived from the sample (37%). Some of the difference might be due to my errors of interpretation, although, as mentioned, cases of "idiocy" were generally more clear-cut in the case files than "imbecility" or "feeblemindedness." As many of the only remaining functional descriptions were those of the nonspecialist referring officials, many of my categorizations inevitably reflected the opinions of these individuals rather than Fitzgerald, Bernstein, or other Rome staff. At least part of the disparity in the frequency of idiocy among the earliest admissions may illustrate the harsher, more dismal judgments of chronicity by those less familiar with mentally retarded people. The other side of that coin, of course, is that Bernstein, especially, was eager to assign admissions to the most promising category possible when presenting a profile of residents who would justify more than simple custodial care.

As one might expect, at least half of those people with multiple disabilities were judged to function at the lowest level of idiocy. At first, the fact that one in five (54 out of 270) of the sample files reported multiple disabilities may seem surprisingly high. This frequency may be due in part to the limitations of behavioral description. For example, a lack of response to visual stimuli could most easily be described as blindness, although it might have been related to cognitive functioning instead of any ocular malfunction. Moreover, in their zeal to justify admission of an individual to Rome, some doctors may have overstated some conditions such as "paralysis of the limbs." Still, the numbers of multiply handicapped people in the files stand in marked contrast with the paucity of attention given to such persons in the public reports of Fitzgerald and Bernstein.

To summarize, a descriptive statistical analysis of the case records substantially confirms the figures upon which the analyses in Chapters 4 and 5 were based. Rome had an older, more handicapped residential population in its first eight years. On the whole, inmates tended to stay at Rome longer than people at other institutions, most of them until they died. From the very first, Rome admitted people who were very mildly retarded. However, the reputation of Rome as a repository for the incurably idiotic was based on significant numbers of individuals with severe, multiple disabilities.

THE PUBLIC AND SEVERE RETARDATION

One of the staples of mental retardation history is that the rise of mental retardation institutions—especially of custodial, congregate asylums—was largely a response to the pleas of parents and other family members for the state to take responsibility for the care of their retarded offspring or relatives. Supposedly, part of the backlog of residents at the early "experimental schools" was due to the refusal of families to accept the return of the youth as they approached adulthood. One pamphlet calling for more and bigger institutions (Department of Public Health and Charities of Philadelphia, 1911) quotes letters from parents trying to get their children admitted to the New Jersey Training School for Children at Vineland, a facility roughly comparable to the Syracuse in terms of its original population. A father from Newton, New Jersey writes: "We are sorry that our boy is losing so much time. Neither I nor my wife can teach him anything, as we cannot speak the language well ourselves. He is the only pupil excluded from the public school, and there are no private schools here in Newton through which he might learn something" (p. 11). The sense of family lives of "quiet desperation" comes through in the words of a mother about her 12-year-old son: "It would break my heart to part with him, but my health is failing fast and the doctor says I must go through an operation" (p. 12). Or this from a father from Paterson, New Jersey: "It is now about two years since first I made application for my son's admission. He is now 15 years old, and instead of getting better, as I had hoped, he is getting worse all the time. He does not realize at all. In short, he is a foolish boy. I feel like a condemned man who is carrying his case to the last court of appeals. If you cannot help me, then, indeed, there is no help for me except that of God almighty" (p. 12)

At least some historians are beginning to question a monochromatic portrait of suffering parents. As usual, this family work has focused more on insane asylums than idiot asylums. Mark Finnane's work (1981, 1985) has outlined a complex family and community response to the growth of asylums in Ireland and Australia. He suggests that rural families were most likely to be suspicious of incarceration. Indeed, he describes a tradition of accommodation and even "superstitious veneration" for the so-called "wandering Idiots" noted in the Irish Census Reports of the nineteenth century (Finnane, 1985, p. 142). Nancy Tome's history (1984) of Thomas Kirkbride and the private Pennsylvania Hospital confirms that many middle- and upper-class families pleaded with Kirkbride to admit their loved ones. However, her examination of Kirkbride's correspondence also reveals the incredible efforts that most families had made to keep the relatives at home. A similar story emerges from Ellen Dwyer's examination of family decisions to have relatives admitted to the Utica and Willard insane asylums in nineteenth-century New York (Dwyer, 1987). She recounts the heroic efforts of many families to keep their relatives at home, despite the types of behavior and physical conditions that argued against it. Most of these histories agree with Dwyer's assessment that "asylums were places of last, not first, resort" for most families (Dwyer, 1987, p. 3).

For the idiot asylums, such evidence comes indirectly, by way of professional complaints about parents who either would not "give up" their children to institutional care, or persistently tried to get them back out after initial placement. In 1915, Elizabeth Irwin of the Public Education Association in New York City, testified before a state commission examining the status of mental retardation services in the state. She reported visiting all of the "ungraded" classes in New

York City in 1912 and 1913 in an effort to convince parents to institutionalize retarded children between the ages of 12 and 16 to institutionalize their children. Her testimony bemoans the family resistance that she repeatedly encountered. Only 20 out of 100 cases agreed to send their children to asylums. Out of those 20, Irwin regretfully reported, only two children stayed in the asylum for more than a year (New York State Commission, 1915, p. 115).

In 1912, the annual report of the Massachusetts School for the Feeble-Minded explained the efforts of parents to get their children discharged from the institution as the unintended consequence of the asylum's successful training. Of course, the asylum leaders treated such developments as a problem to be overcome, not as a recognition of success.

Earlier chapters have argued that there are several more powerful explanations of why custodial institutions arose when they did than simple public demand. The sample of Rome case files suggests that what "public" pressure there was came as much from other segments of the welfare system. At the beginning of the century, poor families often resisted surrender to the almshouse system by using the nearest poorhouse when they chose, as an off-season hostel. At the end of the century, that same spirit of resistance and resilience appears in letters to the Rome officials.

The Family and Rome

Chapter 4 described how Fitzgerald himself was very clear about the incompatibility of a healthy family life and an idiotic child. In a speech to the first New York State Conference of Charities and Correction (Fitzgerald, 1900), he spelled out the "duty" of the state to extract the idiot from the household environment so as to minimize damage to both the disabled person and his or her family. This was especially true "if the parents are poor or in medium circumstances. . . . It is in such families that a large number of children are usually found, and let me impress upon you the fact, that with but few exceptions, it takes more of the time of the mother to look after one idiotic or feeble-minded child than she is able to devote to all her other children. In addition, each idiotic child as soon as it is able to appreciate anything, becomes a source of immoral contamination to other children which is far reaching in its results" (1900, p. 176).

An examination of the family correspondence in the Rome case files suggests that many families were much less convinced than Fitzgerald that the asylum was a felicitous answer to their problems. Certainly, many parents welcomed the relief provided by institutionalization of a disabled son or daughter. Equally certain is that some retarded individuals needed to be rescued from abusive or neglectful families. The case files have several reports of individuals who had been kept locked up in rooms or chained outside by family members. The files also show, however, that many families actively resisted the institutionalization of their loved ones, and continued to argue for their release even after many years at Rome.

Some 72 case files had correspondence of some sort from family members inquiring about their relatives living at Rome. This represents more than 17 percent of the 418 files examined. Given the nature of the population from which the Rome residents were drawn, this percentage strikes me as surprisingly high. Discounting the 30 or 40 files that contain little more than a name and possibly an age, then family correspondence approaches a 1 in 5 frequency. The poignancy of the individual stories in the letters easily outweighs the overall percentages in effect.

"You may rest assured . . ."

The pleas of George G.'s brother (described at the beginning of the chapter) for George's release to live on his farm in Nebraska were not unusual. Nor was Bernstein's reply. The brother of another inmate, Otto G. (no.285), wrote to Bernstein about the possibility of releasing Otto to live with him. Bernstein declined in some of the identical language used in the letter to George G.'s relative. "Your brother [Otto] is surely in no condition to be outside of an institution of this kind. He is unable to talk, disposed to be very uncleanly in his habits and needs constant supervision. You may rest assured he is made comfortable entirely in every way" (no.285).

Within a few years of this letter, Otto died while working as a teamster in the railroad yard of the city of Rome. Apparently, he could work for the railroad although not for his brother. After being notified of Otto's death, his brother wrote again to Bernstein, saying that he could not afford the $25 fee for transporting the body home, and asking politely whether Bernstein or the railroad company could help cover the cost. Never did the brother ask Bernstein the obvious question: How did someone who was kept in the Rome Asylum because of his need for "constant supervision" get killed by a rolling freight car? Despite the circumstances of the accident, and the dignified plea of the brother's letter, Bernstein's letter of reply upbraided the brother for the temerity of his request for more charity, noting that the Rome Asylum had kept Otto for 12 years at no charge to him the brother. Bernstein suggested that the brother visit Otto's grave on the grounds at Rome whenever he could arrange transportation.

If relatives persisted in their requests, Bernstein would sometimes get harsher and harsher in his replies, as in the case of George T. (no.858), who was clearly severely retarded. The file says he could not walk or talk, was not toilet trained, and could not feed himself. He lived on E-8 and E-13 wards, the designated location for the most severely disabled residents, and for the higher-functioning inmates thought to need some discipline. (E-8 was torn down after the 1965 visit of New York Senator Robert Kennedy, and the subsequent public uproar over the conditions there.) In 1913, George's brother from Brooklyn wrote to ask if George could be sent home. Bernstein replied with his boilerplate phrase: "He is kindly treated and everything in our power done for him," then gave the brother a grim prognosis that sounds very different from the optimism of Bernstein's public pronouncements. "We can look for little or no change in his mental condition because of disease processes which are taking place there" (no.858). Bernstein replied to another letter with a stronger description some three months later: "Mentally he is a low grade idiot and will always remain so." In May 1914, Bernstein answered a third inquiry from the brother with his strongest language. "Mentally he is a total blank. He is classed as a low grade idiot. He is quite filthy and he would eat any thing that he can lay his hands on if he was allowed to" (no.858). George died two months later, and his body was returned to his brother.

Bernstein would not even approve family requests for transfers of inmates to facilities closer to home so as to make periodic visits easier (e. g., no.848). Indeed, despite his later experiments with parole and with hiring out inmates for summer jobs, Bernstein even turned down a father's request for his son to make at least a short visit home, if discharge was impossible. "We think it would not be advisable to take James home this summer, as we feel he would be an extream [*sic*] burden for you to car [*sic*] for, and he would derive no special enjoyment from the visit. You may rest assured that he is entirely comfortable in every way" (no.857).

Some successful parents

According to one follow-up study, between 1904 and 1924, at least six sets of parents were persistent and knowledgeable enough to take legal action against the institution, which released their children under order of the New York attorney general (Foley, 1929). Other families apparently tried more informal methods: in 1918, the board of managers threatened to prosecute any families who "kidnapped" their children after the institution had refused to discharge them (Rome, 1918, p. 13).

In case (no.882), the family apparently went directly to the asylum, and the child ("unable to make herself useful in any way") left with them, according to the file, after 10 years at Rome. In another case (no.328), a mother obtained a writ of habeas corpus to force Rome to give up her son. In a third instance (no.881), a woman who took her nine-year-old son home complained in a letter that the child had "sores all over his body" and that his clothes were "shabby." In reply, Bernstein said a special diet meant to treat epilepsy had caused the sores.

Parents of the more severely disabled individuals seemed more likely to inquire about discharge than the parents of more mildly disabled inmates, although the crucial variable might have been age rather than disability. On average, idiots were referred to Rome at an earlier age than imbeciles or feebleminded persons. Parents may have been more likely to request the discharge of comparatively younger children, regardless of functional level. The case records at Rome attest to the existence of a sizable number of families who fought the asylum for control of their relatives.

The Social Agents

The main calls for admission and continued custody of severely retarded individuals in the early days of the Rome Asylum seem from the case record sample to have come not from parents but from superintendents of almshouses and insane asylums. Such requests for admission all claimed chronicity, as mandated by law. What is evident in the case files is how often representatives of the welfare system made their cases by emphasizing the aesthetic and ethical dimensions of chronicity, instead of the economic and professional ones.

The requests for admission to Rome, and the certificates of lunacy are especially useful in documenting these perceptions and categories of chronicity. Although functioning as part of the general welfare system, the welfare representatives could claim no "special" knowledge of feeblemindedness. That, after all, was ostensibly why they were referring people to Rome in the first place. The language and descriptions adopted by the local doctors, county commissioners, and even parents themselves allow some insight into how chronicity was constructed before the application of the professional veneer.

The aesthetics of idiocy

Of the four dimensions of chronicity that I laid out in Chapter 1, I have spent the least time examining how the details of personal appearance often characterized the terms of reference to severely retarded people. Certainly, for the general public, personal appearance had become, if anything, more important during the Victorian era as a key indicator of individual worth. Advertising and consumerism traded on the image of physical health and beauty as equivalent to moral uprightness (Hahn, 1987; Haley, 1978). Equally telling is heightened fascination among the fastidious Victorians for the unusual or entertainingly bizarre in personal appearance. Freak shows flourished (Bogdan, 1988).

Examples from the popular press illustrate how aesthetic evaluations were used to convey the hopelessness of idiocy. In a course of a flowery account of the improvements made at Rome by Fitzgerald, a reporter for the *New York Tribune* turned to physical description when he wanted to show the enormity of the task facing the asylum

officers. "In the first room visited, about twenty men were seated on
benches. . . . The faces of nearly all the men indicated an almost utter
lack of mind. They were looking out with vacant stares as though
they had no thought of anything. The malformation of heads was
remarkable. A diseased condition was stamped upon all of them, and
while evoking sentiments of horror, they also excited one's profound-
est sympathy" (Murlin, 1897, p. 9)

As professionalism came to dominate in the institutional response
to mental retardation, the judgments of personal appearance seem to
have become less appropriate. Assessments based on appearance
were certainly still made: Goddard's descriptions of the bad branches
of the Kallikak family tree show how the eugenicists made much of
such attributions.[3] However, such terms were seen as merely symp-
tomatic of more basic pathology, not as self-contained categories of
chronicity. Common attention might be drawn to the grotesque or the
merely odd; the "objective" professional could go beyond such
simplistic notions to determine "scientifically" the true extent of the
feeblemindedness.

In any case, the certificates of lunacy and the requests for
admission often mentioned impressions of appearance on. Negative
descriptions relied heavily on adjectives of ugliness: "repulsive,"
"slovenly," "sniveling," "brutish," and "stuporous." As the forms
themselves make clear (see the Appendix), toileting skills were
referred to in terms of cleanliness. An incontinent person was
described as "filthy." Indeed, perhaps the second most common
standard of behavior (communication or language skills being first)
was whether someone was "filthy" or "clean."

The ethics of idiocy

The eugenics period is testimony that the moral dimension of
chronicity remained important to professionals. It was also emphasized by local officials who wanted to establish the need for permanent, specialized custody of an individual. For relatively higher-
functioning individuals, the ethical descriptions conveyed a sense of
threat or public danger. In some cases, the threat came in one or
another version of dishonesty, the behavior implied for a person
described as "sly," "deceitful," "lazy," or "uncooperative."

In other cases, the danger is seen as less intentional, less rational, and, presumably, even scarier. Here again, the terms are included not only in the language of the asylum admission forms themselves, but in the words of the officials: "violent," "destructive," "disruptive," and "delusional." One poor fellow was described by the medical examiners as resistant, uncooperative, and deluded because he apparently persisted in believing that "institution officers" were conspiring "to deprive him of his liberty" (no.224). His fear of institutionalization was used as justification for his institutionalization. By way of contrast, the most common positive description of a candidate for admission was the simple phrase that he or she was "clean and quiet."

In at least one case, the examiner seemed to bring a sense of black humor to his behavioral description of an individual he was recommending for incarceration. He first portrays the 17-year-old woman as "a sniveling idiot" who is "indolent, untidy, willful, irritable," who "strikes when opposed." After evidence of such charitable judgments, the examiner ends his remarks: "The patient said that examiners were damned fools and sons of bitches. Statements which we believe to be untrue" (no.192). Whether true or not, the personal opinions of the "patient" were no match for the moral and aesthetic judgments of the official representatives of society. The grotesque should be hidden; the dangerous should be held. Their protests and accusations could be laughed away as well.

THE INFORMAL RECORD OF CHANGE BY 1920

The case records at Rome reveal as much about the people outside the institution as about the people inside. From the admission forms and correspondence, several tensions between institution officials and various segments of the external society emerged more clearly than the oblique references of public documents allowed.

County poorhouse officials virtually competed with each other for Rome's acceptance of their "worst cases" instead of the next county's. Complaints of favoritism or discrimination regularly surfaced in the file correspondence. For his part, Bernstein often complained to the County Commissioners of the poor that they were sending inappropriate people to Rome simply to dispose of them into the state system. Bernstein wanted no severely retarded elderly inmates. In a 1916 letter to his fellow superintendent at the state mental hospital at St. Lawrence, Bernstein vents his suspicions: "I am more and more confirmed in my opinion that certain counties are endeavoring to unload on the State every thing they can. Onondaga County within the last few months has sent three old paralytic women to this institution who could just as well been cared for at the county house or county hospital, or if necessary at county expense in a general hospital for chronic cases. . . . There is no reason why they should fill beds costing from $500 to $1000 in state institutions" (no.891).

Although this is a speculative interpretation, the forms and information that Rome collected also suggest a kind of tension between Syracuse and Rome that would be consistent with Bernstein's chafing at the custodial reputation of his asylum. If "science" needs "data," the logic seemed to be, then the place with the most data must be the most scientific. Many of this era's admissions to Rome came from the Syracuse Asylum.

Running throughout the case files, even the empty ones, is the theme of institutional schizophrenia: either a living laboratory of professionalism and innovation or a moribund warehouse for the storage of humans who were regarded as little more than nature's mistakes. What the case records illustrate even more forcefully than the annual reports is how this split in organizational personality caused tensions in Rome's day-to-day operations. It also recreated in microcosm an entire century of social history in the uses of chronicity and failure.

Chapter Seven The History of Severe Retardation and the Future of Chronicity

It is tempting to describe the early years of the Rome State School as a tale of two cities. Certainly from 1906 to 1920 or so, the experiences of, and attitudes toward, a new admission to Rome varied dramatically, depending on his or her label. If it was not exactly the best of times for those viewed as morons and high-grade imbeciles, many of them undoubtedly had an improved quality of life because of Charles Bernstein's comparatively progressive reform policies of colonies, parole, no sterilization, and intensive vocational training. On the other hand, for those residents of Rome viewed as the most helpless and unproductive, it may well have been the worst of times. Rather than a tale of two cities, perhaps the story is better described as a tale of 40 colonies and a warehouse. In a published article portraying his vision of successful community colonies for his mildly retarded clients, Bernstein—at least by implication—revealed a much more dismal opinion of the very different life for those who remained inside his institution: the bad and the burdensome, the ugly and the useless.

> It is our opinion that the time has come when something much less expensive and many times more wholesome and natural than the physical custody of brick walls and iron enclosures and large per capita expenditures for buildings and yearly maintenance is possible and practicable for a large majority of these cases—that many of them can be rehabilitated and saved for something better than lives of institutional servitude, by careful training in the kinds of work that they are capable of performing. (Bernstein, 1920, p. 1)

For that minority who cannot—even in Bernstein's optimistic opin-ion—be "rehabilitated and saved," the future holds nothing "better than lives of institutional servitude."

The reforms at Rome reached their zenith in the 1920s. Whereas in 1920, Bernstein was still proclaiming the 4:1 ratio of morons and imbeciles to idiots among Rome's admissions (Bernstein, 1920), by the 1935 annual report he was complaining of the burdensome rate of admissions of "paralytics" and "helpless idiots" (Rome, 1935, p. 12). In 1928, Bernstein reported a number of vacancies in the 40 colonies, explaining them as the result of too few suitable "patients" available within the institution (Rome, 1928; Wilber, 1969). The annual reports themselves became increasingly perfunctory documents with only a page or two of commentary by Bernstein to accompany his statistics (although the reports of the other staff—school directors, building supervisors—grew longer).

By the time of his death in 1942, Bernstein must have recognized the unmistakable trend of fewer and fewer services for more and more people that would characterize Rome until the exposés of the mid-1960s. The U-shaped core group of residential buildings were all in place by the 1930s. Some of the colonies were closing. The institutional population in 1942 was 3,900. They were attended by a total staff (administrative, medical, and direct care) of 704. In the next three war years, the number of staff decreased by around 28 percent to around 500 (Wilber, 1969, p. 34), while the residential population increased slightly. The Rome institution's population crested at around 5,200 in 1961. By 1969, the population was close to the levels of the mid-1940s (slightly over 4,000), yet the staff had almost quadrupled, to 1,914 employees (Wilber, 1969, p. 39).

As with the almshouses, as with the "experimental schools" of Howe and Wilbur, so also with Bernstein's Rome.[1] Once again, the pattern of failed reform repeated itself. As before, the unchallenged category of chronicity was available to explain that failure. Bernstein had struggled to make Rome the type of congregate asylum needed to demonstrate his rehabilitative success while simultaneously explain-ing the inevitable failures. The explanation remained in force, larger than ever, long after the demonstration had ended. Once again, chronicity proved more durable than reform.

INVOLUTIONARY CHANGE IN THE NINETEENTH CENTURY

At the beginning of this study, I described my purposes as more integrative and contextual in aim than sequential. The distinction is a fairly common one among historians (Graham, 1983), who often use the terms "synchronic" for the contextual approach and "diachronic" for a more sequential focus. Of course, my history has tried primarily to tell a story, and that implies a certain progression or sequence of change over time. Any historical treatment, it seems to me, must combine elements of both context and sequence, interpretation and chronology. However, I want to return more exclusively to the interpretive context of the dimensions of chronicity that I have tried to weave through my account of the events surrounding the origins of the Rome Custodial Asylum. I will begin by summarizing the patterns of change over time that, I have argued, characterized social policy and practice toward severely retarded people from 1820 to 1920. It is here that parts of my account most obviously differ from some other interpretations of mental retardation history.

Patterns of Change

In his historical account *Growing Old in America,* Fischer (1977) describes three possible patterns of change: evolutionary, revolutionary, and involutionary (see also the treatment of social policy in Rochefort, 1983). Change itself is a constant, of course. However, the rate and direction of change can also undergo fundamental alterations, according to Fischer (p. 100). It is precisely these "deep changes" in the pace and flow of events and attitudes that usually underlie the historian's effort to develop a "periodization" scheme for a particular area of life.

Evolutionary change

In Fischer's organization, the pattern of evolutionary change obtains in periods of slow, steady, linear developments in a specific direction, the preferred pattern of most traditional historical accounts

of mental retardation. In these accounts, the basic revolution occurred with the advent of the Enlightenment era, specifically with the
events surrounding Itard's efforts to teach Victor. Since that time,
traditionalists have argued, despite some inevitable disappointments
and temporary detours (e. g., Kanner, 1964, referring to the eugenics
era as "the great lull"), the basic direction of social response to mental
retardation has been one of steady refinement in the scientific
understanding and treatment of the condition (Adams, 1971;
Baumeister, 1970; Kanner, 1964; Scheerenberger, 1983). For instance, the progress of curriculum and instructional technique supposedly follows this pattern. From the early experiments of Itard
with Victor, through the "physiological treatment" of Seguin, to the
"functional" vocational training and modified academics of the
"ungraded" classrooms of the early 1900s, to the more precise
application of behavior management techniques, the steady progress
of instructional expertise has almost been an article of faith in mental
retardation history (Scheerenberger, 1983).

Revolutionary change

Other accounts have preferred to emphasize the nature and timing
of certain events or discoveries that prompted sudden, revolutionary
changes in the direction of mental retardation policy and practice.
This approach has often produced a description of many more
distinct "periods" of history than the emphasis on evolutionary
change allowed. For example, many versions of revolutionary change
use the beginning of the first public asylum in America specifically
for mentally retarded people (Howe's asylum in 1848) as an obvious
point of redirection in social policy toward state intervention and
institutionalization (Scheerenberger, 1983; Wolfensberger, 1975).
They then find a quick swing to custodialism around 1875, and a
third basic reorientation around the turn of the century (Menolascino
and McGee, 1982; Trent, 1982; Wolfensberger, 1975). For intellectual histories in psychology, the rather sudden, widespread adoption
of the Binet Intelligence Test in America, and the associated "discovery" of the moron, provides another commonly cited set of watershed
events (Zenderland, 1986). Others find the emergence of eugenics in
this period as the key development, one part of which was the rapid

application of a standardized sorting instrument (Wolfensberger, 1975).

Involutionary change

The third type of pattern, the involutionary, has been drawn upon the least in mental retardation history. Rather than a gradual evolution of events in a particular direction, or a series of sudden, dramatic shifts in development, the involutionary approach finds events and policies becoming more detailed and more intricate, but not producing essential change. In Fischer's marvelous phrase, an involutionary pattern of change is one where things become "more elaborately the same" (Fischer, 1978, p. 101). It is this characterization that best summarizes the sequence of developments described in this study. At least from the narrower point of view of severe retardation, social policy and practice in America from 1820 to 1920 did not fundamentally change. Generalized abandonment became specialized, and the justification of the outcome became more professionalized, but the basic outcome remained unchanged.

Emphasizing a pattern of involution leads to some ostensible disagreement with many existing historical accounts. Over the course of institutional development and centralization of services, society's approach to those individuals judged to be "incurable," "helpless" idiots essentially became "more elaborately the same." That is why the case study of the early years of Rome is instructive. It presents a recapitulation of policy developments of the preceding 75 years. The specific contentions defended here may be summarized in a few statements:

1. Segregation and institutionalization of retarded people did not begin in the mid–nineteenth century with the opening of the specialized asylums by Howe and Wilbur. Public incarceration and custodialism began with the spread of the city and county almshouses during the earlier Jacksonian era. Indeed, for most of the century, many more retarded people lived in almshouses than in the more well-known specialized asylums. Of course, the vast majority of retarded people never lived in an almshouse or an asylum, but remained "at large" in the community.

2. There was no "golden age" from 1850 to 1860 or so, when benign, humanitarian reformers operated small, school-like residential facilities. From the perspective of severely retarded people, the early "experimental schools" may even be seen as making things worse. Their exclusion from these schools lent, for the first time, a professional endorsement to their economic, moral, and aesthetic failure. It turned their failure into what I have called chronicity. Whether or not Howe and Wilbur were well-intentioned, visionary individuals, the outcome of their two-tiered division of curable and incurable retarded people was to move mildly retarded children into the realm of educability for the first time, and to leave the rest of the retarded population more firmly ensconced in chronicity than before.

3. The triumph of the congregate, custodial asylum in the last quarter of the nineteenth century seems inadequately explained as the unforeseeable consequence of specific mistakes and reluctant accommodation of public wishes. Rather, the development of the large, public, self-contained institutions in the last quarter of the nineteenth century seems almost unavoidable, given the standards of professionalism and productivity. They represented the continued need for categories of incurable idiots to remain available as an explanation for failure. Failure was held to be a natural limitation of individuals, not a social inequity of incremental reform. Specialized failure had a specialized function, whose practical outcome was simply more elaborate custodialism: involuted abandonment.

4. It was not the general case that families actively pushed for more institutions or passively accepted them as the officially required thing to do. There is evidence that some families actively fought the efforts of public officials to institutionalize their children. Other parents fought valiantly to regain control of their children even after they had been institutionalized. The role of poor families in the "triumph" of institutions and custodialism in the nineteenth century is much more complex than usually recognized.

A Tapestry of Change

Fischer presents his three patterns of change as more or less mutually exclusive. For example, a period of involutionary change might be followed by a brief period of revolutionary upheaval in perspective and behavior, but the upheaval would then subside into a period of evolutionary development. However, there is nothing in this approach to patterns that prohibits seeing more than one pattern of change playing out at the same time for different aspects of an area, such as mental retardation in general. The public might be evolving in its attitudes while professionals are going through a dramatic revolution in perspective.

For me, one of the values of Fischer's identification of the three patterns of change is that it encourages the historian to look for more than one pattern when characterizing the developments being described. The result can be the discovery of strands of change weaving in and out of different patterns, thus creating something closer to the complicated tapestry of cultural history. In a sense, what I am arguing for here is to "contextualize" what is essentially a "sequentializing" tool of historical analysis. The risk to this "change"—if you will—in Fischer's approach is losing the insight of the generalization in pursuit of more finely grained analysis. Sometimes historians try to turn floodlights into lasers and end up completely in the dark.

In this case, the risk is worth it. I think there is evidence to support characterizations of the history of mental retardation in America as comprising simultaneous patterns of evolutionary and involutionary change, accompanied by episodic bursts of revolutionary redirection. Indeed, the position I would defend is that each of the three patterns aptly characterizes a different strand of nineteenth-century mental retardation history. For example, I think one could argue that a traditional intellectual history would justifiably characterize the midcentury writings and policies of Howe, Wilbur, and Seguin as representing a revolutionary change in how an emerging professional specialty viewed mild mental retardation. However, if one expands the focus to include the intellectual developments across the entire area of social welfare, then the developments in concepts about mild retardation tend to flatten into the broader path of evolutionary change that began much earlier than 1850. If one expands the focus in a different direction to include severe as well as mild retardation, then the pattern becomes one of increasing intricacy typical of involution.

What I argue here need not be as directly confrontational with previous histories as some of the points I have made might appear. In terms of overall patterns of sequential change, I would finally make only two modest, general claims. First, the involutionary pattern of change has been neglected in previous accounts of mental retardation history. Second, involutionary change is ultimately the most helpful way to characterize the sequence of developments affecting severely retarded people from 1820 to 1920.

ABANDONMENT AND CHRONICITY

This study has presented a contextual interpretation more than a chronological description. I laid out the structure of that interpretation as the dimensions of chronicity (Table 1.1).

The major development in the area of mental retardation in the last half of the nineteenth century was not the triumph of custodialism but its medicalization through the creation of chronicity. This, in turn, was intimately associated with the rise of a new professional class of institutional experts, and its quest for respectability as a medical specialty. (Although teaching and training were part of this therapeutic perspective, educational specialization did not gain a separate identity until the ungraded classes had been established in the public school systems, after the turn of the century and beyond the walls of the medically dominated institutions.)

The efforts of Charles Bernstein personify this struggle for respectability. The case study of Rome illustrates well the connection between incipient professionalism and the identification of a population requiring service. In a process repeated many times in the nineteenth and early twentieth centuries, superintendents of idiot asylums struggled to establish a social perception of their positions as scientific, unique, and effective. As one historian described the same process for insane asylum leaders, it was "the rise of an occupational group whose future depended upon the curative abilities of its institutional base" (Gitlin, 1982, p. 331).

As Howe, Wilbur, Kerlin, Bernstein, and every other prominent asylum superintendent in the nineteenth century seem to have recognized, at least tacitly, professional prestige cannot base itself on a simple model of custodial housekeeping (Larson, 1977). Anyone can do that. At the same time, however, establishing credibility requires moderation in claims for improvement through "professional treatment" (a stumbling block for Howe and Wilbur in particular). As the example of Rome illustrates, the social pressure to accept an unteachable, chronic class and simultaneously to assert one's expertise through remedial achievements with the inmates made the official disappearance of separate, purely custodial facilities almost inevitable. The teachable classes could establish the efficacy of Bernstein's methods. The unteachable classes provided a "saving remnant," as it were, by which to explain the inevitable failures: those who failed did so because they were unteachable, not because they had not been taught. At the turn of the century this could proceed only within large, *congregate* asylums, comprising every level of disability or deviance. Separate facilities for incurable or unteachable segments could not persist if the superintendents' were to preserve their hope of a secure professional status.

If Bernstein could not live with a facility limited to unteachable idiots, neither could he live with a facility without them. Had an unteachable class not existed, in other words, Bernstein would have had to create one. Classification and diagnosis is one of the best ways of rationalizing a profession. Even without results from treatment, such differentiation discovers categories where none had existed before. There is something new to be expert about.

Such differentiation in the therapeutic dimension also served a control function within the asylum. At Rome, the low-grade or helpless idiot class functioned as a visible destiny for inmates who badly behaved or performaned inadequately (recall the infamous E-8 ward at Rome). The Rome Asylum reproduced the social stigma of institutionalization itself within the microcosm of asylum society. Through such a process, possibly unintentional, professionalism created both the cured and the incurable, the taught and the unteachable. Moreover, it provided a supposedly organic, individualized explanation of social inequity, moral condemnation, and aesthetic rejection that the culture was quick to endorse.

How Failure Becomes Chronicity

What this analysis suggests is that chronicity is not only a concept that develops over time but one that varies in use according to who adopts it. Chronicity is a social creation or category, not a biological given. This does not deny the reality of physiological limitations, but simply places the interpretation of that reality squarely in the social domain, not on the individual. The historian needs to ask how "chronicity" is used, not what it means.

One version of that question is to ask whether chronicity existed as a category before its various dimensions emerged. The answer proposed in this study is that, at least for severe retardation, the separate dimensions of failure existed prior to their assimilation within the concept of chronicity. There were poor people before there was chronic uselessness. There were people viewed as wicked or pitiable before their behavior was seen as incorrigible. What happened to *create* chronicity was the fourth dimension; therapeutic failure.

Chronicity is more than failure. Chronicity adds the element of permanence, of hopelessness, to economic, moral, or aesthetic limitations. The permanence is supplied by the professional dimension, as the perspective shifts from judgmental values to therapeutic "science." The therapeutic dimension provides the supposedly *factual* basis to which the value judgments of the other dimensions may then be tied. Therapeutic failure merged with the other three dimensions to create or construct this larger social interpretation of personal irredeemability. That interpretation, once afoot, then circled back to influence the original three dimensions in terms of language and emphasis.

Productivity and Chronicity

This interpretation of the rise of chronicity can create a misinterpretation of the importance of professionalism in the events of the nineteenth century. Traditionalists tend to like the role of clinical judgment. The increasing control of decisions by expert analysis rather than by political exigency or emotional preference is—in this interpretation—the best feature of the twentieth century-rise of scientific specialization and objectivity in treatment. The more recent criticism of this "cult of expertise" as influenced by a need for legitimacy and the preservation of explanatory failure finds as much to fear as to welcome in the recognition of therapeutic sovereignty. Obviously, the analysis here supports the critical perspective on professionalism. The possibility remains, however, that in analyzing the dangers of the medicalization of social problems, one can overemphasize the power of the clinical perspective. In such a situation, the critics of professionalism end up sharing the assumption of its defenders: that clinical expertise is the actual basis for programmatic decisions. As a result, both sides of the debate have perpetuated a "myth of clinical judgment" (Biklen, 1988), which fails to distinguish scientific rhetoric from political reality.

This is especially true in a history of institutionalization. The professional dimension of failure *justified* the specialized incarceration of low grades, but did not prompt it. The combination of economic, moral, and aesthetic dimensions prompted social abandonment of individuals as failures. Abandonment does not require an asylum, however, as demonstrated by responses such as "outdoor relief," the almshouse, even the family attic. Professionalism and the therapeutic dimension influenced the path of official abandonment, but not the ultimate destination or outcome. In many ways, the triumph of clinical judgment and the therapeutic perspective was one of rhetoric. The preferred strand of discourse shifted, but the other dimensions remained influential.

This is especially true of the influence of capitalism. The economic dimension of failure was present in the nineteenth century as a strand of discourse in which the powerful described the weak in terms of social prominence. Certainly the emphasis on individual productivity as a standard of honor became increasingly strong in the last quarter of the century. The evolution from commercial to industrial capitalism, with the associated merger of wage labor and mass production, ensured that the image of the happy worker would be pushed at all levels of society. Selling one's labor—not skill, but raw productive capacity to perform interchangeable jobs—became not only an unavoidable reality for most workers, but a moral responsibility as well (Braverman, 1974; Katz, Doucet, and Stern, 1982).

The meaning of this economic analysis for severely retarded

people in the nineteenth century is not a simple determinant of who was institutionalized and who was not. Moral and aesthetic judgments played important parts as well. Of course, one can simply push the argument back one stage and contend that the moral and aesthetic criteria, while important, were themselves ultimately created by the existing economic structure and its control of social relationships. That argument will not be settled here, but the schematization of chronicity presented in Chapter 1 is most consistent with the more flexible theory of "cultural hegemony."[2] Social relations are not a one-dimensional process moving in an economic lockstep through history. But neither do attitudes float along in some classless, moral jetstream, unaffected by the structural arrangements of the society beneath it. Moral judgment and the control of the state, aesthetic perceptions and the pursuit of harmony, both reflect and influence the structure of social interactions.[3]

The story of the Rome institution that emerged especially from the case records shows this multidimensional interaction. A strict economic determinism seems unable to explain adequately the low rate of institutionalization for people labeled feebleminded in the nineteenth century. One can speculate that the presence of mentally retarded people in the community was simply not perceived as an active threat to the marketplace (Braverman, 1974). Especially for people labeled as idiotic or imbecilic, the moral and aesthetic judgments usually preceded economic judgments. This is not to say that economic criteria of personal productivity were not applied or not important; they were. For the most severely retarded segment, however, they seem more crucial inside the institution than in the events leading up to admission.

What the records at Rome showed was that the case for admission was most often made in moral and aesthetic terms, not economic or therapeutic terms. Outsiders, when making the case for admitting an individual to Rome, usually argued in terms of behavior that was dangerous or burdensome, or in terms of appearance that was offensive. Once inside the asylum, however, the way one "earned" his or her way back out into society was through a combination of treatment and productive potential.

To put the contention negatively, one feature of the emerging therapeutic perspective was the official deemphasis of ethical and aesthetic judgments and the emphasis of economic and "scientific" criteria. Even professionals could still legitimately draw ethical conclusions from their diagnostic premises, of course. That is what the eugenics period demonstrated with a vengeance. However, professional respectability meant that one's specialized discourse stayed close to the "objective" question of whether a person could be taught or treated so as to succeed in the marketplace.

From this perspective, Bernstein's reform efforts developed as economically based: Who could be made "useful"? Bernstein accepted the "single standard of honor" (Lasch, 1973) of self-support and possessive individualism that decreed personal productivity to be the badge of citizenship. The essence of professional expertise, and the way Bernstein justified his value to society, was through economic rehabilitation, or determination that such improvement was impossible. Some of his institutional charges could, in fact, become productive, said Bernstein, and, therefore, deserved acceptance back into society. Beyond all the more immediate reasons—inadequate funding, the Depression, overcrowding—for the ultimate failure of Bernstein's reform efforts, this implicit acceptance of the economic dominion over social participation doomed his approach from the start. It allowed the myth of clinical judgment to ratify the economic categories of exclusion.

Some Remaining Questions

This study raises as many questions as it answers, and that is all to the good. Historical research in the broad area of disabilities is just beginning to come into its own as a significant part of understanding the causes and the experience of disability. It may be useful to summarize some of the immediate directions that such historiography could take, at least in terms of the topics that were inadequately explored here.

Differential rates of institutionalization

I speculated in several of these chapters on why there may have been such a difference in the percentage of *identified* people in various disability and dependency categories who wound up in some sort of institutional setting. The main focus here has been on the contrast between the relatively high institutionalization rates reported for the insane and the relatively low rates for the feebleminded. I have suggested that those identified as feebleminded—especially before the "discovery" of the moron—were simply so far beyond the pale of marketplace expectations that mere community presence did not represent a threat to the maintenance of a pliant workforce. Indeed, one could argue that the closest comparisons would be small children and elderly people rather than those labeled insane. For these groups as well, one could argue, expectations of productivity were low or nonexistent. Moreover, families may have felt that maintaining such members at home was an acceptable "burden." The insane, on the other hand, were largely able-bodied adults who presumably had been subject to "typical" expectations of productivity and self-sufficiency. As such, their continued presence in the community may have been seen as potentially more disruptive economically.

This line of speculation needs to be explored and challenged. As a theory, it directs itself more to the context of explanation than to the context of discovery. I am not maintaining that city fathers or county commissioners sat down and consciously divided the town's dependent poor in terms of who was thought potentially productive and who was not. Additional interpretation, however, would benefit from answers to several questions of a more concrete nature. How does age of onset of disability compare, not only for those in the institutions but also for those identified as insane or feebleminded in the community? How do other disability groups (e.g., deaf, blind, physically disabled, and epileptic individuals) compare to feebleminded people in terms of rates of institutionalization? Finally, did the rates vary in other countries?

History of chronicity across disability categories

The logic of the analysis presented here suggests that a fruitful direction for future research would be to cut across traditional diagnostic, clinical categories, and compare the experiences of, and policies toward, people with severe or chronic disabilities regardless of the specific etiology. With mental retardation, the overwhelming historiographic tendency has been to focus on issues and events that affected mainly people with comparatively mild or moderate levels of cognitive delay. However, if the arguments here about the dimensions of chronicity and the uses of failure are robust interpretations of the historical context of disability, then they should presumably have some application to other versions of chronicity. Expanding the application to additional populations could make important modifications to the model. Such an analysis would be relevant to the current policy direction toward service categories that—at least officially—are functionally oriented rather than categorical. The definition and influence of "developmental disabilities" specifically comes to mind.

History of family and community life

Overlapping with some of the previous suggestions is the need for historians to break out of the institution and greatly increase our understanding of how families with disabled members, mild or severe, have functioned in their communities, at all levels of society. (Demos, 1981; Farber, 1986; Ferguson and Ferguson, 1987) Mental retardation history has suffered from the "drunk and the streetlight" syndrome. Just as the drunk looks for lost keys where the light shines brightest instead of where he probably lost them, so have historians spent disproportionate amounts of time on the rise of the asylum, where most retarded people never lived. Superintendents wrote the most accessible articles; the case records were for asylum admissions The point is not that research into institutional life and policy should stop. On the contrary, as I hope this study has demonstrated, there is much about the role of asylums and the people who lived and worked there that we need to better understand. However, there is desperately little information about what daily life for the majority of retarded people who lived in the towns and cities of our country might have been like (Groce, 1985; 1992; Rosenkrantz and Vinouskis, 1978; 1979h) How did families manage to keep their severely retarded children at home, as many of them apparently did? What differences existed across class lines, urban-rural lines, racial and ethnic lines?

One promising source for some energetic scholar would be the Soundex Indexes used by Friedberger (1981) in his study of the decision to institutionalize. These indexes of the 1900 Federal Census Manuscripts were created in the 1930s for the initial determination of Social Security benefits. If one has an independent list of names of people labeled retarded, then one can link the two data bases for sociodemographic information about otherwise historically invisible families (see Stephenson, 1980, for a more detailed methodological description). One obvious linkage is between asylum admissions and the Soundex Indexes. However, one could also use almshouse case records to identify idiots and imbeciles who remained close to their communities if not actually with their families. After the turn of the century, student registration lists in the ungraded classrooms (especially in the larger cities with special education departments) might provide another source. Finally, of course, one could turn to the manuscript censuses themselves, for a more tedious but potentially fascinating glimpse of both official notice of disability by the census takers, and the family composition where disabled people resided. Both the 1880 and the 1890 censuses would be especially intriguing sources in this regard as the last two national attempts to identify all retarded people in the country (subsequent censuses restricted their surveys to hospital and institutional populations).

The comparison of public and private asylums

Important work in the history of mental illness has been done in comparing developments at small, private mental hospitals, with those at the large public insane asylums that followed (Digby, 1985; Scull, 1981a; Tomes, 1984). Similar comparisons in mental retardation would be helpful. Small facilities such as the one first begun by Wilbur in Massachusetts, or one in Amityville on Long Island, presumably served a paying clientele. Such facilities might provide a way to better understand how middle- and upper-class families dealt with feeblemindedness in the nineteenth and early twentieth century. Other facilities such as Elwyn, in Pennsylvania, and Vineland, in New Jersey, were semiprivate hybrid organizations that might serve as useful intermediary settings. Only one short article (Doll, 1970) has discussed these private facilities, yet they would seem to offer a potentially useful comparison and contrast with the public asylums on any number of points.

Regional comparisons

This study is similar to many in the history of mental illness and mental retardation in its focus on developments in the Northeast region of the United States. There are substantial reasons for this emphasis that go beyond the undeniable benefit of more available evidence. While some unpublished dissertations investigate developments in the Midwest (e.g., Levstik, 1981; Slater, 1987), few studies exist of the South or the West. Studies in the South, in particular, would allow a racial comparison in terms of institutionalization and family responses. Did the developments in the Northeast recur in the establishment and development of western institutions, or were the later facilities able to skip steps or avoid some stages altogether? Did the lower population density and frontier quality of life in some of the states affect attitudes and practices of settlers towards the care of their disabled relatives? The differences in the stage of economic development, and the prevalence of wage labor, between the industrial states and the farm states could offer an interesting application of the economic dimension of chronicity.

CURRENT REFORMS AND SPHERES OF FAILURE

The editors of an anthology of articles written largely in defense of institutions for mentally retarded individuals (Crissey and Rosen, 1986a) usefully summarize the latest explanation of why society should preserve the institutional setting for a certain segment of the retarded population. The defense should sound familiar.

> To promote the institution as a viable option requires an examination of the unique potential of the institutional setting to provide opportunities not provided as well or as easily within other settings. . . . Care can vary according to degree of need but it is assumed that those persons requiring greatest care will be the most severely afflicted, manifesting multiple problems of impairment and requiring the broadest range of professional team involvement. (Crissey and Rosen, 1986b, p. 174)

Skeptics of the possibility of a *"good"* institution will see in such arguments simply the latest version of professionals preserving a place for the explanatory failures. Similar versions of this plea for segregated, congregated residential services can currently be found within literature about educational, vocational, and recreational services. Indeed, after the legislative and judicial activism of the late 1960s and early 1970s, such calls for professional "traditionalism" in services now seem to be increasing.

However, the relevance of this history of social policy and practice may be even greater for the current generation of progressive reformers than for the traditionalists within mental retardation and developmental disabilities. It is dangerous to make current events the occasion for drawing "lessons" from history. It risks the implication that historical homework has no value until graded by the contemporary policy makers and service providers for its direct applicability to some immediate issue. Nonetheless, those individuals struggling with the frustrations and delays of significant change in implementing the reforms promised now for almost two decades should look to the past at least for the comfort of common experience, if not the caution against repeated mistakes.

Is Failure Avoidable?

Failure became transformed into chronicity through the application of the therapeutic perspective. Chronicity is created by the merger of professional judgment with the other dimensions of failure. The prominence of this judgment is currently enshrined official policy and in law. However, professional judgment ratifies only; it does not originate success or failure. The problem is that professionalism has some very powerful reasons of self-protection to endorse the continued presence of a percentage of failure, poverty, custody, and hiddenness that economic, ethical, and aesthetic dimensions seem to demand.

The analysis in Michael Walzer's *Spheres of Justice* (1983) is that differences in outcome have been allowed to spread across rightly distinct spheres of life (to greatly simplify an extended argument). As a society, we use a notion of "simple equality" of opportunity that refuses to acknowledge the complexity of individual abilities and social domains. As a result, our society allows criteria that have no relevance to influence success or failure in different domains. The influence of money in political campaigns, to take a mundane example, allows the criteria of the marketplace to influence who gets chosen for political office. Walzer uses a passage from Pascal's *Pensées* to explain his basic point: "Tyranny is the wish to obtain by one means what can only be had by another. We owe different duties to different qualities: love is the proper response to charm, fear to strength, and belief to learning" (cited in Walzer, 1983, p. 18).

Monopoly within one domain or sphere of social life is often bad enough, as the economic inequities in this country demonstrate. However, the *domination* that ensues when power cuts across domains is even worse. Walzer argues that we should fight dominance more than monopoly.

In a similar analysis, one could argue that the future of current reform efforts depends on a two-stage effort that begins with the recognition of something like "spheres of failure." The first stage of reform must be a struggle against the dominance of failure across all of the dimensions of life for severely retarded people. Indeed, a shorthand way to define chronicity as developed in this account is simply "dominance of professionalized failure." The effort must be to break down the totality of chronicity into the independent dimensions of evaluation: aesthetics, ethics, and economics. The judgment that someone is economically unproductive becomes a discrete evaluation, unrelated to moral worth or personal attractiveness (Bogdan and Taylor, 1989; Ryan, 1977). The key to this disintegration of chronicity is the dismissal of the professional explanation of therapeutic failure.

The question arises as to whether some type of failure is not unavoidable. The dimensional structure outlined here may have emerged from particularly discriminatory and oppressive social circumstances, but the continuums of success-failure that they represent would seem difficult to avoid in even the most humane of societies. There will always be a need to label some behavior as morally better or worse. Realistically speaking, would not even the most egalitarian society still have room for economic winners and losers, with the losers even so being well off? Regardless of what standard is used, it seems essential to identify what is beautiful around us.

It probably will never be enough, therefore, to diminish the influence of professionalism over service outcomes, to circumscribe its officially recognized sphere of influence. Such a step challenges cross-dimensional dominance but does not oppose intradimensional monopoly. A total reform effort must recognize that limiting the license of expertise may merely remove the rhetorical cover from the real power of the other dimensions in the lives of disabled people.

The Second Stage of Reform

Why should all retarded people be poor, even with supported employment? Economic failure should not be—even rhetorically—the consequence of a professional diagnosis. The converse is also true: economic success will not be permanently secured by therapeutic approaches to improve productivity. What reformers must confront more fully is that economic failure itself must be directly opposed.

The second stage of reform, then, is to challenge directly the economic arrangements in this society that seem to influence the most inappropriate versions of moral and aesthetic failure as well. It is here that many of our current reform efforts fall short, neglecting to challenge directly the defense of economic inequity in terms of individual merit. Instead, some of our most promising reforms currently seem to endorse a capitalistic definition of people's worth by the sale of their labor rather than by the gift of life itself. In our well-intentioned eagerness to have severely retarded people join this system (Will, 1984), perhaps we echo the past in too readily accepting this "commodification" of culture.

Even the language of our reforms seems unintentionally to convey this sense of acceptance of the structural inequities. We speak of "clients" and "consumers" (and increasingly of "customers") as though the highest ideal in service reform is something akin to selling soap at the local supermarket. One perceptive critic has made this point of the futile incrementalism in calls for "independent living," or "self-advocacy:

> The problem with consumer choice, self-reliance and related principles, is that their use often dodges the issues of power and structure in social life. The

consumer cannot be sovereign within a world in which the mechanics of power are located elsewhere. . . . Consumer choice and self-reliance are worthy principles, but outside the context of a comprehensive political strategy they can, especially in the present context, become an excuse for public neglect to pass itself off as benevolent minimal government, leaving the mechanics of social and economic disadvantage undisturbed. (Williams, 1983, p. 1006)

The struggle must be not only to make disabled people appear more normal, but also to overturn the culturally enforced notions of "body beautiful," and "individual appeal." The reform efforts must seek not only to lessen the burden and danger of severely retarded individuals, but to move beyond a utilitarian ethic that allows us to respond to social injustice with individual mercy but not with structural change.

The challenge of reform, then, is to avoid confronting the dominance of chronicity while accepting a monopoly of failure in the evaluative spheres of life. To do otherwise risks the perpetuation of abandonment, if only of a few. Society, if unchallenged, will always find a use for consistent failure, an individual fate that justifies abandonment.

Appendix Admission Forms
to the
Rome and Syracuse
Asylums

Form of Request for Admission to the Rome State Custodial Asylum

According to the form prescribed by the Board of Managers of the Rome State Custodial Asylum, October 28, 1895, and by resolution of said Board that date ordered to go into effect immediately, under the authority of Chapter 59 of the Laws of 1895.

To the Superintendent of the Rome State Custodial Asylum:

I hereby request that _____ who is idiotic or mentally deficient and resides in town of _____ in the County of _____ the State of New York, be admitted as an inmate to said Asylum.

Dated the _____ day of _____ 18_____.

(To be signed by the applicant.)   _____

Supt. of Poor _____ County

Statement

(The family physician, parents, friends or Superintendent of Poor are requested to state the facts called for below to the best of their knowledge and belief. If any particular is unknown the fact should be stated.)

1. Age _____ years; sex _____; civil condition _____; color _____; occupation _____; religion _____;

   Nativity _____ (of father ___ _____

   (of mother _____

   Education ___ _____ (None

   (Reads

2. When was mental peculiarity first noticed?
3. What is the bodily condition of patient? (If there is any deformity of body or limbs, so state.)
4. Is there any defect of the special senses? (If so, describe it.)
5. Is the patient subject to epilepsy? (If so, state frequency of attacks.)
6. Is the patient violent, dangerous, destructive, irritable or passionate? (If so, give instances.)
7. Was the patient ever an inmate of an Asylum or Hospital for the insane? (If so, was patient discharged as recovered, improved or unimproved and when did such discharge take place?)
8. Is the patient cleanly or otherwise in dress and personal habits?
9. Has the patient any morbid habit? (If so, describe it.)

10. Is the patient addicted to the use of tobacco or narcotic drugs of any kind? (If so, state to what extent.)
11. What is supposed cause of present mental condition?
12. Is there any history of insanity, epilepsy, chorea, or defects of vision, hearing or speech or any nervous affection in the family of father or mother? (If so, describe.)
13. How many brothers and sisters has the patient had?
14. Was there any bodily deformity or mental deficiency in the other children? (If so, describe.)
15. Other facts indicating idiocy or mental deficiency? (State if there has been any change in the patient's mental condition.)
16. Name of parents or nearest relative?
17. Residence and P. O. address.

New York Asylum for Idiots

Syracuse, New York

Syracuse, _____ _____ 188__

Let every Question be answered as minutely as possible by the Parents or Friends of Applicants for Admission to the Asylum.

1. What is the applicant's name?
2. What is the applicant's age and date of birth?
3. Where was _he born?
4. Was _he born at the full period of gestation?
5. Were there any extraordinary circumstances attendant upon delivery? If so, describe them.
6. What has been the general health and the bodily condition of the applicant?
7. What is now the general health of the applicant?
8. Does _he walk?
9. At what age did _he begin to walk?
10. At what age was any peculiarity first noticed?
11. In what manner did peculiarity first manifest itself?
12. Is there any peculiarity in the form or size of head? If so, describe.
13. Is there any infirmity of body or limbs, any paralysis, or any striking peculiarity? If so, describe fully.
14. Is _he now subject, or has _he ever been subject, to epilepsy, convulsions, or fits of any kind? If so, describe fully.
15. Is _he of average size for h__ age?
16. Is _he active and vigorous? Does _he run about and notice things, or is _he indolent?
17. Is _he nervous?
18. How is h__ appetite? Is _he gluttonous?
19. What is the state of the sense of taste? Is _he particular about what _he eats, or will _he swallow things without regard to taste?
20. Are sight and hearing good?
21. Is he [fond] of music?
22. Does he recognize color?
23. What colors does he know by name?
24. Does he recognize form?
25. Does _he notice pictures to distinguish them?
26. Does _he understand language?
27. Does _he understand a command?
28. Can _he do an errand?
29. Does _he talk?

30. At what age did _he commence to talk?
31. Is there any peculiarity or defect of speech? If so, describe.
32. Does _he use understandingly such words as or and if?
33. Please give several specimens of h__ mode of talking, and be careful to put down the words exactly as _he uses them.
34. Does _he know the alphabet?
35. Does _he read? How much?
36. Does _he count? How many?
37. What are h__ habits with regard to personal cleanliness?
38. Does _he soil or wet the bed?
39. Does _he soil or wet day clothing?
40. Can _he dress and undress h__self?
41. Can _he feed h__self?
42. Does _he use a spoon, or knife and fork?
43. Can _he tie h__ shoe strings in a regular knot?
44. Can _he do any work? and what kind?
45. Does _he hide, break, or destroy?
46. Does _he sleep well and quietly?
47. Is _he obedient?
48. Is _he passionate, or of good temper?
49. Has _he any other unfortunate habits?
50. How does _he amuse h__self?
51. What cause has been ascribed for h__ mental deficiency?
52. Has _he had the usual diseases of childhood—measles, scarlatina, whooping cough, &c?
53. Has _he been vaccinated?
54. Of what country was father of the applicant a native?
55. What was the general bodily condition and health of the father? Was he vigorous and healthy, or the contrary?
56. Was the father of the applicant scrofulous, or was he subject to fits?
57. Were all his senses perfect?
58. Was he always a temperate man?
59. About how old was he when the applicant was born?
60. Was there any known peculiarity in the family of the father of the applicant?— that is, were any of the grandparents, parents, uncles, aunts, brothers, sisters, or cousins, blind, deaf, or insane, or inflicted with any infirmity of body or mind?
61. If dead, at what age did the father die and of what disorder?
62. Where was the mother of the applicant born?
63. What was the general bodily condition of the mother of the applicant? strong and healthy, or the contrary?
64. Was she scrofulous, or ever subject to fits?
65. Were all her senses perfect?
66. Was she always a temperate woman?

67. About how old was she when the applicant was born?
68. How many children had she before the applicant was born?
69. How many since?
70. How many have died, and of what disease?
71. Was there, or is there any deformity of body, or mental deficiency in the other children? If so, describe fully.
72. What was the state of the mother's health during the time she was pregnant with the applicant?
73. Was she subject to any bodily injury or severe sickness or to any extraordinary mental emotions or fright, great sorrow, or the like?
74. Was she related by blood to her husband? If so, in what degree—first, second, or third cousins?
75. If dead, at what age did she die, and of what disorder?
76. Was there any known peculiarity in her family?—that is, were any of her grandparents, parents, uncles, aunts, sisters, brothers, children, or cousins, either blind or deaf or insane, or afflicted with any infirmity of body or mind?
77. Please state any facts that may have a bearing on the case.
78. Name of parent or guardian
79. Residence, P. O. address

The Family Physician, or the one best acquainted with the family and the child, is requested to fill out and sign the following certificate.

_____188__

_____Citizen of New York, Physician, and practitioner in the town of _____ hereby certify, that I have examined _____ and find that _____ is not insane, but is so deficient in mental ability, that _____ cannot be taught in Common Schools as others of _____ age,
_____ bodily health is _____, and _____ has no contagious disorder.

Signed _____

N.B.—The Physician is earnestly requested to review the above questions, and to state in writing his opinion of the *cause* of the person's mental deficiency. To state whether the child is or has been epileptic. Also to mention any organic or functional peculiarity that he may have observed. It may be greatly for the advantage of the applicant, that the physician should send in writing, a full and minute account of the case, with his own thoughts and suggestions about it; especially any facts in answer to Questions Nos. 60 to 76 inclusive, which may be within his knowledge. Such letters will be considered confidential, and may be sent directly to the Superintendent.

This circular, when properly filled out, is to be mailed to

Superintendent of the N. Y. Asylum for
Idiots,
Syracuse, New York

Notes

INTRODUCTION

1. Portions of this section appeared earlier, in a somewhat different version, in an article in the journal *Social Policy* (P. Ferguson, 1987).

2. Emphasis added; an abbreviated but more easily accessible statement of their position is available in Ellis et al., 1981. A similar argument is put forward by Marie Skodak Crissey and Marvin Rosen (1986b).

CHAPTER 1

1. This does not include the thousands of individuals labeled mentally retarded who continue to live in nursing homes for the elderly, even though many of them are youth and young adults. Lakin and his colleagues reported over 30,000 such individuals in their report for 1989 (Lakin, White, Prouty, Bruininks, and Kimm, 1991). Recent federal legislation has targeted the removal of these individuals from such inappropriate settings, but again the actualization of the policy remains far from complete.

2. In 1912, the superintendent of the Craig Colony for Epileptics (opened in 1894 in upstate New York) estimated that 98 percent of the epileptic individuals institutionalized at his facility were "feeble-minded." But he appeared to mean simply that "these persons cannot be expected to enter into the life of the community as a normal person should" (Shanahan, 1912, p. 156). No matter how one interprets his comments, they are undoubtedly an exaggeration by almost anyone's standards today.

3. The quotation is actually cited by John Wisdom (1965, p. 87) from a presentation that Wittgenstein made. However, the thinking behind the slogan is perhaps most accessibly presented in Wittgenstein's so-called *Blue and Brown Books* (Wittgenstein, 1958). William Bouwsma (1981) discusses this change in focus as it affects intellectual history and the search for meaning.

CHAPTER 2

1. For convenience, I will abbreviate the citations in the text for this information, other than some specific surveys and signed reports, as "NYSBC" followed by the year of the report being cited (e. g., NYSBC, 1867, p. xxv).

2. A facility designated as an insane asylum opened in Williamsburg, Virginia, in the eighteenth century. However, it remained small and uninfluential, run by a single family, and generally isolated from institutional developments even in other parts of the South. It is the kind of "first" that is more misleading than helpful in terms of the evolution of institutions that followed. However, it is an interesting story in its own right. For more information, see Dain's institutional history of its first 100 years of operation from 1766 to 1866 (Dain, 1971). There are a number of works of varying usefulness on the development of insane asylums during the eighteenth and nineteenth centuries, including Norman Dain (1964), Albert Deutsch (1937), Richard Fox (1978), and the various writings of Gerald Grob (1966, 1973, 1977, 1983, 1991) and David Rothman (1971, 1978, 1980). However, despite my disagreement with his analysis of deinstitutionalization, Andrew Scull's work in this area (1975, 1976, 1977, 1979, 1981, 1984, 1989) remains my preference.

CHAPTER 3

1. For convenience, I will abbreviate citations in the text for institutional reports by listing only the location name (e.g., Syracuse or Rome for annual reports from the asylums located in those cities). In some cases, I will use the name of the facility instead, as being more familiar than the location (e. g., "Elwyn" for a prominent, semiprivate institution outside Philadelphia). This practice will prevent confusion about the repeated changes in official names that took place at all of the asylums as linguistic fashion and social policy developed.

CHAPTER 5

1. There is some confusion on this point in some historical accounts of Fernald's position. Sloan and Stevens (1976, p. 77), for example, seem to badly misread what Fernald is really arguing. James W. Trent (1993) provides a much better analysis of the context of the positions on sterilization held by Fernald and others. Other good discussions of the positions and practices of leading eugenicists toward people who were mentally retarded are provided by Philip Reilly (1983, 1991), L. J. Ray (1983), Peter Tyor (1972), and Philip Jenkins (1984).

2. In New York, as in most other states, superintendents could not legally stop families from taking their relatives out of institutions unless the original admissions had been court-ordered. By 1912, Homer Folks, well-known leader of the Charity Aid Society, and others around the country were pressing for legislation that would have given states the right to retain inmates deemed "unfit" for home life, even though families had requested their discharge (Folks, 1912, p. 177). Even without legal backing, as I will discuss in Chapter 6, Bernstein rejected family requests for return of a relative, and he strongly implied that his permission for such discharges was required.

CHAPTER 6

1. All of the citations from the case files in this chapter identify the source of information by file number only.

2. The word "archives" is stretching the point. At the time I examined them, the files were kept in file cabinets in a damp, unused basement room. Some other historical materials were kept upstairs (e.g., volumes of *The Herald*, an institution newspaper published for many years, which included letters and other items from inmates themselves). The unfortunate state of the Rome case files was not at all unusual, and better than in some other New York asylums. Dwyer (1987) reports finding the case files in a similar condition at the Willard State Hospital. The early files from Wilbur's days at the Syracuse State School had been lost to fire.

3. Stephen Gould (1981) has documented that appearance was important enough for someone to alter some of the photographs in Goddard's book *The Kallikak Family* (1912), in a way that made the eyes of the "bad" strand of Kallikaks look darker and more foreboding. However, Zenderland (1986), while not disputing that the photos look doctored, points out that part of Goddard's argument about the most mildly retarded element was that they could not be spotted by appearance and that only experts could tell the morons from the rest of us. Moreover, Fancher (1987) has argued that it was common practice at the time to retouch photographs, and that nothing out of the ordinary was done to the Kallikak photographs.

CHAPTER 7

1. One might also include a similar outcome in the mental hospitals and the failed vision of people like Thomas Kirkbride in Philadelphia. Two of the best sources for these stories are Laura Gitlin, *The Professionalization of Medical Superintendents and the Treatment of the Poor in the United States: The Issue of Incurability, 1840–1870* (1982), and Nancy Tomes, *A Generous Confidence: Thomas Story Kirkbride and the Art of Asylum-keeping, 1840–1883* (1984). Gitlin's dissertation in particular was very helpful in developing my analysis of chronicity and incurability.

2. The term, of course, comes from Antonio Gramsci (1971), and its applications to historical analysis are discussed by Lears (1985).

3. To some extent, Andrew Scull's criticisms of David Rothman anticipate my criticisms of Wolfensberger (1975) on this point. Scull (1981a, 1981b) thinks that Rothman's revisions (especially his *Discovery of the Asylum*, 1971) of whiggish institutional history ultimately fail as alternative interpretations because they remain at the level of stated intentions. There is, says Scull, no adequate recognition of the actual behavior and social structure, even class divisions, that must ground any interpretation of what people say. Wolfensberger makes much the same mistake by

remaining at the level of stated intentions of institutional leaders. This type of intellectual history lends itself to a parody of scholarly debate as a "battle of quotations," with each opponent contending that his or her citations are more accurate indications of official intentions.

Bibliography

NOTES ON SOURCES

The material needed to formulate answers to the questions that I asked in this study came from three basic types of primary sources, as well as secondary sources.

The New York State Board of Charities

A major source of information on the legacy of the almshouse discussed in Chapter 2 was the annual reports of the New York State Board of Charities. Every year the board reported on inspections by its members of each of the county almshouses. The descriptions and censuses of these facilities illustrated the role of the almshouses in the evolution of the concepts of chronicity and custodialism. The information these reports contain on the location of, and attitudes toward, severely retarded people throughout the nineteenth century has barely been touched in histories of mental retardation. Even though the board did not exist before 1867, it reprinted several earlier reports of the status of the almshouses.

The board's annual reports contain information on other institutions besides the almshouses. Each year brief commentary and recommendations on state provisions for the idiot asylums were combined with very useful fiscal and demographic information. The board reports also contain studies sponsored by the board, including major surveys by Hoyt (New York State Board of Charities, 1873) and Willard (1865), which were drawn upon in Chapter 3. In short, these reports constitute the single most inclusive picture of institutional practices for all dependent populations in New York State.

Institutional Annual Reports

The idiot asylums in New York, Massachusetts, and Pennsylvania were among the earliest state asylums in the country. The superintendents of these facilities remained prominent participants in the professional debates that accompanied the spread of the idiot asylums to other states. People such as Wilbur at Syracuse, Howe and Fernald at South Boston (later Waverly), and Kerlin and Barr at Elwyn used their annual reports to elaborate their notions of what mental retardation was, and what the role of the asylum should be. Later, at the Rome State School, Bernstein would also write much more than simple facts and figures in trying to convince both legislators and the general public of his various concerns. Much of Chapters 3, 4, 5, and 6 drew upon these annual reports for both words and numbers about life in institutions. In fact, when it comes to severely retarded inmates of these institutions, the reports are as revealing for what they do not say as for what they do.

In addition to the annual reports, the superintendents wrote numerous articles in the effort to bring legitimacy to their small but growing profession. These articles contain little information about the earliest leaders (Howe, Wilbur, Seguin), but significant information about the time after establishment of a professional organization in 1876 (Sloan and Stevens, 1976; Trent, 1982). Bernstein of Rome did not write many articles (although he published different versions of the same basic article in three or four places), but often contributed to discussions or other forums for group debates.

Rome Case Files

Finally, for the case study of the first 20 years of the Rome Idiot Asylum, I relied heavily on information from the case files for more than 400 of the first 1,000 admissions. These case files varied from single pages bearing no more than a name and number to amazing accumulations of decades of official descriptions, parental correspondence, and demographic data. Some had matrons' reports on the inmates' disciplinary record and health status. Some had photographic material. All of this material was examined with basic interpretive techniques for emerging themes and categories. The results of this process constitute the body of Chapter 6.

Secondary Sources

Much of the important historical research in this general area has been done in the history of mental illness, not mental retardation. The most influential interpretations of both the rise of mental asylums and the modifications during the Progressive era are found in this literature. Much of the research is suggestive of similar developments in the field of mental retardation. Over the last 150 years, many of the changes in mental retardation practice seem mainly to echo practices initiated some 10 to 20 years earlier in mental illness circles. The various dimensions of chronicity seem to apply equally well to either population. Nonetheless, there are also some important, but unexamined, differences: widely disparate proportions of institutionalization; different levels of professionalization among superintendents; and different definitions of custodialism. Both the similarities and differences required that throughout my analysis of developments for severely retarded people, I make a conscious comparison with contemporaneous events in mental illness to test the interpretive schemes I wanted to defend. In particular, as mentioned in Chapter 1, the social construction of chronicity—by the state, by economic forces, and by the asylum superintendents—cuts across disability categories, yet retains curious variations for each type of facility (Gitlin, 1982).

ANNUAL REPORTS

Signed articles or sections within annual reports are included in the main reference list that follows.

Rome State Custodial Asylum (Rome, New York), 1895–1942

New York State Idiot Asylum (Syracuse, New York), 1852–82

Newark State Custodial Asylum for Feeble-Minded Women (Newark, New York), 1882–1900

New York State Board of Charities (Albany, New York), 1868–1901

New York State Department of Mental Hygiene (Albany, New York), 1919–30

New York State Commission for the Feeble-Minded (Albany, New York), 1918–23

New York City Board of Charities and Correction (New York, New York), 1876–81

Massachusetts School for the Feeble-Minded (Waverly, Massachusetts), 1890–1914

REFERENCES

Adams, Margaret. 1971. *Mental Retardation and Its Social Dimensions.* New York: Columbia University Press.

Altschuler, G. C., & J. M. Saltzgaber. 1984. "Clearinghouse for Paupers: The Poorfarm of Seneca County, New York, 1830–1860." *Journal of Social History* 17(4): 573–600.

American Association on Mental Retardation. 1992. *Mental Retardation: Definition, Classification, and Systems of Support.* 9th ed. Washington, D.C.: AAMR.

Barr, Martin W. 1910. *Mental Defectives: Their History, Treatment and Training.* Philadelphia: P. Blakiston's Son & Co.

Barr, Martin W., & E. F. Maloney. 1920. *Types of Mental Defectives.* Philadelphia: P. Blakiston's Son & Co.

Baumeister, A. A. 1970. "The American Residential Institution: Its History and Character." In A. A. Baumeister & E. C. Butterfield, eds. *Residential Facilities for the Mentally Retarded*, pp. 1–28. Chicago: Aldine.

Bellamy, G. Thomas, Larry E. Rhodes, David M. Mank, & Joyce M. Albin. 1988. *Supported Employment: A Community Implementation Guide.* Baltimore: Paul H. Brookes. History, 18, 79–89.

Berkowitz, Edward D. 1984. History, Public Policy and Reality. *Journal of Social History* 18:79–89.

———. 1992. Disabled Policy: A Personal Postscript. *Journal of Disability Policy Studies* 3(1): 1–16.

Bernstein, Charles 1903. Discussion [of Mason paper]. *Proceedings of the New York State Conference of Charities and Correction* 4:201–9.

———. 1912a. Discussion [of Fernald paper]. *Journal of Psycho-Asthenics* 17(3): 99–111.

———. 1912b. Reply and discussion [of Davenport paper]. *Proceedings of the New York State Conference of Charities and Correction* 13:143–47

———. 1912c. Discussion. *Proceedings of the New York State Conference of Charities and Correction*, 13:190–97.

———. 1917. Minutes. *Proceedings and Addresses of the 41st Annual Session of the American Association for the Study of the Feeble-Minded*, p. 29.

————. 1920. "Colony and Extra-institutional Care for the Feeble-Minded." *Mental Hygiene* 4(1): 1–28.

Biklen, Douglas. 1988. "The Myth of Clinical Judgment." *Journal of Social Issues* 44(1): 127–40.

Billings, J. S. 1895. *Report on the Insane, Feeble-Minded, Deaf and Dumb, and Blind in the United States at the Eleventh Census: 1890.* Washington, D.C.: Government Printing Office.

Blanton, R. L. 1976. "Historical Perspectives on Classification of Mental Retardation." In N. Hobbs, ed., *Issues in the Classification of Children.* Vol. 1, pp. 164–93. San Francisco: Jossey-Bass.

Bledstein, Burton J. 1976. *The Culture of Professionalism: The Middle Class and the Development of Higher Education in America.* New York: Norton.

Blustein, Bonnie E. 1981. " 'A Hollow Square of Psychological Science": American Neurologists and Psychiatrists in Conflict." In A. T. Scull, ed. *Madhouses, Mad-Doctors, and Madmen: A Social History of Psychiatry in the Victorian Era,* pp. 241–70. Philadelphia: University of Pennsylvania Press.

Bogdan, Robert. 1986. "Exhibiting Mentally Retarded People for Amusement and Profit, 1850–1940." *American Journal of Mental Deficiency* 91(2): 120–26.

————. 1987. "The exhibition of Humans with Differences for Amusement and Profit." *Policy Studies Journal* 15(3): 537–50.

————. 1988. *Freakshow: Presenting Human Oddities for Amusement and Profit.* Chicago: University of Chicago Press.

Bogdan, Robert, & S. J. Taylor, 1982. *Inside Out: The Social Meaning of Mental Retardation.* Toronto: University of Toronto Press.

————. 1989. "The Social Construction of Humanness: Relationships with Severely Disabled People." *Social Problems* 36(2): 135–48.

Bouwsma, William J. 1981. "Intellectual History in the 1980s: From History of Ideas to History of Meaning." *Journal of Interdisciplinary History,* 12(2): 279–91.

Braddock, David 1987. *Federal Policy toward Mental Retardation and Developmental Disabilities.* Baltimore: Paul H. Brookes.

Braddock, David, J. I. Haney, Richard Hemp, & Glenn T. Fujiura. 1988. "Public Expenditures for Developmental Disabilities: Analyses of Nationwide Trends in Funding." In L. W. Heal, J. I. Haney, & A. R. N. Amado, eds. *Integration of Developmentally Disabled Individuals into the Community.* 2nd ed.. Baltimore: Paul H. Brookes.

Braddock, David, & Dale Mitchell. 1992. *Residential Services and Developmental Disabilities in the United States: A National Survey of Staff Compensation, Turnover and Related Issues.* Washington, D.C.: American Association on Mental Retardation.

Bragar, Madeline C. 1977. "The Feebleminded Female: An Historical Analysis of Mental Retardation as a Social Definition, 1890–1920." *Dissertation Abstracts International* 39(2): 807A. University Microfilms no. 78-13297.

Braverman, Harry. 1974. *Labor and Monopoly Capital: The Degradation of Work in the Twentieth Century.* New York: Monthly Review Press.

Brenzel, Barbara M. 1983. *Daughters of the State: A Social Portrait of the First Reform School for Girls in North America, 1856–1905.* Cambridge: MIT Press.

Brockett, L. P. 1855. "Idiots and Institutions for Their Training." *American Journal of Education* 1(4): 593–608.

Brown, B. 1847. "The Treatment and Cure of Cretins and Idiots, with an Account of a Visit to the Institution on the Abendberg in Switzerland." *American Journal of the Medical Sciences* 14:109–117.

Brown, George. 1884. "In memoriam — Hervey B. Wilbur, M.D." *Proceedings of the Association of Medical Officers of American Institutions for Idiotic and Feeble-Minded Persons* 9:291–95.

Buckley, James T., & G. T. Bellamy. 1985. "National Survey of Day and Vocational Programs for Adults with Severe Disabilities: A 1984 Profile." In Philip M. Ferguson, ed. *Issues in Transition Research: Economic and Social Outcomes* pp. 1–12. Eugene: University of Oregon, Specialized Training Program.

Cashman, Sean D. 1984. *America in the Gilded Age: From the Death of Lincoln to the Rise of Theodore Roosevelt.* New York: New York University Press.

Cohen, Patricia C. 1981. Statistics and the State: Changing Social Thought and the Emergence of a Quantitative Mentality in America, 1790 to 1820." *William and Mary Quarterly* 38(1): 35–55.

Cohen, Stanley, & Andrew T. Scull. eds. 1983. *Social Control and the State.* New York: St. Martin's Press.

Crissey, Marie S., & Marvin Rosen. eds. 1986a. *Institutions for the Mentally Retarded: A Changing Role in Changing Times.* Austin, Tex.: Pro-ed.

———. 1986b. "Summing Up: The Case for Institutions." In Marie S. Crissey & Marvin Rosen, eds. *Institutions for the Mentally Retarded: A Changing Role in Changing Times*, pp. 171–78). Austin, Tex.: Pro-ed.

Dain, Norman. 1964. *Concepts of Insanity in the United States, 1789–1865.* New Brunswick, N.J.: Rutgers University Press.

———. 1971. *Disordered Minds: The First Century of Eastern State Hospital in Williamsburg, Virginia, 1766–1866.* Williamsburg, Va.: Colonial Williamsburg Foundation.

Danielson, Louis C., & G. Thomas Bellamy. 1989. "State Variation in Placement of Children with Handicaps in Segregated Environments." *Exceptional Children* 55(55): 448–55.

Demos, John. 1970. *A Little Commonwealth: Family Life in Plymouth Colony.* New York: Oxford University Press.

———. 1981. "History and the Formation of Social Policy toward Children: A Case Study." In David J. Rothman & Stanton Wheeler, eds. *Social History and Social Policy*, pp. 301–24). New York: Academic Press.

Department of Public Health and Charities of Philadelphia. 1911. *The Feeble-Minded World.* Bulletin no. 4. Philadelphia: DPHCP.

Deutsch, Albert. 1937. *The Mentally Ill in America: A History of their Care and Treatment.* New York: Columbia University Press.

Digby, Anne. 1985. *Madness, Morality and Medicine: A Study of the York Retreat, 1796–1914*. New York: Cambridge University Press.

Dix, Dorothea L. 1844. Memorial to the Legislature of the State of New York. *New York Assembly Documents, no. 21*. Albany: State of New York.

Doll, Edgar A. 1964. *Trends in Mental Evaluation of the Mentally Retarded*. Paper presented at the Institute on Mental Retardation, Bordentown, N.J.

Doll, Eugene E. 1962. "A Historical Survey of Research and Management of Mental Retardation in the United States." In E. P. Trapp & Philip Himelstein, eds. *Readings on the Exceptional Child: Research and Theory*, pp. 21–68. New York: Appleton-Century-Crofts.

———. 1970. "A Historical View of the Private Residential Facility in the Training and Study of the Mentally Retarded in the United States." *Mental Retardation* 85: 3–8.

Drew, Clifford J., Don R. Logan, & Michael L. Hardman. 1988. *Mental Retardation: A Life Cycle Approach*. 5th ed. New York: Macmillan.

Dwyer, Ellen. 1987. *Homes for the Mad: Life Inside Two Nineteenth-Century Asylums*. New Brunswick, N.J.: Rutgers University Press.

———. 1992. "Stories of Epilepsy, 1880–1930." In Charles E. Rosenberg & Jane Golden, eds. *Framing Disease: Studies in Cultural History*, pp. 248–72. New Brunswick, N.J.: Rutgers University Press.

Eberlein, H. D. (1943) 1978. "When Society First Took a Bath." In Judith W. Leavitt, & Ronald L. Numbers, eds. *Sickness and Health in America: Readings in the History of Medicine and Public Health*, pp. 331–41. Madison: University of Wisconsin Press.

Ehrenreich, John H. 1985. *The Altruistic Imagination: A History of Social Work and Social Policy in the United States*. Ithaca, N.Y.: Cornell University Press.

Eisner, Elliot W. 1988. "The Primacy of Experience and the Politics of Method." *Educational Researcher* 17(5): 15–20.

———. 1991. *The Enlightened Eye: Qualitative Inquiry and the Enhancement of Educational Practice*. New York: Macmillan.

Ellis, Norman R., David Balla, Otto Estes, Sue A. Warren, C. E. Meyers, John Hollis, Robert L. Isaacson, Bobby E. Palk, & Paul S. Siegel. 1981. "Common Sense in the Habilitation of Mentally Retarded Persons: A Reply to Menolascino and McGee." *Mental Retardation* 19(5): 221–25.

Fancher, Raymond E. 1987. "Henry Goddard and the Kallikak Family Photographs: 'Conscious Skulduggery' or 'Whig History'?" *American Psychologist* 42(6): 585–90.

Farber, Bernard. 1968. *Mental Retardation: Its Social Context and Social Consequences*. Boston: Houghton Mifflin.

———. 1986. "Historical Context of Research on Families with Mentally Retarded Members." In James J. Gallagher & Peter M. Vietze, eds. *Families of Handicapped Persons: Research, Programs, and Policy Issues* pp. 3–23. Baltimore: Paul H. Brookes.

Ferguson, Dianne L. 1987. *"Curriculum Decision Making for Students with Severe Handicaps: Policy and Practice."* New York: Teachers College Press.

Ferguson, Dianne L., & Philip M. Ferguson. 1986. "The New Victors: A Progressive Policy Analysis of Work Reform for People with Very Severe Handicaps." *Mental Retardation* 24(6): 331–38.

Ferguson, Philip M. 1987. "The Social Construction of Mental Retardation: Notes on the Relationship of Minority Group Status and Cognitive Limitations." *Social Policy* 18(1): 51–56.

Ferguson, Philip M., & Dianne L. Ferguson. 1987. "Parents and Professionals." In Peter Knoblock, ed. *Understanding Exceptional Children and Youth*, pp. 346–91. Boston: Little, Brown.

Ferguson, Philip M., Michael Hibbard, James Leinen, & Sandra Schaff. 1990. "Supported Community Life: Disability and the Renewal of Mediating Structures," *Journal of Disability Policy Studies* 1(1): 8–39.

Fernald, Walter E. 1892. "Some of the Methods Employed in the Care and Training of Feeble-Minded Children of the Lower Grades." *Proceedings of the Association of Medical Officers of American Institutions for Idiotic and Feeble-Minded Persons* 17:450–57.

———. 1893. "The History of the Treatment of the Feeble-Minded." *Proceedings of the National Conference of Charities and Correction* 20:203–21.

———. 1912. "The Burden of Feeble-Mindedness." *Journal of Psycho-Asthenics* 17(3): 85–99.

———. 1924. "Thirty Years Progress in the Care of the Feeble-Minded." *Journal of Psycho-Asthenics* 29:206–19.

Fiedler, Leslie. 1978. *Freaks: Myths and Images of the Secret Self.* New York: Simon & Schuster, Touchstone Books.

Figlio, Karl 1978. "Chlorosis and Chronic Disease in Nineteenth-Century Britain: The Social Constitution of Somatic Illness in a Capitalist Society." *Social History* 3(2): 167–97.

Finnane, Mark. 1981. *Insanity and the Insane in Post-Famine Ireland.* London: Croom Helm.

———. 1985. "Asylums, Families, and the State." *History Workshop* 20(Autumn): 134–38.

Fischer, D. H. 1977. *Growing Old in America: The Bland-Lee Lectures Delivered at Clark University.* New York: Oxford University Press.

Fish, William B. 1891. "Report of the Committee on Custodial Care of Adult Idiots." *Proceedings of the National Conference of Charities and Correction* 18:98–106.

———. 1892. "Custodial Care of Adult Idiots." *Proceedings of the Association of Medical Officers of American Institutions for Idiotic and Feeble-Minded Persons* 17:203–11.

Fitzgerald, John. 1900. "The Duty of the State Towards Its Idiotic and Feeble-Minded." *Proceedings of the New York State Conference of Charities and Correction* 1:172–78.

Foley, Roy W. 1929. "A Study of the Patients Discharged from the Rome State

School for the Twenty Year Period Ending December 31, 1924." *Journal of Psycho-Asthenics* 34:180–207.

Folks, Homer. 1912. "Report of the Committee on the Mentally Defective in Their Relation to the State." *New York State Conference of Charities and Correction* 13:172–79.

Fox, Richard W. 1978. *So Far Disordered in Mind: Insanity in California, 1870–1930.* Berkeley: University of California.

Friedberger, Mark. 1981. "The Decision to Institutionalize: Families with Exceptional Children in 1900." *Journal of Family History* 6(4): 396–409.

Geertz, Clifford. 1980. "Blurred Genres: The Refiguration of Social Thought." *American Scholar* 49(2): 165–79.

Gerber, David A. 1992. "Volition and Valorization in the Analysis of the 'Careers' of People Exhibited in Freak Shows." *Disability, Handicap and Society* 7(1): 53–69.

Gettelman, Marvin. 1975. "Philanthropy as Social Control in Late 19th Century America: Some Hypotheses and Data on the Rise of Social Work." *Societas* 5(1): 49–59.

Gitlin, Laura N. 1982. "The Professionalization of Medical Superintendents and the Treatment of the Poor in the United States: The Issue of Incurability, 1840–1870." *Dissertation Abstracts International* 43(6): 2128A. University Microfilms no. 82-25713.

Goddard, H. H. 1912. *The Kallikak Family: A Study in the Heredity of Feeble-Mindedness.* New York: Macmillan.

Goetz, Lori, Mellanie Lee, Stacey Johnston, & Robert Gaylord-Ross. 1991. "Employment of Persons with Dual Sensory Impairments: Strategies for Inclusion." *Journal of the Association for Persons with Severe Handicaps* 16(3): 131–39.

Gorwitz, K. 1974. "Census Enumeration of the Mentally Ill and the Mentally Retarded in the Nineteenth Century." *Health Services Reports* 89:180–87.

Gould, Stephen J. 1981. *The Mismeasure of Man.* New York: W. W. Norton.

Graham, O. L., Jr. 1983. "The Uses and Misuses of History: Roles in Policymaking." *Public Historian* 5(2): 5–19.

Gramsci, Antonia. 1971. *Selections from the Prison Notebooks of Antonio Gramsci.* Quentin Hoare & Geoffrey N. Smith, trans. New York: International Publishers.

Graney, Bernard J. 1979. "Hervey Backus Wilbur and the Evolution of Policies and Practices toward Mentally Retarded People." *Dissertation Abstracts International* 40(12): 6229A. University Microfilms no. 801337.

Greene, Maxine. 1986. "Qualitative Research and the Uses of Literature." *Journal of Thought* 21(3): 69–83.

Griesenger, William. 1867. *Mental Pathology and Therapeutics.* C. Z. Robertson & J. Rutherford, trans. London: New Sydenham Society.

Griffin, J. D., & Cyril Greenland. 1981. "Institutional Care of the Mentally Disordered in Canada: a 17th Century Record." *Canadian Journal of Psychiatry* 26(4): 274–78.

Grob, Gerald N. 1966. *The State and the Mentally Ill: A History of the Worcester State*

Hospital in Massachusetts, 1830–1920. Chapel Hill: University of North Carolina Press.

———. 1973. *Mental Institutions in America: Social Policy to 1875.* New York: Free Press.

———. 1977. "Rediscovering Asylums: The Unhistorical History of the Mental Hospital." *Hastings Center Report* 7(4): 33–41.

———. 1983. *Mental Illness and American Society, 1875–1940.* Princeton, N.J.: Princeton University Press.

———. 1986. "Mental Retardation and Public Policy in America: A Research Agenda." *History of Education Quarterly* 26(2): 307–13.

———. 1991. *"From Asylum to Community: Mental Health Policy in Modern America."* Princeton, N.J.: Princeton University Press.

Groce, Nora. 1985. *Everyone Here Spoke Sign Language: Hereditary Deafness on Martha's Vineyard.* Cambridge: Harvard University Press.

———. 1992. " 'The Town Fool': An Oral History of a Mentally Retarded Individual in Small Town Society." In Philip M. Ferguson, Dianne L. Ferguson, & Steven J. Taylor, eds. *Interpreting Disability: A Qualitative Reader,* pp. 175–96. New York: Teachers College Press.

Hahn, Harlan. 1987. "Advertising the Acceptably Employable Image: Disability and Capitalism." *Policy Studies Journal* 15(3): 551–70.

Haley, Bruce. 1978. *"The Healthy Body and Victorian Culture."* Cambridge: Harvard University Press.

Haller, Mark H. 1984. *Eugenics: Hereditarian Attitudes in American Thought.* 2nd ed. New Brunswick, N.J.: Rutgers University Press.

Harvey, Beth. 1992. *"Cultural Diversity, Families, and the Special Education System: Communication and Empowerment."* New York: Teachers College Press.

Haskell, R. H. 1944. "Mental Deficiency over a Hundred Years: A Brief Historical Sketch of Trends in this Field." *American Journal of Psychiatry* 100(Special Centennial Anniversary Issue): 107–18.

Hebberd, R. W. 1912. "The Development of State Institutions for the Mentally Defective in this State for the Next Decade." *Proceedings of the New York State Conference of Charities and Correction* 13:179–90.

Hecht, Irene W. D., & Frederick Hecht. 1973. "Mara and Benomi Buck: Familial Retardation in Colonial Jamestown." *Journal of the History of Medicine* 28:174–75.

Henning, D., & N. Bartel. 1984. *Deinstitutionalization: A Study of Community Program Directors' and Superintendents' Attitudes.* Philadelphia: Temple University Press.

Hofstadter, Richard. 1955. *Social Darwinism in American Thought.* Rev. ed. Boston: Beacon Press.

Hollander, Russell. 1986. "Mental Retardation and American Society: The Era of Hope." *Social Service Review* 60(3): 395–420.

Howe, Samuel G. 1851. "On Training and Educating Idiots: The Second Annual Report Made to the Legislature of Massachusetts." *American Journal of Insanity* 8(2): 97–118.

———. 1972. *On the Causes of Idiocy; Being the Supplement to a Report by Dr. S. G. Howe and the Other Commissioners Appointed by the Governor of Massachusetts to Inquire into the Condition of the Idiots of the Commonwealth, dated February 26, 1848, with an Appendix.* New York: Arno Press.

Hurd, Henry. 1916. *The Institutional Care of the Insane in the United States and Canada.* Baltimore: Johns Hopkins University Press.

Ireland, William W. 1900. *The Mental Affections of Children: Idiocy, Imbecility, and Insanity.* 2nd ed. Philadelphia: P. Blakiston's Son & Co.

Jarvis, Edward. (1855) 1971. *Insanity and Idiocy in Massachusetts: Report of the Commission on Lunacy, 1855, by Edward Jarvis* Cambridge: Harvard University Press.

Jenkins, Philip. 1984. "Eugenics, Crime and Ideology: The Case of Progressive Pennsylvania." *Pennsylvania History* 51(1): 64–78.

Jimenez, Mary A. 1987. *Changing Faces of Madness: Early American Attitudes and Treatment of the Insane.* Hanover, N.H.: University Press of New England.

Johnson, Alexander. 1896. "Permanent Custodial Care." *Proceedings of the National Conference of Charities and Correction* 23:207–19.

Jones, R. E. 1963. "Correspondence of the A.P.A. Founders." *The American Journal of Psychiatry* 119(12): 1121–34.

Kanner, Leo. 1964. *"A History of the Care and Study of the Mentally Retarded."* Springfield, Ill.: Charles C. Thomas.

———. 1967. "Medicine in the History of Mental Retardation: 1800–1965." *American Journal of Mental Deficiency* 72(2): 165–70.

———. 1976. "The Origins of Public Education: A Reassessment." *History of Education Quarterly* 16(4): 381–407.

———. 1978. "Origins of the Institutional State." *Marxist Perspectives* 1(4): 6–22.

———. 1983. *Poverty and Policy in American History.* New York: Academic Press.

———. 1984. "Poorhouses and the Origins of the Public Old Age Home." *Milbank Memorial Fund Quarterly/Health and Society* 62(1): 110–40.

———. 1986. *In the Shadow of the Poorhouse: A Social History of Welfare in America.* New York: Basic Books.

Katz, Michael B., Michael J. Doucet, & Mark J. Stern. 1982. *The Social Organization of Early Industrial Capitalism.* Cambridge, Mass.: Howard University Press.

Kerlin, Isaac N. 1884. "Provision for Idiotic and Feeble-Minded Children." *Proceedings of the National Conference of Charities and Correction* 11:246–63.

———. 1886. "Report of the Committee on Provision for Idiotic and Feeble-Minded Persons." *Proceedings of the National Conference of Charities and Correction* 13:288–97.

Keyssar, Alexander. 1986. *Out of Work: The First Century of Unemployment in Massachusetts.* Cambridge: Cambridge University Press.

Kiernan, William E., & Robert H. Bruininks. 1986. "Demographic Characteristics." In William E. Kiernan & Jack A. Stark, eds. *Pathways to Employment for Adults with Developmental Disabilities*, pp. 21–50. Baltimore: Paul H. Brookes.

Kiernan, William E., Bryan C. Smith, & Mark B. Ostrowsky. 1986. "Developmental Disabilities: Definitional Issues." In William E. Kiernan & Jack A. Stark, eds. *Pathways to Employment for Adults with Developmental Disabilities,* pp. 11–20. Baltimore: Paul H. Brookes.

Kiernan, William E., & Jack A. Stark, eds. 1986. *Pathways to Employment for Adults with Developmental Disabilities.* Baltimore: Paul H. Brookes.

Kitsuse, John, & Aaron V. Cicourel. 1963. "A Note on the Official Use of Statistics." *Social Problems* 11(2): 131–39.

Klebaner, Benjamin J. 1976. *Public Poor Relief in America: 1790–1860.* New York: Arno Press.

Knight, G. H. 1891. "Colony Care for Adult Idiots." *Proceedings of the National Conference of Charities and Correction* 18:107–8.

Kregel, John, & Paul Wehman. 1989. "Supported Employment: Promises Deferred for Persons with Severe Disabilities." *Journal of the Association for Persons with Severe Handicaps* 14(4): 293–303.

Kuhlmann, Frederick. 1916. "Part Played by the State Institutions in the Care of the Feeble-Minded." *Journal of Psycho-Asthenics* 21(1/2): 3–24.

———. (1940–41). "One Hundred Years of Special Care and Training." *American Journal of Mental Deficiency* 45(1): 8–24.

Lakin, K. Charles. 1979. *Demographic Studies of Residential Facilities for the Mentally Retarded: An Historical Review of Methodologies and Findings.* Minneapolis: University of Minnesota, Department of Psycho-educational Studies.

Lakin, K. Charlie, Robert H. Bruininks, & Barbara B. Sigford. 1981. "Early Perspectives on the Community Adjustment of Mentally Retarded People." In Robert H. Bruininks, C. Edward Meyers, Barbara B. Sigford, & K. Charlie Lakin, eds. *Deinstitutionalization and Community Adjustment of Mentally Retarded People.* Monograph no. 4, pp. 28–50. Washington D.C.: American Association on Mental Deficiency.

Lakin, K. Charlie, Bradley K. Hill, & Robert H. Bruininks. 1988. "Trends and Issues in the Growth of Community Residential Services." In Michael P. Janicki, Marty W. Krauss, & Marsha M. Seltzer, eds. *Community Residences for Persons with Developmental Disabilities: Here to Stay,* pp. 25–42. Baltimore: Paul H. Brookes.

Lakin, K. Charlie, Bradley K. Hill, Florence A. Hauber, Robert H. Bruininks, & Laird W. Heal. 1983. "New Admissions and Readmissions to a National Sample of Public Residential Facilities." *American Journal on Mental Deficiency* 87(1): 1–8.

Lakin, K. Charlie, Carolyn C. White, Robert W. Prouty, Robert H. Bruininks, & Christina Kimm. 1991. *Medicaid Institutional (ICF-MR) and Home and Community Based Services for Persons with Mental Retardation and Related Conditions.* Report no. 35. Minneapolis: University of Minnesota, Center on Residential Services and Community Living.

Lane, Harlan. 1976. *The Wild Boy of Aveyron.* Cambridge: Harvard University Press.

Larson, Magali S. 1977. *The Use of Professionalism: A Sociological Analysis.* Berkeley: University of California Press.

Lasch, Christopher. 1973. *The World of Nations: Reflections on American History, Politics, and Culture,* pp. 3–17. New York: Knopf.

Lears, T. J. Jackson 1985. "The Concept of Cultural Hegemony: Problems and Possibilities." *American Historical Review* 90(3): 567–93.

Leavitt, Judith W., & Ronald L. Numbers, eds. 1978. *Sickness and Health in America: Readings in the History of Medicine and Public Health.* Madison: University of Wisconsin Press.

Lerman, Paul. 1982. *Deinstitutionalization and the Welfare State.* New Brunswick, N.J.: Rutgers University Press.

Levstik, Frank R. 1981. "A History of the Education and Treatment of the Mentally Retarded in Ohio, 1787–1920." *Dissertation Abstracts International* 42(2): 822A. (University Microfilms no. 81-15130).

Lowell, Josephine S. 1882. "Report on the Public Charities of New York City." *Fifteenth Annual Report of the New York State Board of Charities.* Albany: Weed, Parsons.

Luckin, Bill. 1983. "Towards a Social History of Institutionalization." *Social History* 8(1): 87–94.

McDonnell, John, Barbara Wilcox, Shawn M. Boles, & G. Thomas Bellamy. 1985. "Transition Issues Facing Youth with Severe Disabilities: Parents' Perspective." *Journal of the Association for Persons with Severe Handicaps* 10(1): 61–65.

McGaughey, Martha J., William E. Kiernan, Sheila A. Lynch, Robert L. Schalock, & Donna R. Morganstern. 1991. *National Survey of Day and Employment Programs for Persons with Developmental Disabilities: Results from State MR/DD Agencies.* Boston: Children's Hospital, Training and Research Institute for People with Disabilities.

MacMillan, Donald L. 1982. *Mental Retardation in School and Society.* 2nd ed. Boston: Little, Brown.

Mann, Lester. 1979. *On the Trail of Process: A Historical Perspective on Cognitive Processes and Their Training.* New York: Grune and Stratton.

Marks, Russell. 1974. "Lewis M. Terman: Individual Differences and the Construction of Social Reality." *Education Theory* 24(4): 336–55.

Mayer, John A. 1983. "Notes towards a Working Definition of Social Control in Historical Analysis." In Stanley Cohen & Andrew Scull, eds. *Social Control and the State,* pp. 17–38. New York: St. Martin's Press.

Menolascino, Frank J., & John J. McGee. 1982. "The Psychological Rights of the Child and Handicapping Conditions." *Viewpoints in Teaching and Learning* 58:87–98.

Mercer, Jane. 1973. *Labeling the Mentally Retarded.* Berkeley: University of California Press.

Midelfort, H. C. Erik. 1987. *Melancholy and the transformation of the insanity defense.* Paper presented as part of the Gaston Lectures, Center for the Humanities, University of Oregon, Eugene, Ore., January.

Millias, Ward W. 1942–43. "Charles Bernstein, 1872–1942: Bernstein as a Humanist." *American Journal of Mental Deficiency* 47(1): 17–19.

Mills, C. Wright. 1959. *The Sociological Imagination.* New York: Oxford University Press.

Mohl, Raymond. 1971. *Poverty in New York 1783–1825.* New York: Oxford University Press.

Mottus, Jane E. 1983. *New York Nightingales: The Emergence of the Nursing Profession at Bellevue and New York Hospital, 1850–1920.* Rochester, N.Y.: UMI Research Press.

Murlin, E. L. 1897. "Rome State Custodial Asylum: How Oneida County's Miserable and Unhealthy Institution was Transformed into a Useful Dispenser of the State's Charity—Improvements in Buildings and Management." *New York Tribune,* October 10, p. 4.

New York State Commission. 1915. *Report of the State Commission to Investigate Provision for the Mentally Deficient.* Albany: J. B. Lyon Company.

Partlow Review Committee. 1978. Report of review, unpublished memorandum, October.

Piven, Frances F., & Richard A. Cloward. 1972. *Regulating the Poor: The Functions of Public Welfare.* New York: Vintage Books.

Platt, Anthony. 1969. *The Child Savers: The Invention of Delinquency.* Chicago: University of Chicago Press.

Pollock, Horatio M., & E. M. Furbush. 1921. "Patients with Mental Disease, Mental Defect, Epilepsy, Alcoholism and Drug Addiction in Institutions in the United States, January 1, 1920." *Mental Hygiene* 5(1): 139–69.

Powell, F. M. 1887. "The Care and Training of Feeble-Minded Children." *Proceedings of the National Conference of Charities and Correction* 14:250–60.

Quincy, J. (1821) 1971. "Report of the Committee on the Pauper Laws of This Commonwealth." In *The Almshouse Experience: Collected Reports.* New York: Arno Press.

Radbill, Samuel X. 1976. "Reared in Adversity: Institutional Care of Children in the 18th Century." *American Journal of Diseases of Children* 130:751–61.

Ray, Isaac. 1846. "Observations on the Principal Hospitals for the Insane, in Great Britain, France and Germany." *American Journal of Insanity* 2(4): 289–389.

Ray, L. J. 1983. "Eugenics, Mental Deficiency and Fabian Socialism between the Wars." *Oxford Review of Education* 9(3):213–23.

Raymond, C. S. 1948. "The Development of the Program for the Mentally Defective in Massachusetts for the Past One Hundred Years 1848–1948)." *American Journal of Mental Deficiency* 53(1): 80–91.

Reeves, Edith G. 1914. *Care and Education of Crippled Children in the United States.* New York: Russell Sage Foundation.

Reilly, Philip. 1983. "The Surgical Solution: The Writings of Activist Physicians in the Early Days of Eugenical Sterilization." *Perspectives in Biology and Medicine* 26:637–56.

———. 1991. *The Surgical Solution: A History of Involuntary Sterilization in the United States.* Baltimore: The Johns Hopkins University Press

"Report of the Committee Appointed by the Last General Assembly upon the

Subject of Town and State Paupers." (1852) 1976. In *The State and Public Welfare in Nineteenth-Century America: Five Investigations, 1833–1877.* New York: Arno Press.

"Report of Select Committee Appointed to Visit Charitable Institutions Supported by the State, and All City and County Poor and Work Houses and Jails. (1857) 1976. In *The State and Public Welfare in Nineteenth-Century America: Five Investigations, 1833–1877.* New York: Arno Press.

"Report of the Special Joint Committee Appointed to Investigate the Whole System of Public Charitable Institutions of the Commonwealth of Massachusetts during the Recess of the Legislature in 1858." (1859) 1976. *The State and Public Welfare in Nineteenth-Century America: Five Investigations, 1833–1877.* New York: Arno Press.

"Retarded Students Segregated, Study Shows." 1992. *New York Times,* Oct. 18, p. 42.

Reverby, Susan, & David Rosner. 1979. "Beyond the 'Great Doctors.' " In Susan Reverby & David Rosner, eds. *Health Care in America: Essays in Social History,* pp. 3–16. Philadelphia: Temple University Press.

Rhodes, L. E., & Lee Valenta. 1985. "Industry-based Supported Employment: An Enclave Approach." *Journal of the Association for Persons with Severe Handicaps* 10:12–20.

Richards, James B. 1885. "The Education of the Feeble-Minded." *Proceedings of the National Conference of Charities and Correction* 12:174–78.

Riggs, J. G. 1936. *Hello Doctor: A brief Biography of Charles Bernstein, M.D.* East Aurora, N.Y.: Roycroft.

———. 1981b. "Three Centuries of Care of the Mentally Disabled in Rhode Island and the Nation, 1650–1950." *Rhode Island History* 40(4): 111–32.

———. 1983. "Defectives, Dependents, and Delinquents: Images of the Needy and Policy Development." *Dissertation Abstracts International* 44(7): 2264A. University Microfilms no. 83-26028.

Rosenberg, Charles E. 1981. "Inward Vision and Outward Glance: The Shaping of the American hospital, 1880–1914." In David J. Rothman, & Stanton Wheeler, eds. *Social History and Social Policy,* pp. 19–55. New York: Academic Press.

Rosenkrantz, Barbara G., & Maris A. Vinovskis. 1978. "The Invisible Lunatics: Old Age and Insanity and Mid-Nineteenth-Century Massachusetts." In Stuart F. Spicker, Kathleen M. Woodward, & David D. Van Tassel, eds. *Aging and the Elderly: Humanistic Perspectives in Gerontology,* pp. 95–125. Atlantic Highlands, N.J.: Humanities Press.

———. 1979a. "Caring for the Insane in Ante-Bellum Massachusetts: Family, Community, and State Participation." In Allan J. Lichtman & Joan R. Challinor, eds. *Kin and Communities: Families in America,* pp. 187–218. Washington, D.C.: Smithsonian Institution Press.

———. 1979b. "Sustaining 'the Flickering Flame of Life': Accountability and Culpability for Death in Ante-Bellum Massachusetts Asylums." In Susan Reverby & David Rosner, eds. *Health Care in America: Essays in Social History,* pp. 155–82. Philadelphia: Temple University Press.

Rothman, David J. 1971. *The Discovery of the Asylum: Social Order and Disorder in the New Republic.* Boston: Little, Brown.

————. 1978. "The State as Parent: Social Policy in the Progressive Era." In Willard Gaylin, Ira Glasser, Steven Marcus, & David J. Rothman, eds. *Doing Good: The Limits of Benevolence,* pp. 68–95. New York: Pantheon Books.

————. 1980. *Conscience and Convenience: The Asylum and Its Alternatives in Progressive America.* Boston: Little, Brown.

Rothman, David J., & Stanton Wheeler, eds. 1981. *Social History and Social Policy.* New York: Academic Press.

Royfe, Ephraim H. 1972. "A Systems Analysis of an Historic Mental Retardation Institution: A Case Study of Elwyn Institute, 1852–1970." *Dissertation Abstracts International* 33(4): 1474A. University Microfilms no. 72-20211.

Rusch, Frank, ed. 1986. *Competitive Employment Issues and Strategies.* Baltimore: Paul H. Brookes.

Ryan, Joan. 1977. "The Production and Management of Stupidity: The Involvement of Medicine and Psychology." In David Robinson & Michael Wadsworth, eds. *Studies in Everyday Medical Life,* pp. 153–76. Oxford: Oxford University Press.

Ryan, Mary P. 1981. *Cradle of the Middle Class: The Family in Oneida County, New York, 1790–1865.* New York: Cambridge University Press.

Sailor, Wayne, & Douglas Guess. 1983. *Severely Handicapped Students: An Instructional Design.* Boston: Houghton Mifflin.

Scheerenberger, Richard C. 1983. *A History of Mental Retardation.* Baltimore: Paul H. Brookes.

————. 1987. *A History of Mental Retardation: A Quarter Century of Promise.* Baltimore: Paul H. Brookes.

Schneider, David M., & Albert Deutsch. 1941. "*The History of Public Welfare in New York State, 1867–1940.*" Chicago: University of Chicago Press.

Scotch, Richard K. 1984. *From Good Will to Civil Rights: Transforming Federal Disability Policy.* Philadelphia: Temple University Press.

————. 1989. "Politics and Plicy in the History of the Disability Rights Movement." *Milbank Quarterly* 67(Suppl. 2): 380–99.

Scull, Andrew T. 1975. "From Madness to Mental Illness: Medical Men as Moral Entrepreneurs." *European Journal of Sociology* 16(2): 218–61.

————. 1976. "Mad-Doctors and Magistrates: English Psychiatry's Struggle for Professional Autonomy in the Nineteenth Century." *European Journal of Sociology* 17(2): 279–305.

————. 1977. "Madness and Segregative Control: The Rise of the Insane Asylum." *Social Problems* 24(3): 337–51.

————. 1979. "*Museums of Madness: The Social Organization of Insanity in Nineteenth-Century England.*" New York: St. Martin's Press.

————. 1980. "A Convenient Place to get Rid of Inconvenient People: The Victorian Lunatic Asylum." In Anthony D. King, ed. *Buildings and Society: Essays on the Social Development of the Built Environment,* pp. 37–60. London: Routledge and Kegan Paul.

————. 1981a. "The Discovery of the Asylum Revisited: Lunacy Reform in the New American Republic." In A. T. Scull, ed. *Madhouses, Mad-Doctors, and Madmen: The Social History of Psychiatry in the Victorian Era*, pp. 144–65. Philadelphia: University of Pennsylvania.

————. 1981b. "Humanitarianism or Control? Some Observations on the Historiography of Anglo-American Psychiatry." *Rice University Studies* 67(1): 21–41.

————. 1981c. "Progressive Dreams, Progressive Nightmares: Social Control in 20th Century America." *Stanford Law Review* 33:575–90.

————. 1984. *Decarceration: Community Treatment and the Deviant—a Radical View.* 2nd ed. Englewood Cliffs, N.J.: Prentice-Hall.

————. 1989. *Social Order/Mental Disorder: Anglo-American Psychiatry in Historical Perspective.* Berkeley: University of California Press.

Scull, A. T., ed. 1981. *Madhouses, Mad-Doctors, and Madmen: The Social History of Psychiatry in the Victorian Era.* Philadelphia: University of Pennsylvania Press.

Shanahan, W. T. 1912. Discussion [of Davenport paper]. *Proceedings of the New York State Conference of Charities and Correction* 13:154–56.

Shattuck, Roger. 1980. *The Forbidden Experiment: The Story of the Wild Boy of Aveyron.* New York: Farrar Straus Giroux.

Singer, J. D., & J. D. Butler. 1987. "The Education for All Handicapped Children Act: Schools as Agents of Social Reform." *Harvard Educational Review* 57(2): 125–52.

Slater, Kenneth O. 1987. "An Historical Analysis of Public Policy for the Care and Treatment of People Who Are Mentally Retarded in Michigan." *Dissertation Abstracts International* 47(8): 3205A. University Microfilms no. 86-25609.

Sloan, William, & Harvey A. Stevens. 1976. *A Century of Concern: A History of the American Association on Mental Deficiency.* Washington, D.C.: American Association on Mental Deficiency.

Smith, J. David. 1985. *Minds Made Feeble: The Myth and Legacy of the Kallikaks.* Rockville, Md.: Aspen Systems Corporation.

Spitzer, Steven. 1975. "Toward a Marxian Theory of Deviance." *Social Problems* 22(5): 638–51.

Spitzka, E. C. 1878a. "Merits and Motives of the Movement for Asylum Reform." *Journal of Nervous and Mental Diseases* 5:694–714.

————. 1878b. "Reform in the Scientific Study of Psychiatry." *Journal of Nervous and Mental Diseases* 5:200–229.

Starr, Paul. 1982. *The Social Transformation of American Medicine.* New York: Basic Books.

Stephenson, Charles. 1980. "The Methodology of Historical Census Record Linkage: A User's Guide to the Soundex." *Journal of Family History* 5(1): 113–15.

Stewart, W. R. 1911. *The Philanthropic Work of Josephine Shaw Lowell: Containing a Biographical Sketch of Her Life Together with a Selection of Her Public Papers and Private Letters.* New York: Macmillan.

Talbot, Mabel E. 1964. *Edouard Seguin: A Study of an Educational Approach to the Treatment of Mentally Defective Children.* New York: Teachers College Press.

———. 1967. "Edouard Seguin." *American Journal on Mental Deficiency* 72(2): 184–89.

Taylor, Steven J. 1988. "Caught in the Continuum: A Critical Analysis of the Principle of the Least Restrictive Environment." *The Journal of the Association for Persons with Severe Handicaps* 13(1): 41–53.

———. 1992. "The Paradox of Regulations: A Commentary." *Mental Retardation* 30(3): 185–90.

Taylor, Steven J., Douglas Biklen, & James Knoll, eds. 1987. *Community Integration for People with Severe Disabilities*. New York: Teachers College Press.

Tomes, Nancy. 1984. *A Generous Confidence: Thomas Story Kirkbride and the Art of Asylum-Keeping, 1840–1883*. New York: Cambridge University Press.

Tredgold, A. F. 1914. *Mental Deficiency*. 4th ed. New York: William Wood & Company.

Trent, James W., Jr. 1982. "Reasoning about Mental Retardation: A Study of the American Association on Mental Deficiency." *Dissertation Abstracts International* 43(5): 1714A. University Microfilms no. 82-22732.

———. 1993. "To Cut and Control: Institutional Preservation and the Sterilization of Mentally Retarded People in the United States, 1892–1947." *Journal of Historical Sociology* 6(1): 56–73.

Turnbull, H. R., III, ed. 1981. *The Least Restrictive Alternative: Principles and Practices*. Washington, D.C.: American Association on Mental Deficiency.

Twining, William. 1843. *Some Account of Criticism, and the Institution for Its Cure on the Abendberg, near Interlachen, in Switzerland*. London: Parker.

Tyor, Peter L. 1972. "Segregation or Surgery: The Mentally Retarded in America, 1850–1920." *Dissertation Abstracts International* 33(6): 2876A. University Microfilms no. 72-32598.

———. 1977. "'Denied the Power to Choose the Good': Sexuality and Mental Defect in American Medical Practice, 1850–1920." *Journal of Social History* 10(4): 472–89.

Tyor, Peter L., & Leland V. Bell. 1984. *Caring for the Retarded in America: A History*. Westport, Conn.: Greenwood Press.

Tyor, Peter L., & J. S. Zainaldin. 1979. "Asylum and Society: An Approach to Institutional Change." *Journal of Social History* 13(1): 23–48.

U.S. Bureau of the Census. 1923. *Feeble-Minded and Epileptics in Institutions, 1923*. Washington, D.C.: Government Printing Office.

U.S. Bureau of the Census. 1976. *Historical Statistics of the United States: Colonial Times to 1970*. Washington, D.C.: Government Printing Office.

U.S. Department of Education. 1989. *Eleventh Annual Report to Congress on the Implementation of the Education of he Handicapped Act*. Washington, D.C.: Government Printing Office.

Vogel, Morris J. 1979. "Machine Politics and Medical Care: The City Hospital at the Turn of the Century." In Morris J. Vogel & Charles E. Rosenberg, eds. *The*

Therapeutic Revolution: Essays on the Social History of American Medicine, pp. 159–75. Philadelphia: University of Pennsylvania Press.

Wallace, A. F. C. 1978. *Rockdale: The Growth of an American Village in the Early Industrial Revolution.* New York: W. W. Norton.

Wallin, J. E. W. 1917. *Problems of Subnormality.* Yonkers-on-Hudson, N.Y.: World Book Company.

Walzer, Michael. 1983. *Spheres of Justice.* New York: Basic Books.

Warner, A. G. 1971. *American Charities: A Study in Philanthropy and Economics.* New York: Arno Press.

Wehman, Paul. 1988. "Supported Employment: Toward Zero Exclusion of Persons with Severe Disabilities." In Paul Wehman & M. Sherril Moon, eds. *Vocational Rehabilitation and Supported Employment*, pp. 3–16. Baltimore: Paul H. Brookes.

———. 1992. "Transition for Young People with Disabilities: Challenges for the 1990s." *Education and Training in Mental Retardation* 27(2): 112–18.

Wehman, Paul, & J. W. Hill. 1981. "Competitive Employment for Moderately and Severely Handicapped Individuals." *Exceptional Children* 47(6): 338–45.

Wehman, Paul, John S. Kregel, & John Seyforth. 1985. "Transition from School to Work for Individuals with Severe Handicaps: A Follow-up Study." *Journal of the Association for Persons with Severe Handicaps* 10(3): 132–36.

White, Carolyn C., Robert W. Prouty, K. Charlie Lakin, & Ellen M. Blake. 1992. *Persons with Mental Retardation and Related Conditions in State-operated Residential Facilities: Year Ending June 30, 1990 with Longitudinal Trends from 1950–1990.* Report no. 36. Minneapolis: University of Minnesota, Center for Residential Services and Community Living.

Whitney, E. A. 1949–1950. "Mental Deficiency in the 1880's and 1940's: A Brief Review of Sixty Years Progress." *American Journal of Mental Deficiency* 54(2): 151–54.

Wilber, R. C. 1969. *Rome State School: 1894–1969.* Rome, N.Y.: Rome State School.

Wilbur, Hervey B. 1876. "Management of the Insane in Great Britain." In New York State Board of Charities, *Annual Report* no. 9, pp. 175–207.

———. 1878. "The Status of the Work." *Proceedings of the Association of Medical Officers of American Institutions for Idiotic and Feeble-Minded Persons* 3:96–97.

Will, Madeline. 1984. "Bridges from School to Working Life." *Programs for the Handicapped* 2(March/April): 1–5.

Willard, S. D. 1865. "Report on the Condition of the Insane Person in the County Poorhouse of New York." *Assembly Documents*, pp. 1–70.

"The Willard Asylum, and Provision for the Insane." 1865. *American Journal of Insanity* 22(2): 192–212.

Williams, Gareth H. 1983. "The Movement for Independent Living: An Evaluation and Critique." *Social Science and Medicine* 17(15): 1003–10.

Wines, F. H. 1888. *Report on the Defective, Dependent, and Delinquent Classes of the Population of the United States as Returned at the Tenth Census (June 1, 1880).* Washington, D.C.: Government Printing Office.

Winslow, C. E. A. 1937). *A Survey of Methods of Care, Treatment, and Training of the Feeble Minded Together with a Program for the Future.* Summary report. Utica, N.Y.: State Hospital Press, 1–42.

Wisdom, John. 1965. *Paradox and Discovery.* New York: Philosophical Library.

Wittgenstein, Ludwig. 1958. *Preliminary Studies for the "Philosophical Investigations" Generally Known as the Blue and Brown Books.* New York: Harper.

Wolfensberger, Wolf. 1972. *The Principle of Normalization in Human Services.* Toronto: National Institute on Mental Retardation.

————. 1975. *The Origin and Nature of our Institutional Models.* Syracuse, N.Y.: Human Policy Press.

————. 1983. "Social Role Valorization: A Proposed New Term for the Principle of Normalization." *Mental Retardation* 21(6): 234–39.

Yates, J. (1824). 1901. "Report of the Secretary of State in 1824 on the Relief and Settlement of the Poor." In New York State Board of Charities. *Thirty-fourth Annual Report,* pp. 937–1145. Albany: State of New York.

Zenderland, Leila C. 1986. "Henry Herbert Goddard and the Origins of American Intelligence Testing." *Dissertation Abstracts International* 47(7): 2628A. University Microfilms no. 86-24043.

Zigler, Edward, David Balla, & Robert Hodapp. 1984. "On the Definition and Classification of Mental Retardation." *American Journal of Mental Deficiency* 89(3): 215–30.

Zigler, Edward, & Robert M. Hodapp. 1986. *Understanding Mental Retardation.* New York: Cambridge University Press.

Zinn, Howard. 1980. *A people's History of the United States.* New York: Harper and Row.

Zollers, Nancy, John Conroy, C. S. Hess, & E. Newman. 1984. *Transition from School to Work: A Study of Young Adults and their Families in Pennsylvania.* Philadelphia: Temple University, Developmental Disabilities Center.

Index